IMAGES
of America

SURRY

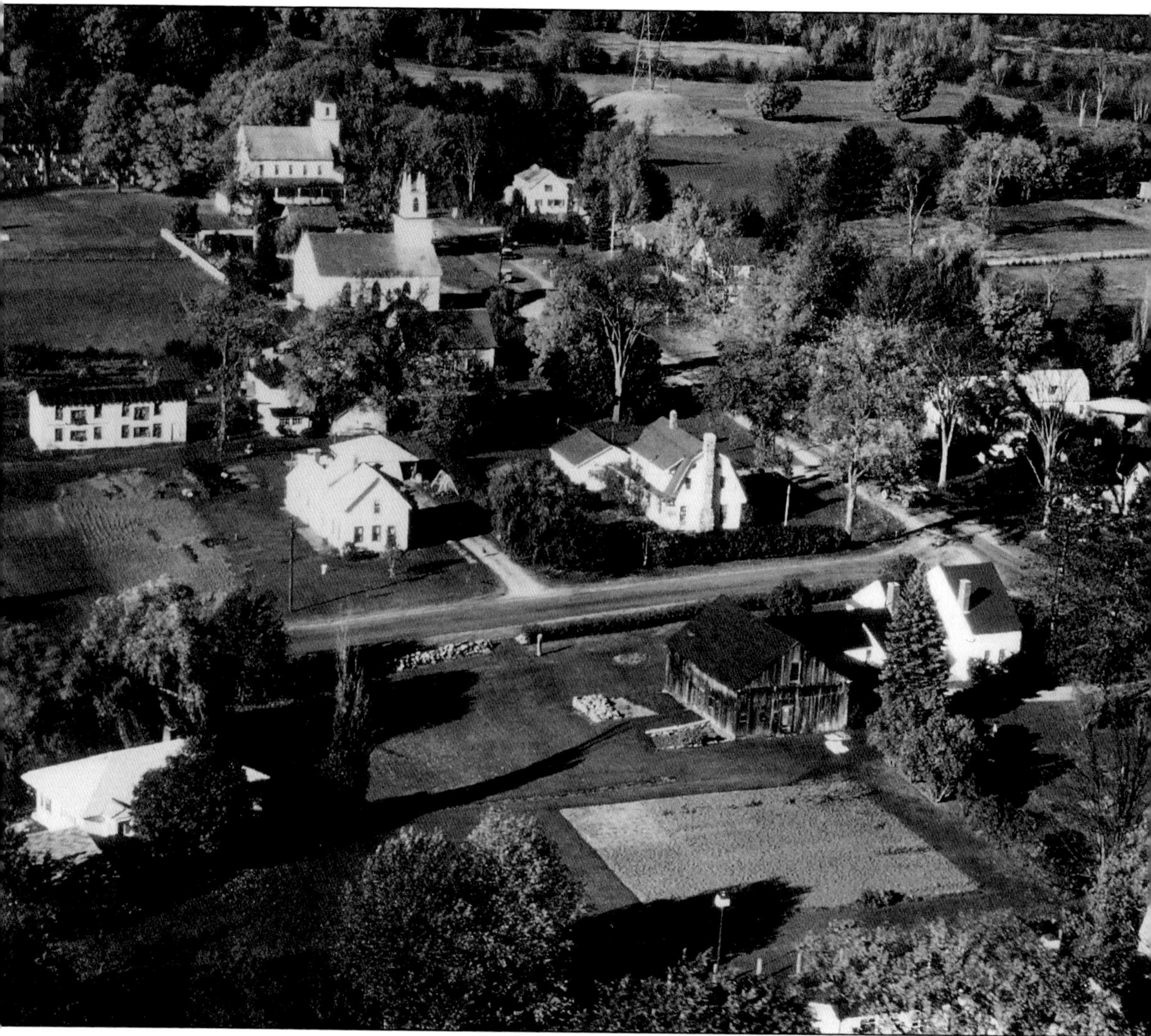

Aerial View of Surry Village, 1975. This view of Surry, taken in 1975, shows the Great Road, the town hall, and Crane's Church.

IMAGES
of America

SURRY

Surry History Committee

ARCADIA
PUBLISHING

ISBN 978-0-7385-0523-7

Published by Arcadia Publishing
Charleston, South Carolina

Printed in the United States of America

Library of Congress Catalog Card Number: Applied For

For all general information contact Arcadia Publishing at:
Telephone 843-853-2070
Fax 843-853-0044
E-mail sales@arcadiapublishing.com
For customer service and orders:
Toll-Free 1-888-313-2665

Visit us on the Internet at www.arcadiapublishing.com

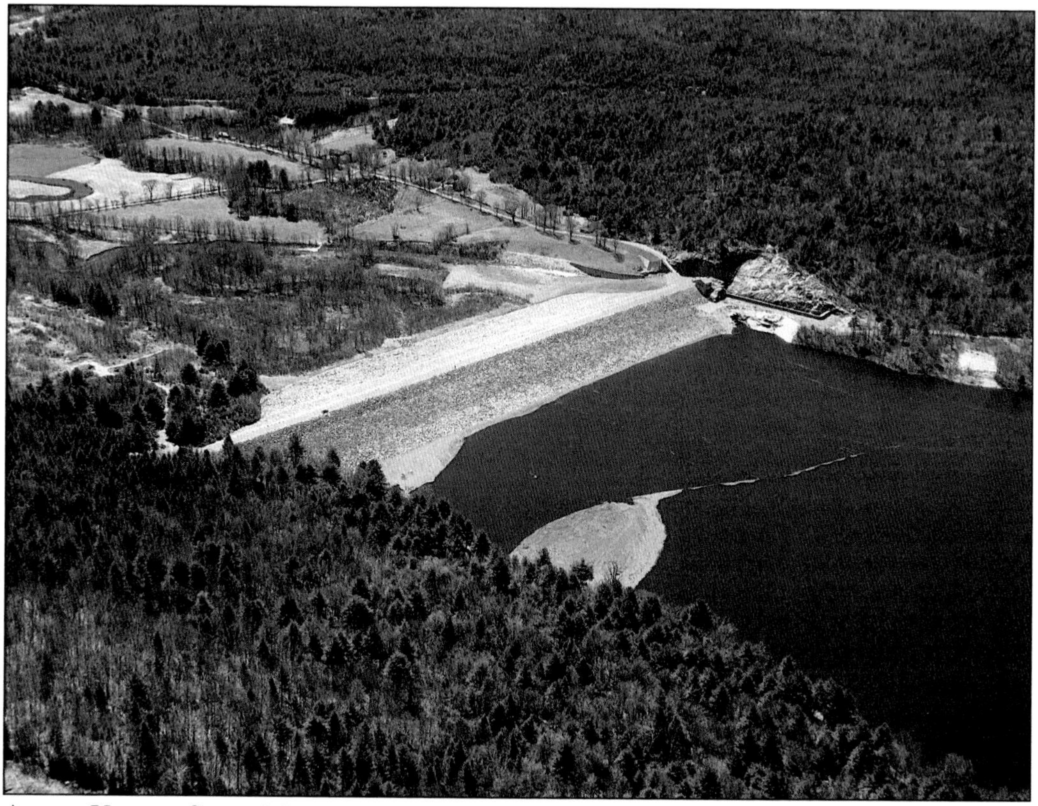

Aerial View of Surry Mountain Dam, 1958. This view of Surry Mountain Dam was taken in 1958. Compare this photograph with its companion image on pages 88 and 89.

Contents

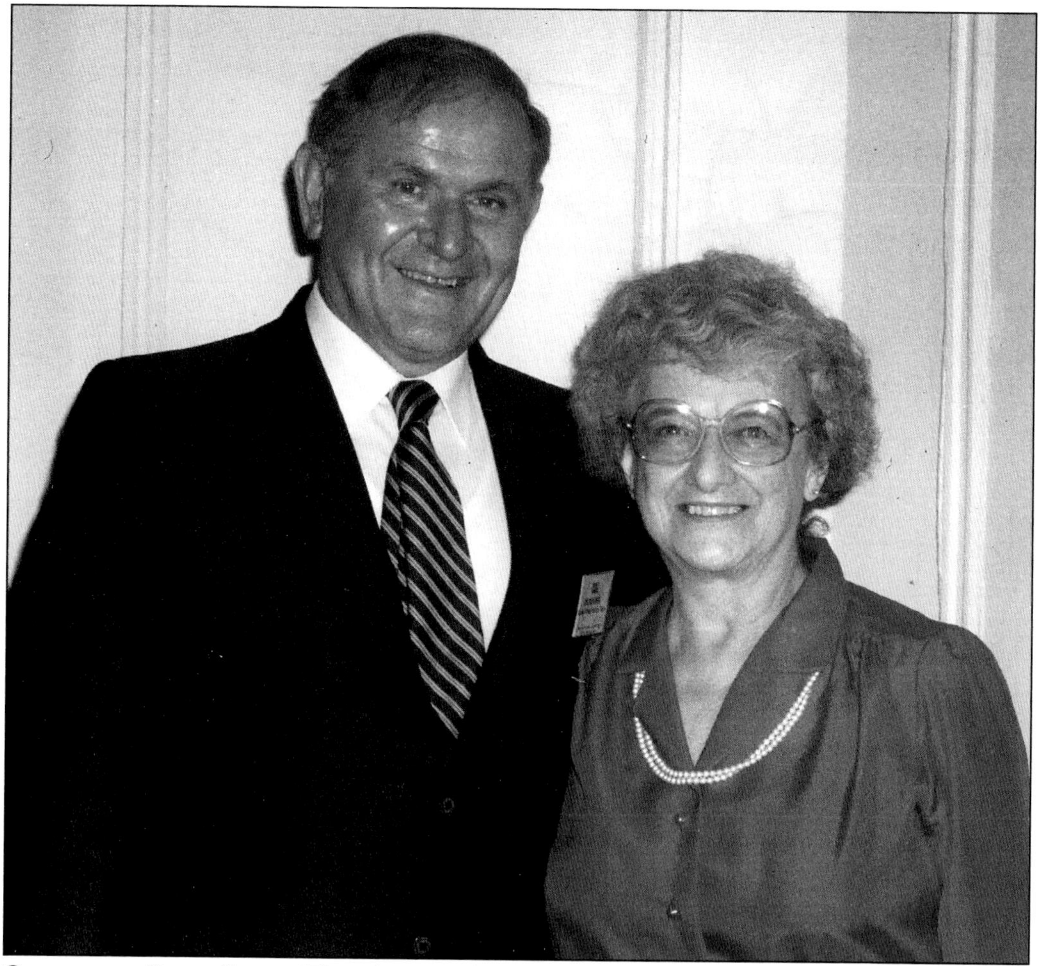

Calvin and Ruth Frink. This photograph of the Frinks was taken in 1982 at a conference at Bretton Woods.

The Surry History Committee dedicates this volume to Calvin and Ruth Frink, without whose leadership and generosity it would not have come into being. Calvin Frink invited volunteers 10 years ago to begin the task of bringing Frank Kingsbury's History of the Town of Surry *up to date—that is, to bring the genealogies, property transfers, municipal records, and the like through the 75 years of the 20th century since Kingsbury's* History. *A loyal group of 12 has worked for a decade on that research, inspired and enriched by the documents, maps, photographs, and historical ephemera regarding the town of Surry that Frink has patiently gathered over decades.*

This pictorial history is the first installment of that research. Meanwhile, the Frinks have led busy public lives filled with service. Calvin Frink's contributions total more than 100 service-years to his town, and they are enumerated in chapter 5. Ruth Frink has supported her husband's busy schedule throughout while logging her own impressive record of 30 years of volunteering at Cheshire Medical Center, 27 years with the Surry Fireman's Auxiliary, 12 years serving variously as tax collector and supervisor of the checklist and ballot counter, and a decade or so volunteering with 4-H and the Parents' Club. The Frinks are a model to all in their devotion to each other through 57 years of marriage and their magnanimous commitment to community.

Introduction

Surry is the pictorial chronicle of an archetypal New England town. Surry has it all—river and mountain, field and forest, mill and mine. Meetinghouse and church still anchor the village center, fulfilling without interruption their historical functions. Surry's history encompasses turnpike, railroad, even plans for a canal. As public education has consolidated and modernized throughout the 20th century, Surry's older district school buildings have nonetheless survived into the present, converted to alternative uses.

The town is the scene of a major undertaking by the U.S. government: construction of a flood-control dam, which changed landholding patterns, uprooted lives, and transformed the economy of a diminutive agricultural town. This book publishes photographs from the files of the Army Corps of Engineers, documenting the dam from layout to completion, from footings to spillway. It also records a "lost Surry," the collection of homesteads that, because of their location on prime floodplain, had to be sacrificed to the good of the larger community.

Surry portrays the life and environment of a diminutive but charming Yankee township. As towns go, it was a bit of an afterthought. Early settlers of the Ashuelot Valley above Keene discovered that they had little physical contact with the two towns within whose borders they lived: Gilsum and Westmoreland. Surry Mountain to the east and Westmoreland hills to the west bracketed the Ashuelot corridor, leaving Peter Hayward and 21 other early proprietors sufficiently estranged that they petitioned for independent corporation. Far from resisting the petition, the parent towns endorsed the alteration of boundaries, absolving them of civic responsibilities "over the hills." Petition was granted by John Wentworth, provincial governor, and council, and Surry was thereby born on March 9, 1769, taking as one third of its territory the Westmoreland Leg, and two thirds from Gilsum, the western slopes of Surry Mountain and the entirety of the valley between. The name adopted is that of a southern county in England, Surrey, the purported ancestral locus of many of the founding settlers. One wonders how these south-of-England identifiers felt two years later when the county of which they were part incorporated as Cheshire, a west country region of considerable cultural difference from Hampshire and Surrey, which thus far had served as sources of reference.

As created in the ninth year of the reign of King George III, Surry loosely resembled an index card standing on end. Measuring 3.25 by 5.5 miles, it encompassed 12,212 acres, making it one of the smallest townships in the county; so, too, in population—Surry's census has never exceeded 900 persons.

What it lacks in numbers, Surry reclaims in spirit. This is a community. It has survived the decline of turnpikes and the displacement of dam and reservoir. It has inspired extraordinary records of public service from generations of individuals, continuing into the present. In our age of sprawl and rampant individualism, could this be the historical model we have left behind, to our detriment?

A word about history and pictures: we characterize this book as a pictorial chronicle intentionally, for it is important that this is photograph-driven narrative rather than a comprehensive history that happens to be illustrated. We depict what the available photographs happen to show, with the intention of captioning in a way that establishes threads of continuity and provides context for understanding. Entire topics are necessarily excluded (for example, the canal idea, service in the Revolutionary War, and temperance) because pictorial evidence was not available. We welcome any comments and corrections, for we do have the luxury of moving on to publish an update of the written history as well.

Although the subject may be small in scale, the photographs published here reveal a community of hardy, optimistic, resourceful New Englanders, forging better lives for themselves and their children in challenging circumstances. Surry is a microcosm of central and northern New England, as the certainties of agricultural subsistence gave way to reduced yields and economic innovations from the larger world beyond. Surry has adapted and survived, not only to the loss of agricultural self-sufficiency but also to the radical change of place and identity that came with the construction of the flood-control dam in 1940. Through it all, as the pictures demonstrate, townsfolk kept smiling, children played, and improvements and reforms continued—all in a setting that can only be termed a natural blessing. Welcome to Surry.

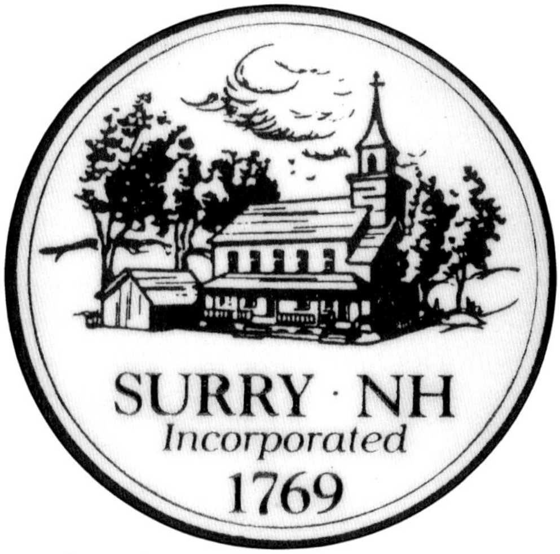

The Seal. The Surry town seal was developed by the Surry History Committee in 1990–1991.

Surry History Committee

Constance Blewett
Frederick Breton
Sheila Breton
Susan Farrell
Mary Fosher
Calvin Frink
David Harvey
Marilyn Jarvis
Mabel Rhoades
Bruce Smith
Kenneth Smith
Beth Stillings
Christopher Warman

One
Land and Water

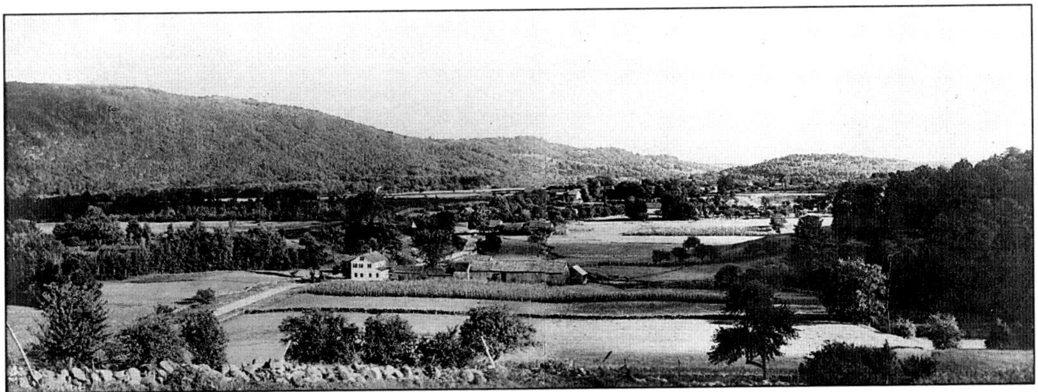

Surry Landscape. The earliest images of Surry are overwhelmingly the work of one individual, James E. Harvey. A fourth-generation descendant of pioneer settler Capt. Thomas Harvey (1740–1826), James Harvey made his living as a professional photographer in eastern New England for 30 years, until he retired to Surry in 1919. Once back in town, he undertook a systematic documentation of his birthplace by camera, leaving us a remarkable window upon a fading world. His images were frequently made into postcards, many surviving to the present. The community was simultaneously being chronicled in the *History of the Town of Surry, 1769–1922*, by Frank B. Kingsbury (1925). Kingsbury in fact used Harvey photographs to illustrate his volume. While the picture ofttimes equates to the proverbial thousand words, the ironic reality is that it is Kingsbury's written identifications and Kingsbury's researched facts that enable us to *understand* Harvey's memorable images. Welcome, then, to this view of Surry, a turn-of-the-century American Pastoral, as captured by the lens of James Ellsworth Harvey.

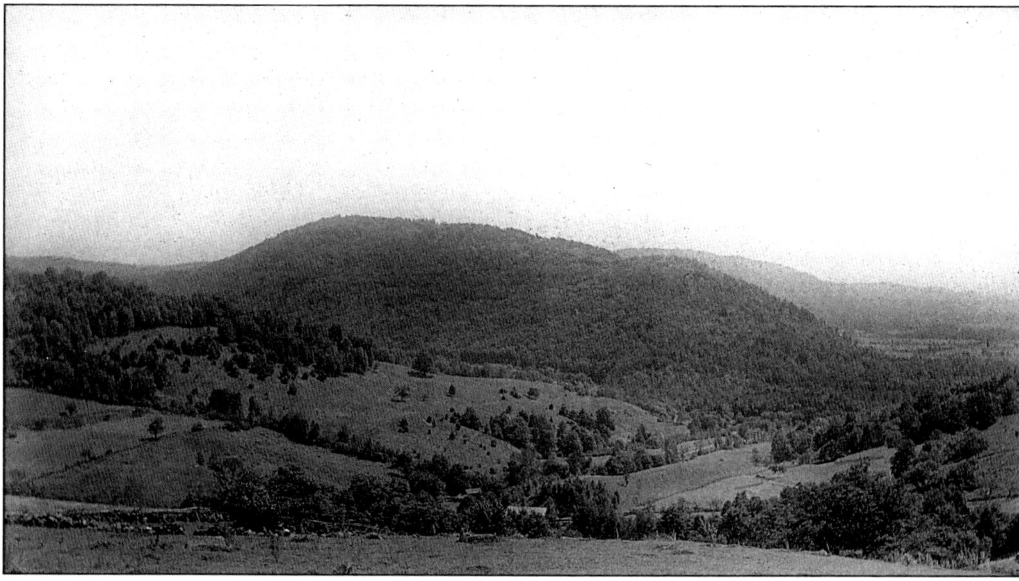

THE LAND, 1910. The rolling topography of Surry makes it one of the more scenic landscapes of southwestern New Hampshire. The continuing agricultural uses of the hillsides (grazing, hay mowing, and so on) made for splendid vistas, as yet unobstructed by resurgent forest. This scene is reminiscent of a time (*c.* 1850) when central New England was 85 percent cleared of forest. Today the ratio is reversed.

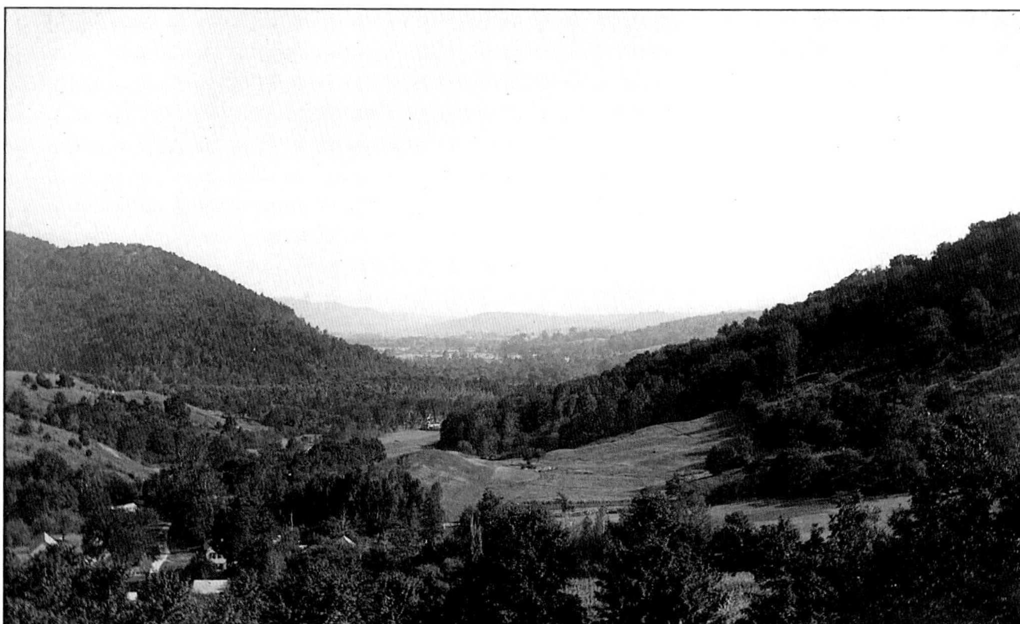

THE VALLEY. The last glacial sheet reconfigured the prehistoric Lake Hitchcock, antecedent to the Connecticut River, by scraping mountains to their bedrock cores, distributing stone and till across the landscape, and gouging a 50-mile drainage channel from Washington to Hinsdale (applying contemporary landmarks) that came to be named Ashuelot. This view southward invokes the geologic forces of ice and water and granite. The settlement of Surry is a mere outpost on a glacial timeline.

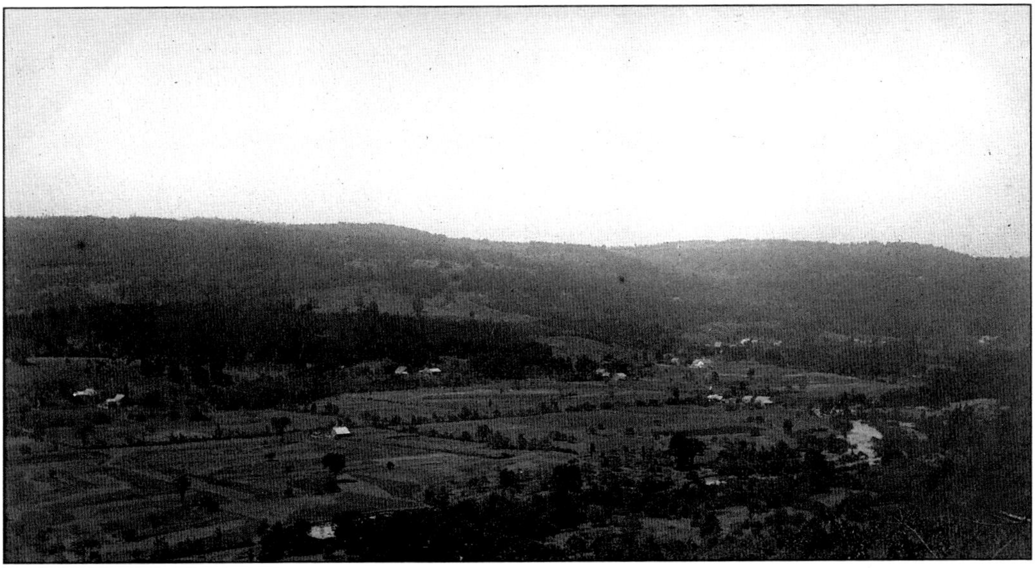

A DOMESTICATED LANDSCAPE. This idyllic image shows a settled agricultural village whose denizens work the rich alluvial soils of the floodplain to the fullest and still tend some upland mowings and pastures. Notice the several monarchical elm trees, in glorious maturity prior to the devastations of Dutch elm blight.

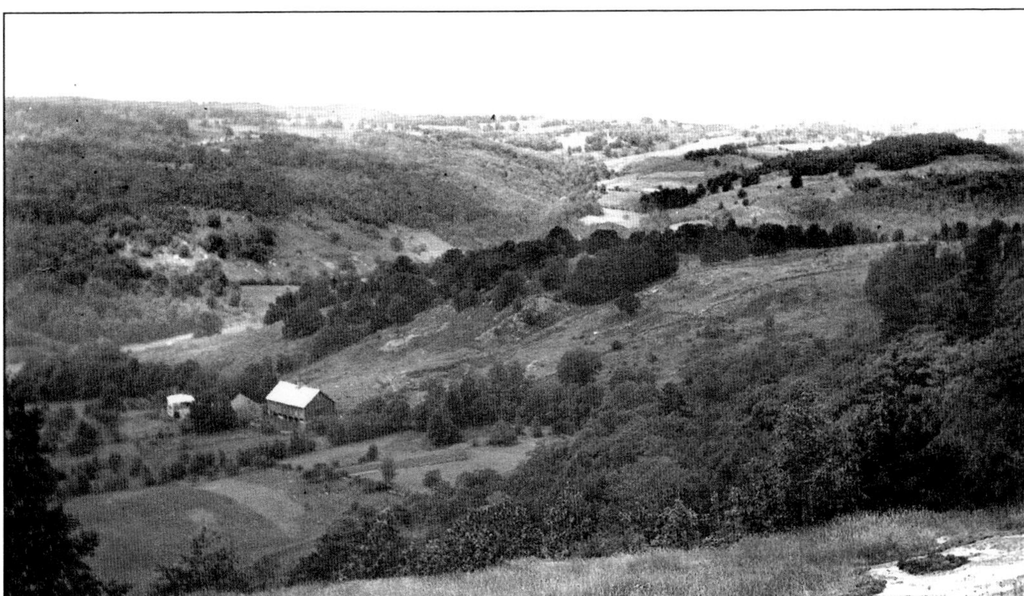

WEST HILL. This view down onto the Reed Farm shows the extent to which pastures remained open even into the 20th century. One hundred years later, nature has reclaimed much of this land in second- and third-growth forest.

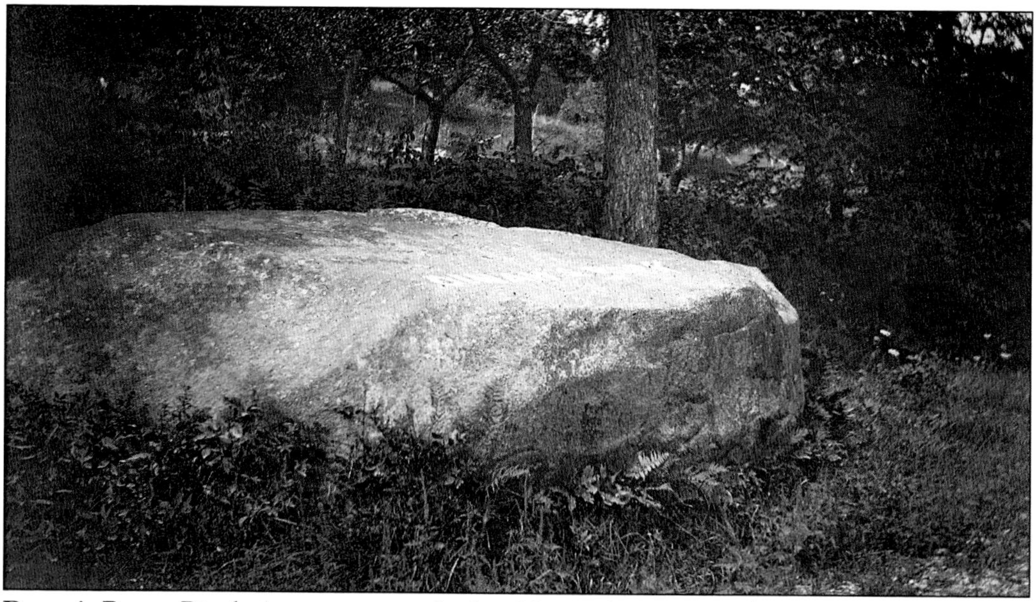

Dinah's Rock. Dinah Armstrong was the last Native American to live in the town of Surry, and the town supported her in her last years and final illness. On her good days, she was fond of sitting on this rock, midway between her dwelling and the village center, engaging the passing Anglo citizenry as they went about their business. She died in her 70s in 1812. The rock was inscribed "Dinah's Rock" by Wallace Wilcox in 1884.

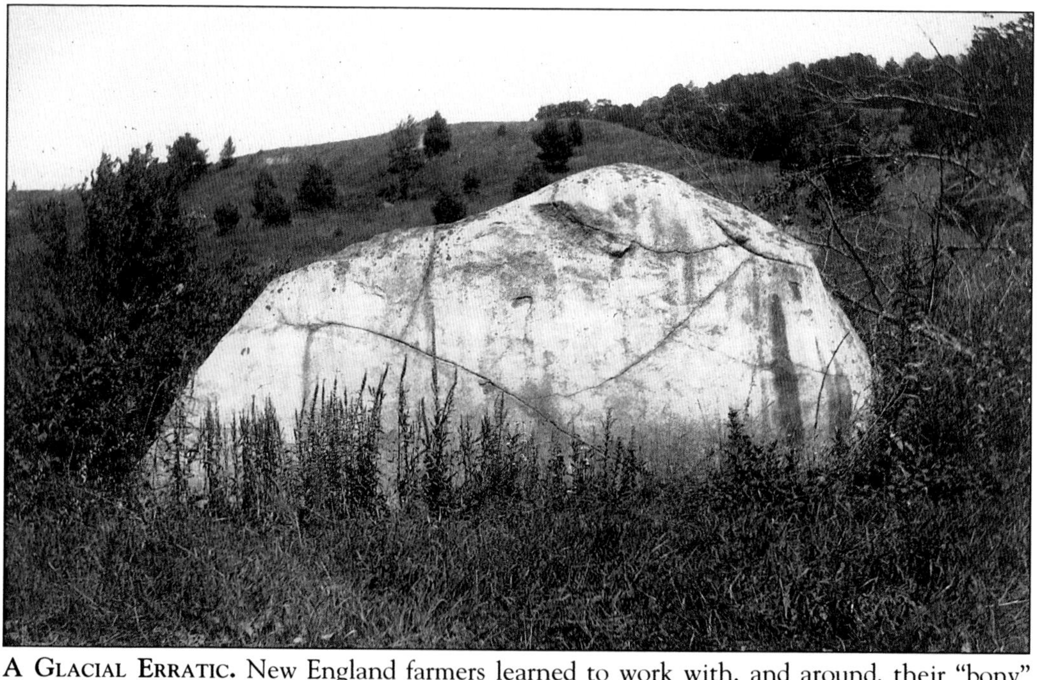

A Glacial Erratic. New England farmers learned to work with, and around, their "bony" natural inheritance. Some boulders, regardless of how rounded their surfaces from grinding and scraping under enormous glacial pressures, were simply too large to remove or bother with splitting. This Gilsum Road erratic is perhaps one of the many from Mount Ascutney (Vermont) that punctuate the surface of Cheshire County.

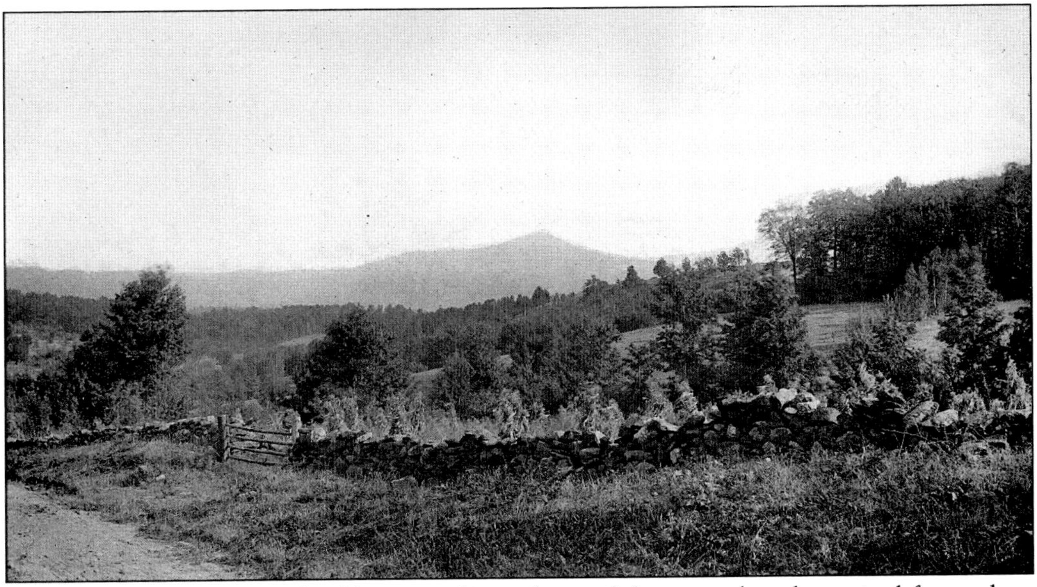

THE STONE FENCE. Lesser boulders were levered out of the ground as the annual freeze-thaw cycle heaved them to the surface and assembled in piles in the fields. Sledding such rock to the perimeter wall on a stone boat made good winter work for man and beast. Simple bar ways set rails in wooden posts; an industrious farmer using a star drill might fashion granite posts instead. Mount Monadnock looms in the background.

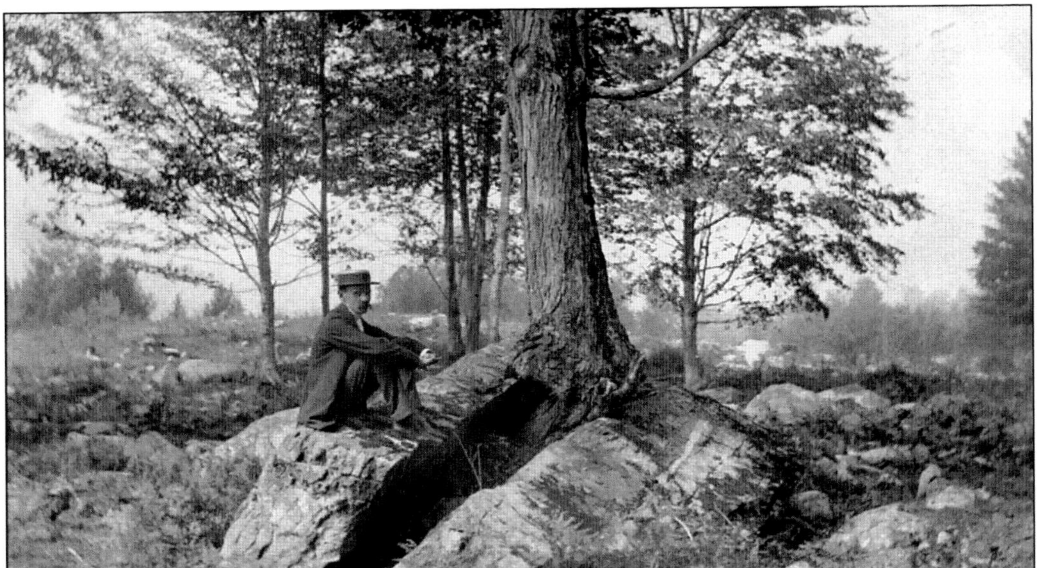

THE DUEL. James Harvey was sufficiently impressed by this silent contest of vegetable versus mineral that he placed an urbane cousin atop the ledge for a documentary shot. Where he found evidence of geological transformation, we perhaps read "radon."

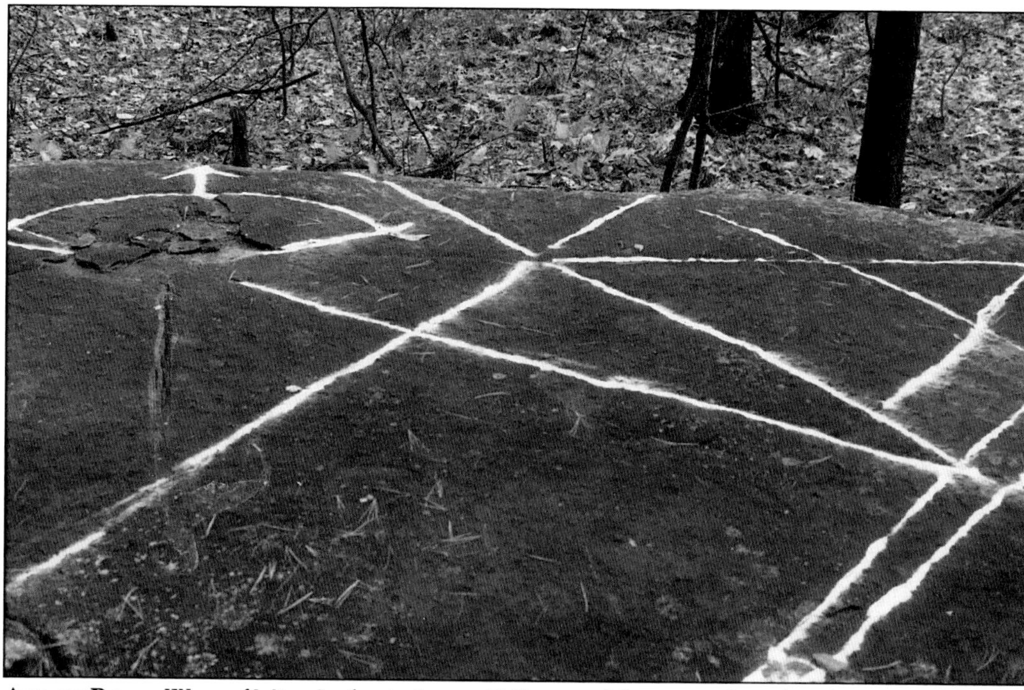

ARROW ROCK. West of Mine Ledge is Arrow Hill, site of these weathered etchings. Highlighted by limestone, the drawn bow surely (?) betokens Indian messaging. But what of the others? Citing family, Kingsbury attributes all to the ax work of William B. Mason, a "peculiar" (heavy reader) but physically powerful man who lived and worked with his brother Elijah (see Masonian Skidder, page 31). On a hike in Hinsdale, William Mason fatally reversed the curse of Sisyphus by pushing a boulder downhill, suffering a heart attack, and dying at age 80.

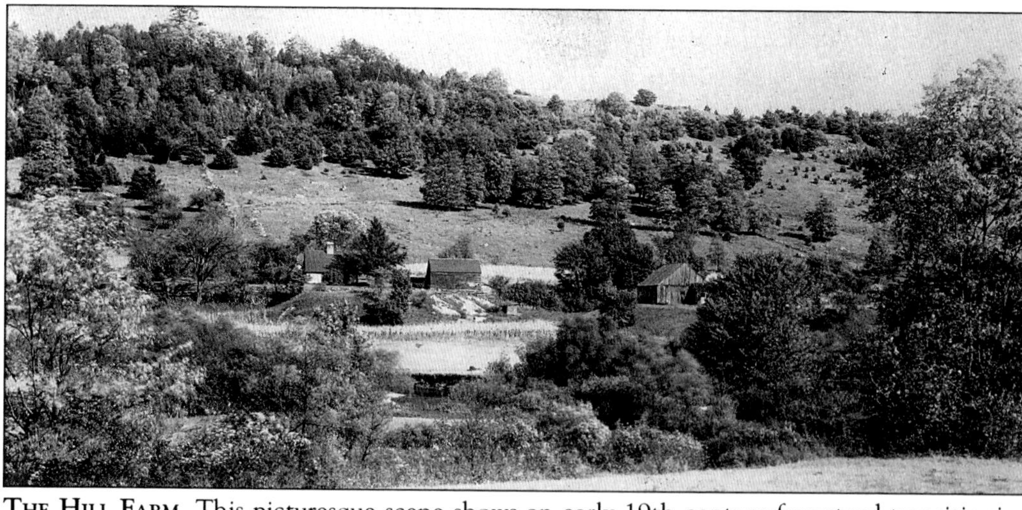

THE HILL FARM. This picturesque scene shows an early-19th-century farmstead transitioning to less intensive use of the land. A modest center-chimney Cape-style house, with full-sized English barn and lesser outbuildings, is situated atop landfill, apparently dredged from the farm pond in the middle foreground. The hillside beyond has two vertical stone fences, indicating original mowing if not planting, but it is now only grazed, permitting the resprouting rootstock to erupt as trees within a decade.

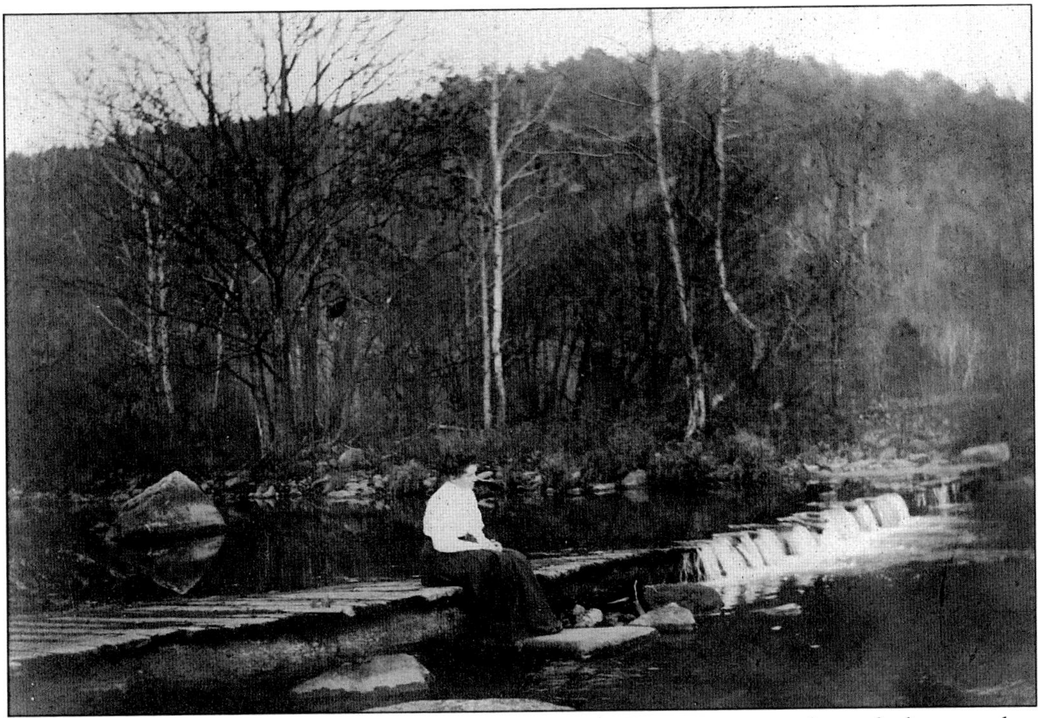

The River and the Maiden, 1908. Kate Hannah Porter, sister-in-law of photographer James E. Harvey, muses on the passing of "time and tide." The last-born child (1865) of Dr. William Henry Porter, successful physician and public citizen of Surry, she remained at her familial home for the entirety of her life.

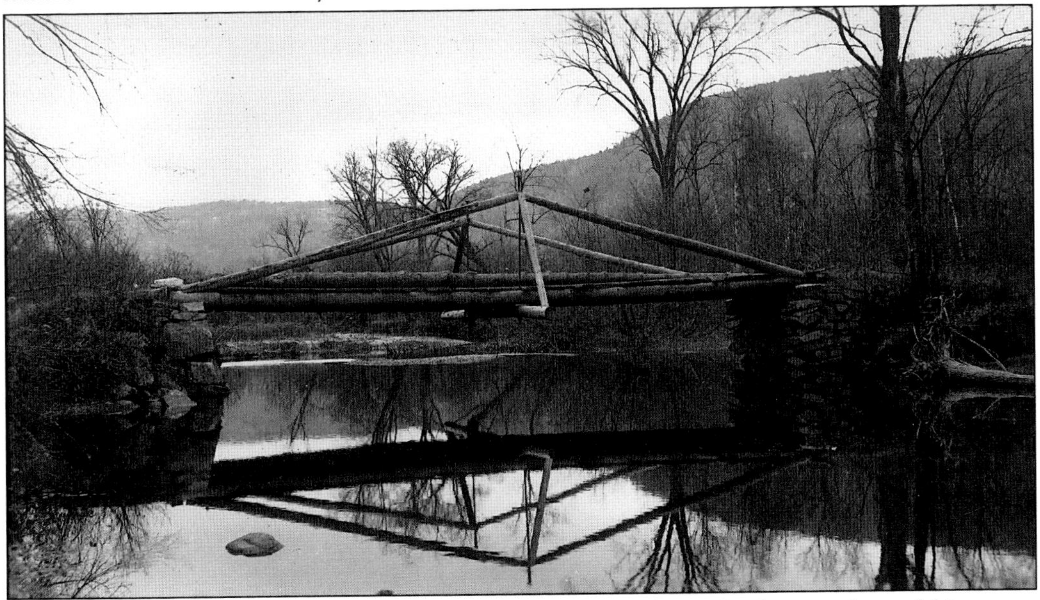

The Keller Bridge. A placid Ashuelot River courses beneath the simplest of king post bridges, on the J.N. Keller Farm, in the southern end of Surry. The view is upstream, with Surry Mountain on the right (east). The open bridge and calm waters combined to make a favored swimming hole.

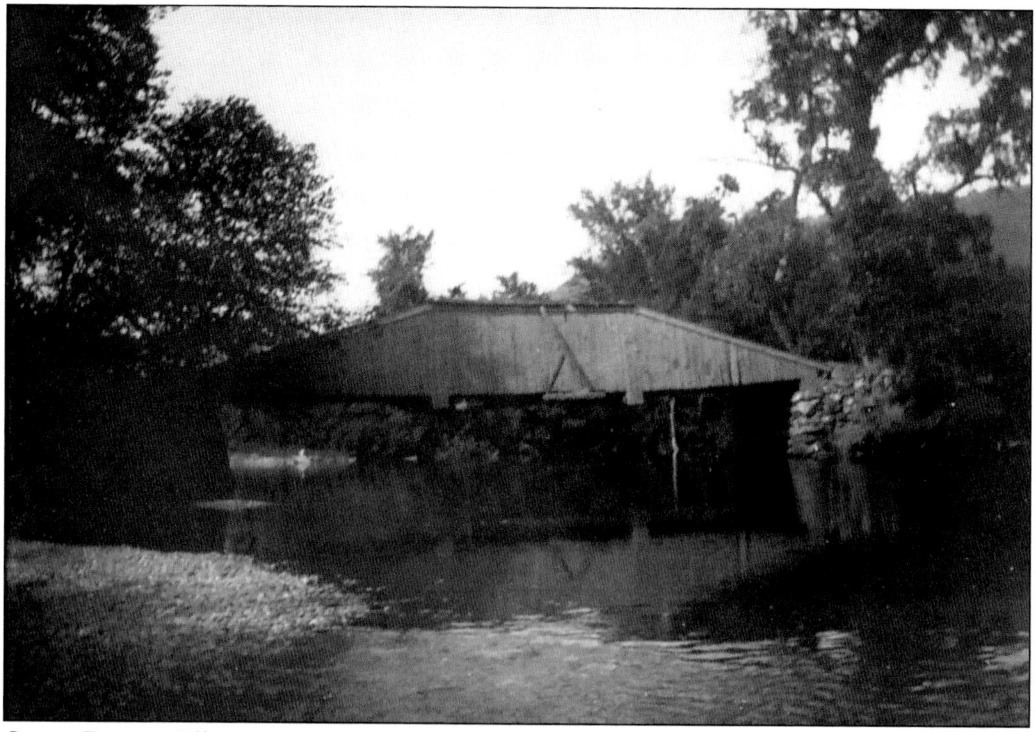

Great Bridge. Effecting a traverse of a deep and rushing river has been an engineering miracle throughout history. Small wonder Romans named their chief priest Pontifex Maximus, derived from *pons*, bridge (whence "pontiff"). Here is Surry's Great (or Red) Bridge, on the East Surry Road. This Wilder truss model was built c. 1890. Earlier versions had served the Cheshire Turnpike, from 1805 to 1840, whereby the substantial footings. The span is 60 feet.

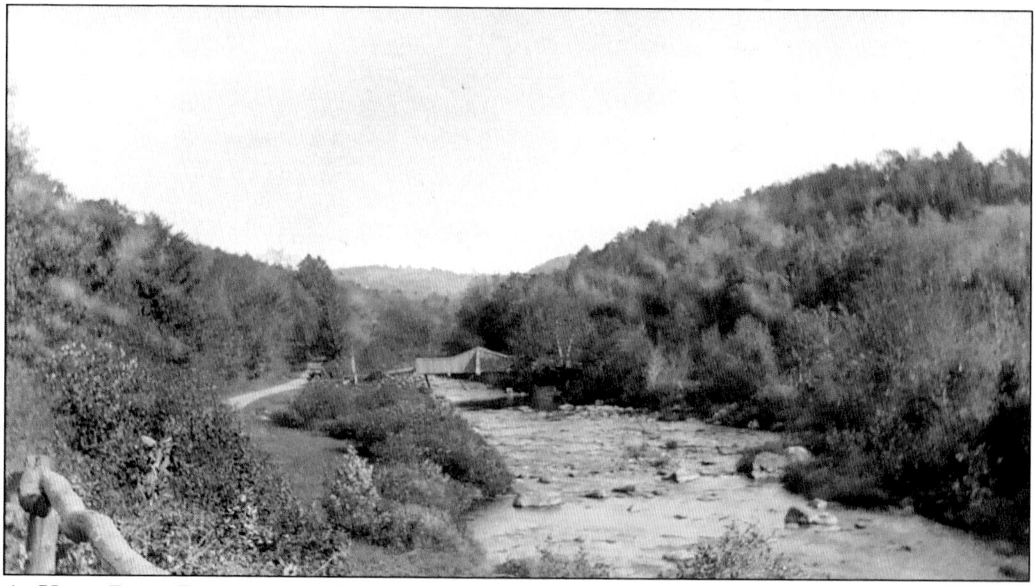

A King Post Bridge. Another bridge spanning a shorter distance upstream is built in the simpler king post style, the thrust of the center being carried to the abutments by the tripod superstructure.

A Boy's Delight. A leaking milldam, an old mill, the cool embrace of overarching foliage on a steamy midsummer day—what more could a 10-year-old boy on frog patrol want . . .

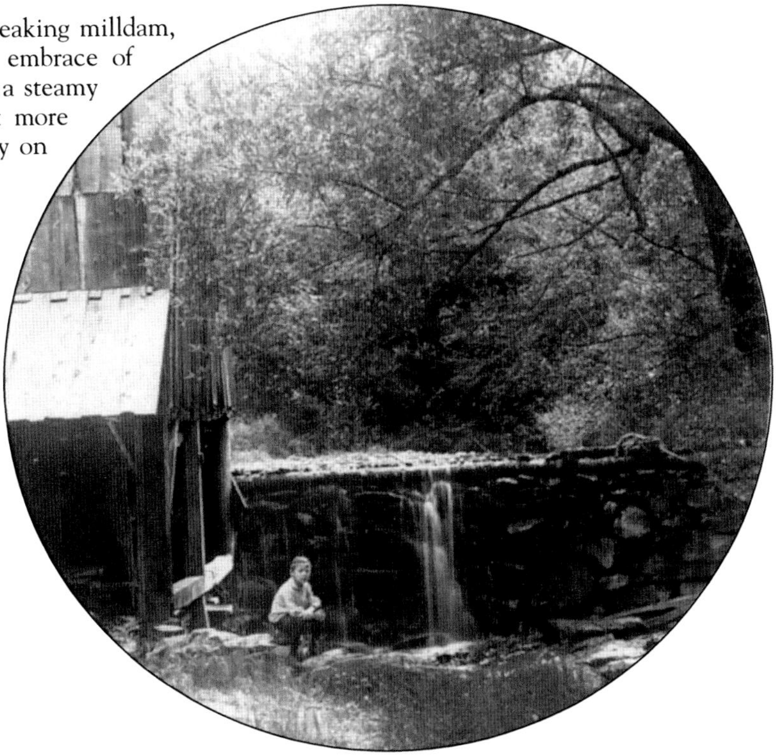

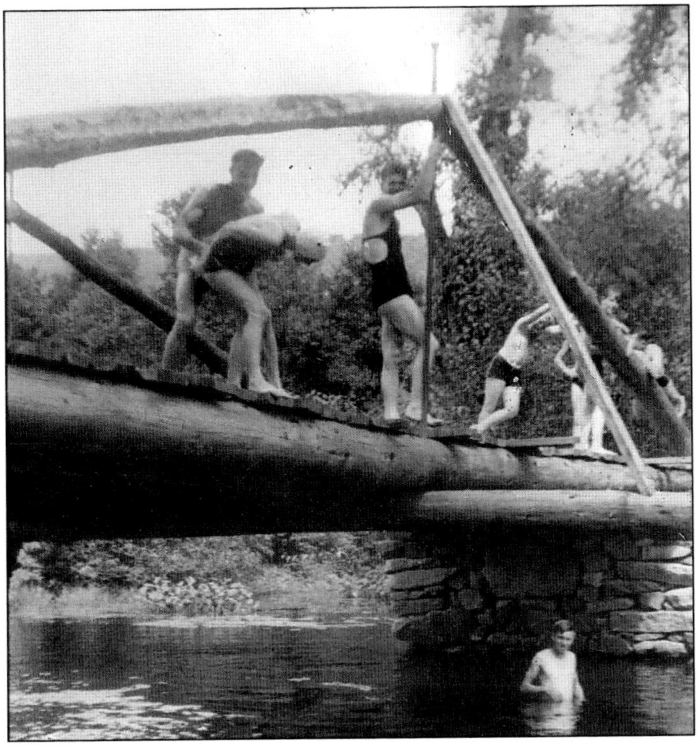

The Swimming Hole. . . . except the push and pull of turf battles on a bridge with school chums. Absent the side framing, this crude king post provides an ideal platform for the competitive instincts of these preadolescents.

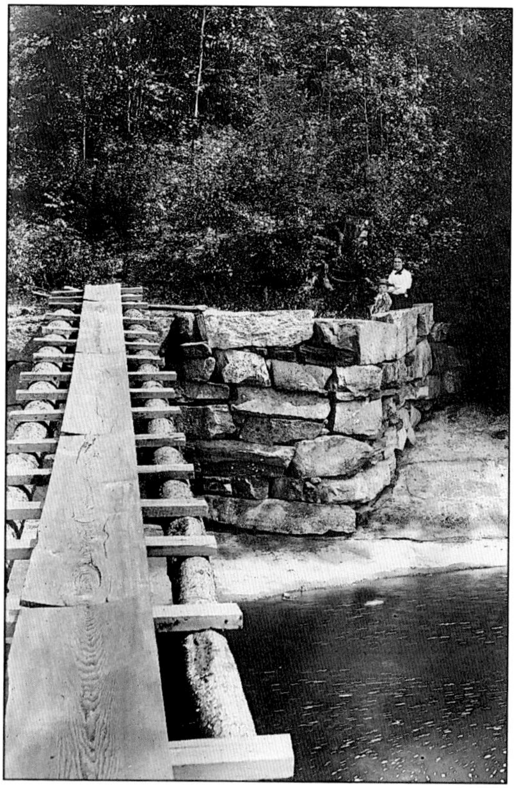

A Footbridge. Here is a marker of a community in transition. Where quarried footings once supported a substantial bridge, we now find a *reductio ad absurdum:* planking laid atop milled struts, providing a minimal footbridge to the opposite abutment, already grown in enough to render invisible the roadbed that formerly approached.

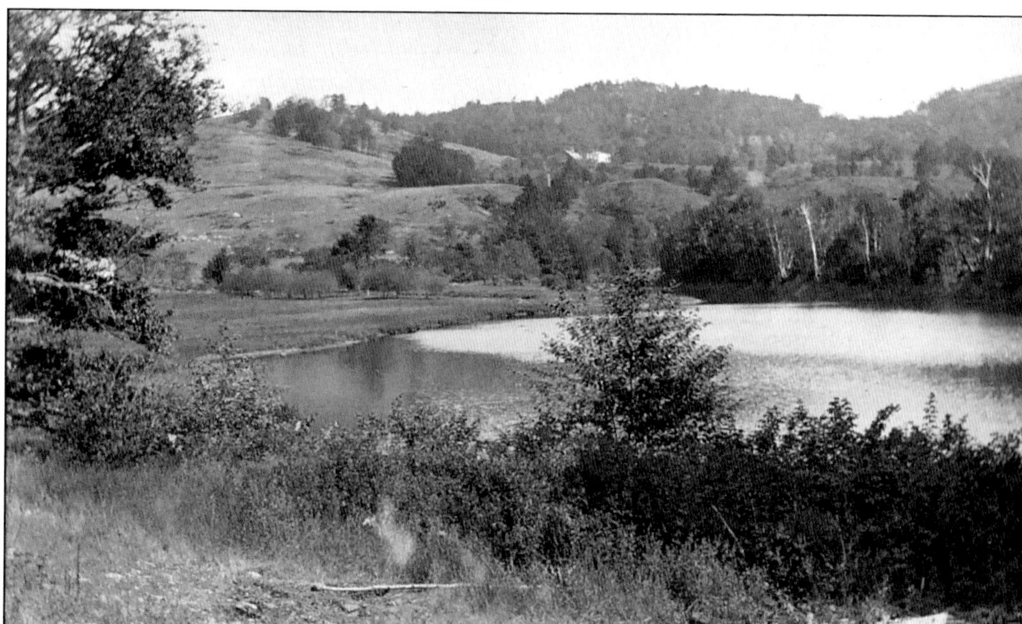

A Farm Pond. Surry's hilly profile creates swift drainage to the Ashuelot River at the bottom, leaving little opportunity for natural wetlands, swamps, and the like. Farmers found it necessary to excavate their own farm ponds, such as this one, to serve their livestock and occasional irrigation needs. Unmaintained, most of these ponds have reverted to boggy swales.

THE 40-FOOT FALLS. An example of Surry's precipitous drainage to the valley floor is this long-favored site, the waterfall of Merriam (Harvey) Brook. It attracted admirers winter as well as summer, in photographer James E. Harvey's day and in ours.

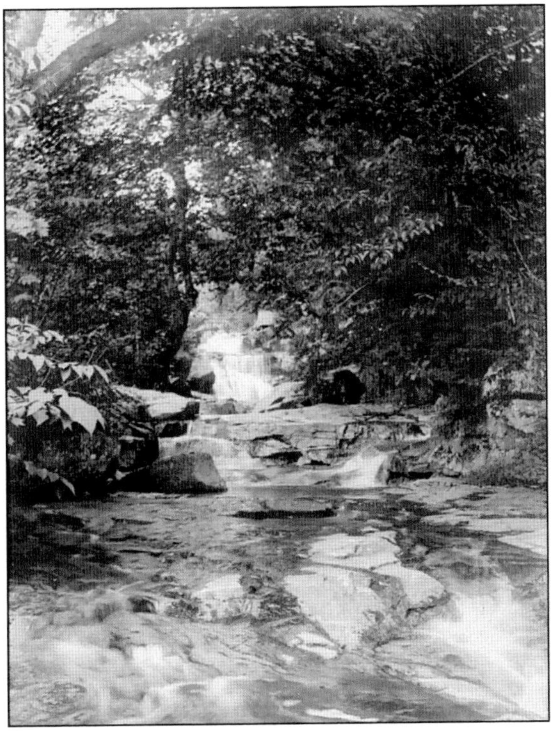

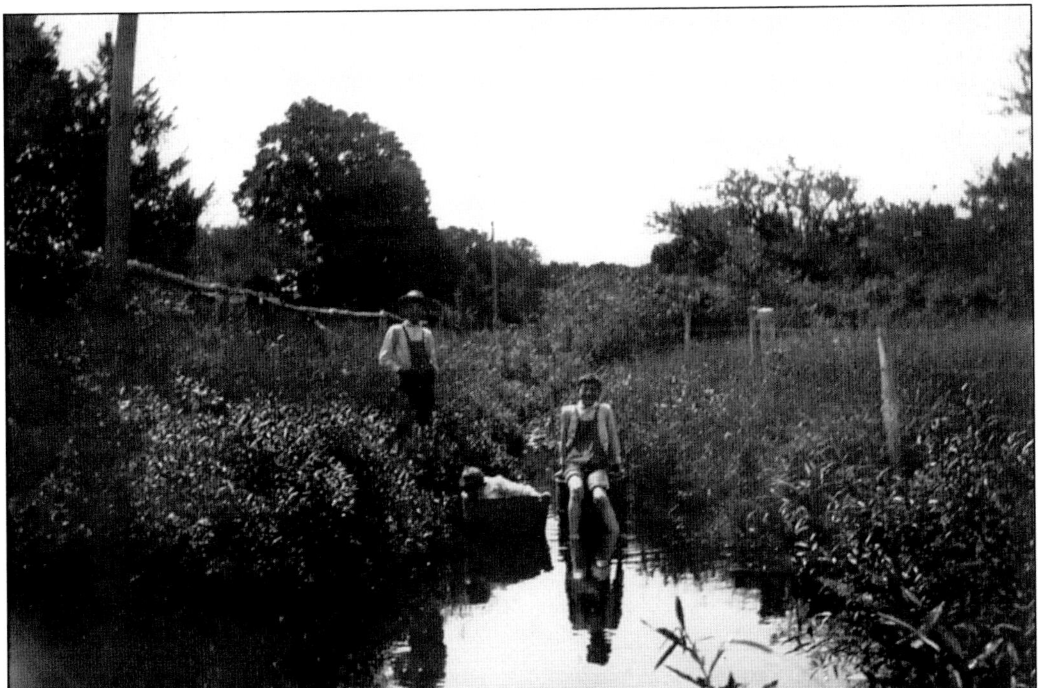

THE BOYS' LIFE. The biodiversity of a farm pond would often include adolescent specimens of *homo sapiens*, exploring for amphibians, reptiles, aquatic insects, and other treasures, and not above acting out the Moses in the Bulrushes saga recounted the previous Sunday.

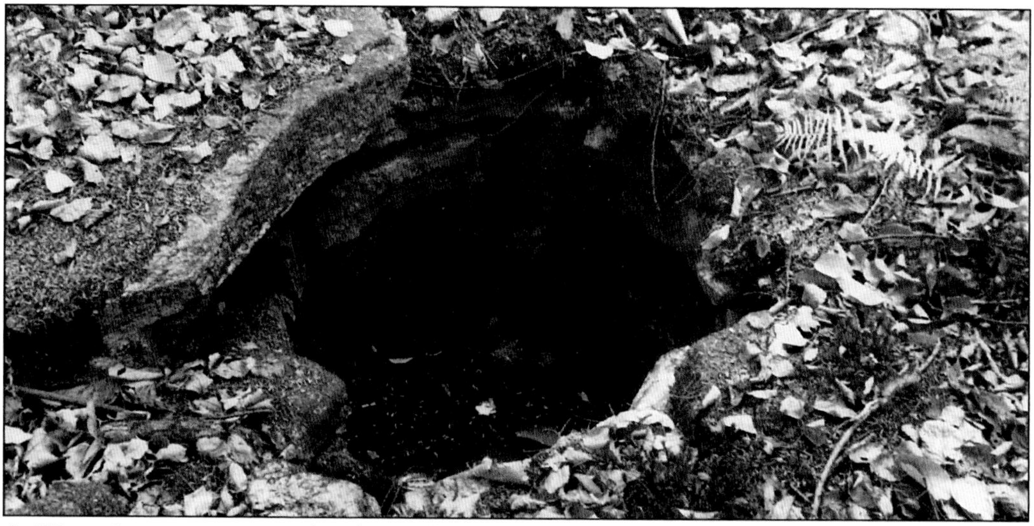

A Well. It is easy to regard a dug well as merely a hole sunken sufficiently deep to tap the water table. But homesteaders' wells are domestic works of engineering, with stone-lined walls substantial enough to withstand the tendency to collapse inward and the expansion-contraction forces of New England seasonal progression. Consider the artfulness with which this well (abandoned) attains closure for fitting of a stone well cap—all without a dollop of mortar.

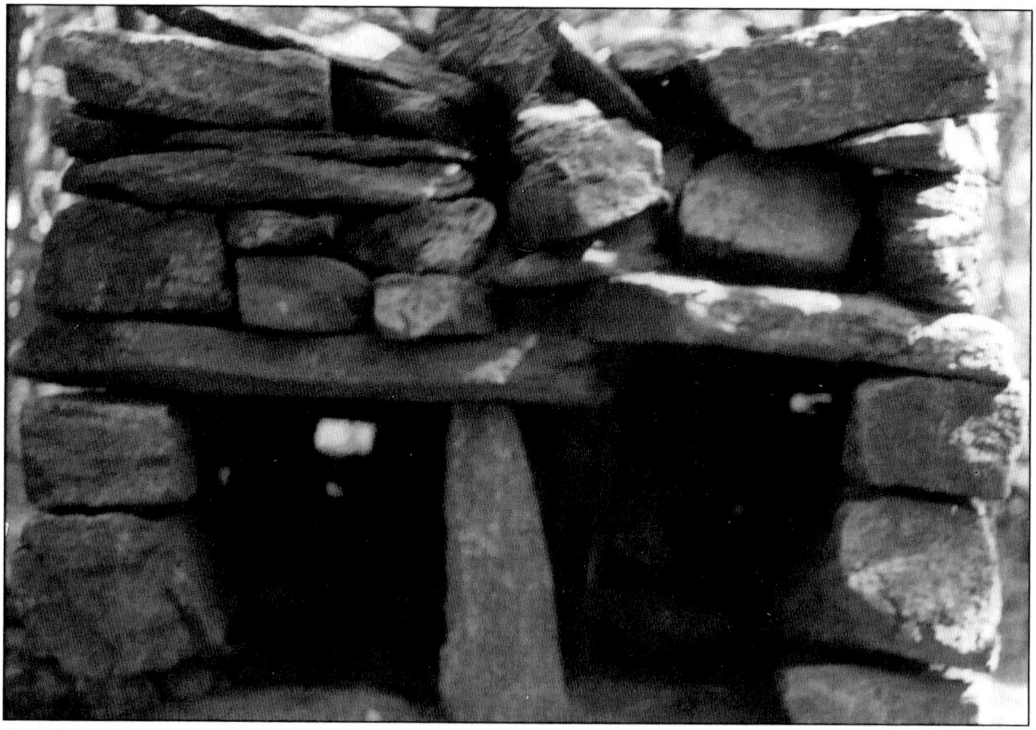

A Monument. On top of Surry Mountain are several stone "monuments," with varying accounts of origin. We find persuasive the tales of village boys carrying up a pair of stones each time they climbed the hill, providing the materials for cairn building. This one clearly took the shape of a cache for keeping fuelwood dry.

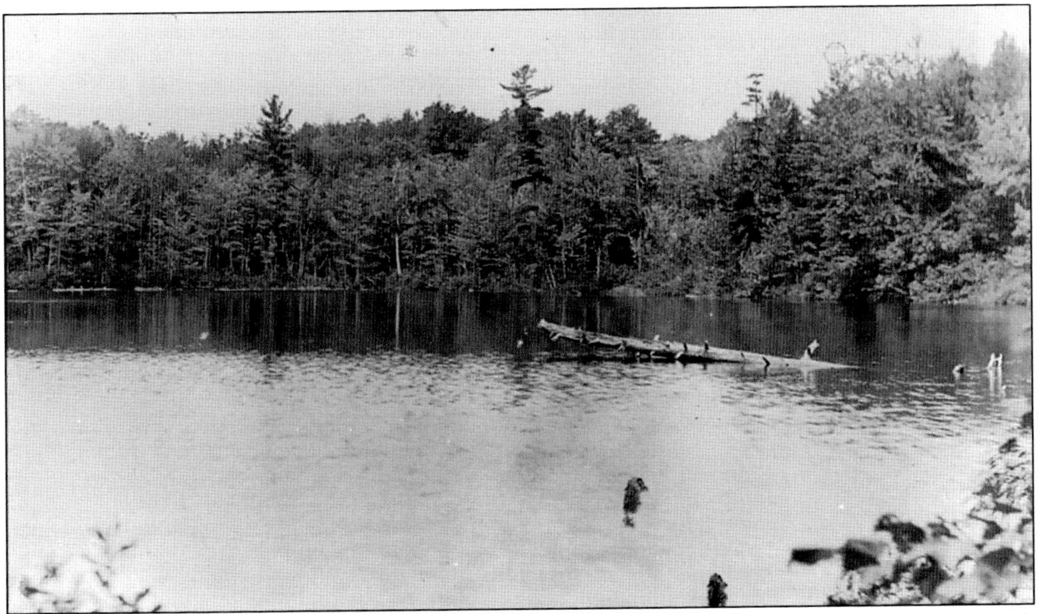

Lily Pond. The second most significant body of water after the Ashuelot River is Lily Pond. It lies unseen in a saddle atop Surry Mountain, more than 700 feet above the valley floor. The pond is a solitary tarn, ringed by a spongiform shoreline and a palisade of chisel-pointed trees, the work of generations of beaver.

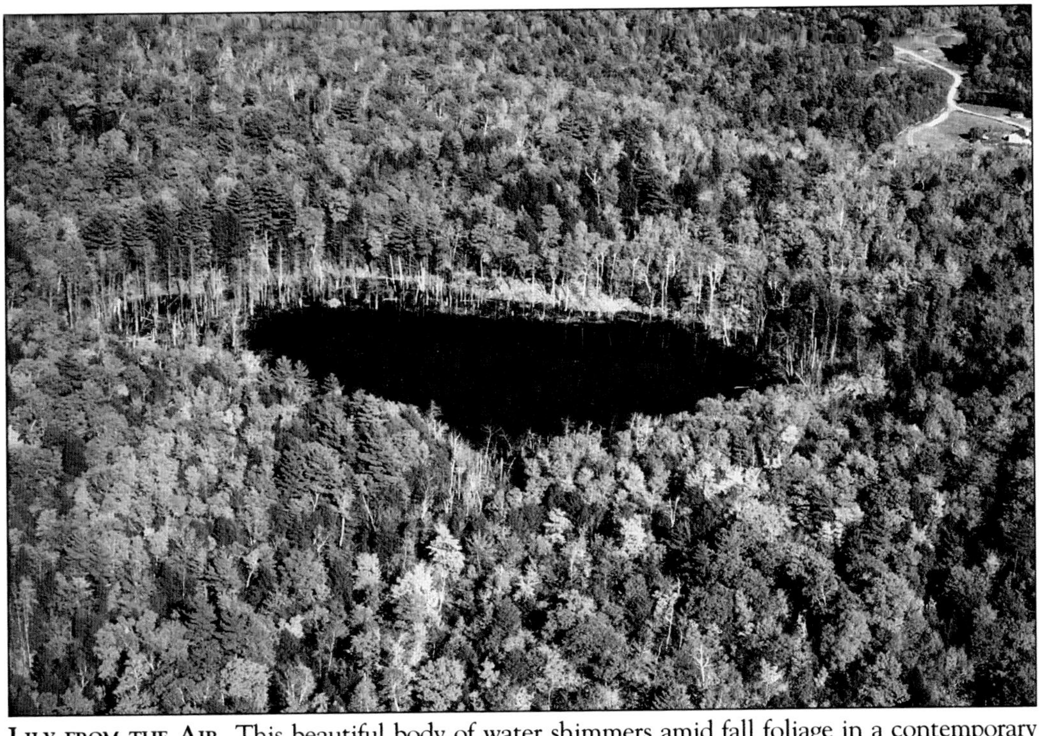

Lily from the Air. This beautiful body of water shimmers amid fall foliage in a contemporary photograph, a special place irrespective of vantage point. Spring fed from the ledges above, Lily Pond has an outlet that over centuries has sculpted other natural phenomena (following).

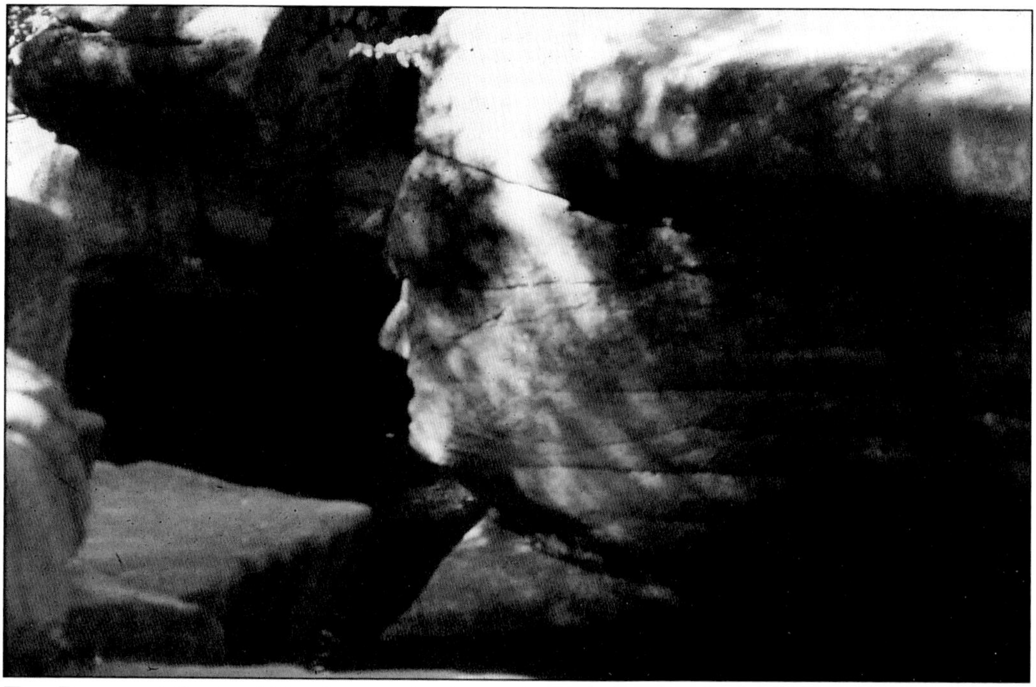

The Profile. Lily Pond Brook cascades down the western slope, washing and shaping Surry's own mountain profile. Unlike New Hampshire's "Old Man" at Cannon Mountain, this one does not require cabling and sutures to maintain its visage.

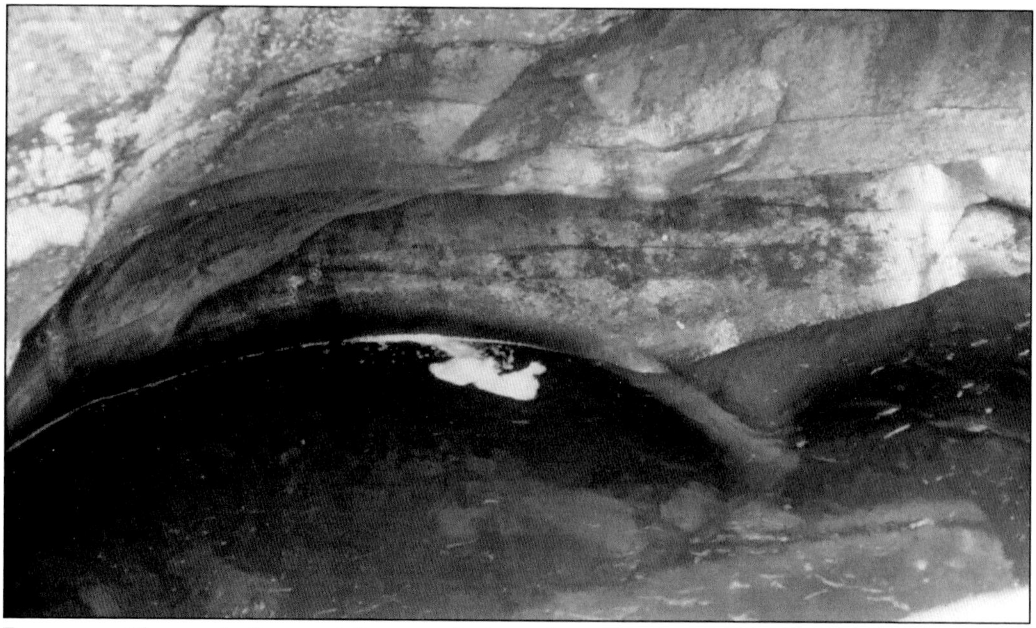

Potholes. The steady flows and frequent freshets that surge down Lily Pond Brook have etched a curious geological phenomenon of natural potholes. These are smooth, symmetrically shaped basins scoured out of the ledge walls and floor by whirling gravels in the torrent. Of the dozen or so potholes (best visible from the south edge) in the brook, some are as large as five feet deep and as many feet in diameter.

Two

PUBLIC LIFE AND LIVELIHOOD

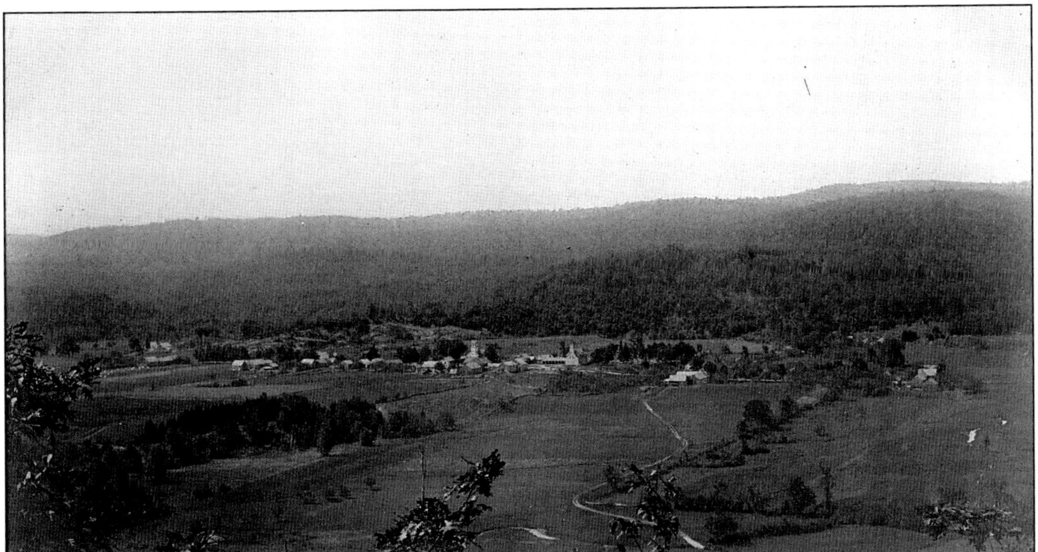

SELF-SUFFICIENCY. Surry in 1900, like most agricultural villages of northern New England, was in decline. Soils were thinning, and second-growth forests were becoming commodity woodlots competing with rail-borne timber from the west. Even pine, so useful as stock for containers (boxes, pails, firkins, and the like), soon faced competition from metal and cardboard products. Many children envisioned their futures elsewhere. Once-thriving taverns on the turnpikes had lost their patronage to the railroad, which now sped past Surry in minutes. Population, which stood at about 100 heads of households in 1850, prior to the Civil War, remained substantially the same at the close of World War I. Mining had been tried, and failed. The Ashuelot River had powered a few mills, but only the gristmills and sawmills had staying power. Artisans filled niches (shoemaker, tanner, wheelwright, carpenter, blacksmith), and those with education filled others (teacher, minister, librarian). Fields were returning to forest, and once-handsome homes were falling upon hard times. But if our vantage point shows a trend line of decline, James E. Harvey's images nonetheless show a town of proud self-sufficiency, of spacious houses sheltering generations through the rigor of New Hampshire winters, of industrious individuals forging lives of quiet respectability, with a place for sport and play. Behind every image is a natural world of unusual beauty and interest.

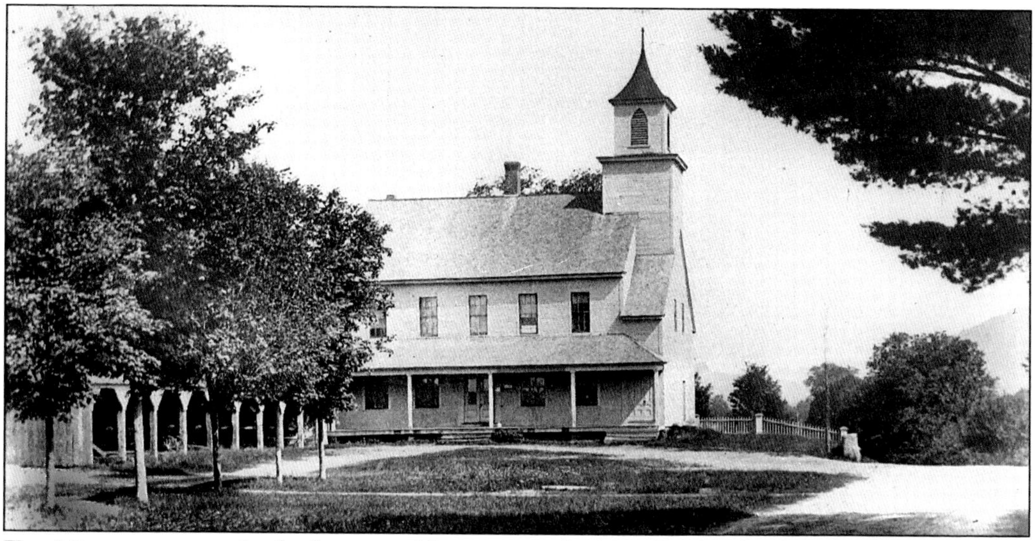

The Meetinghouse. As the largest public space in the New England village, the meetinghouse served both civil and religious purposes. Surry's meetinghouse, built in stages beginning in 1771, retained its dual identity through 1839, whereupon it served exclusively secular purposes. It is architecturally authentic in retaining the entrance in the center of the long side. (Meetinghouses that became churches generally moved entrances to the gable end to accommodate the preaching, rather than deliberative, functions.) Town meeting has been conducted in this building annually since 1772.

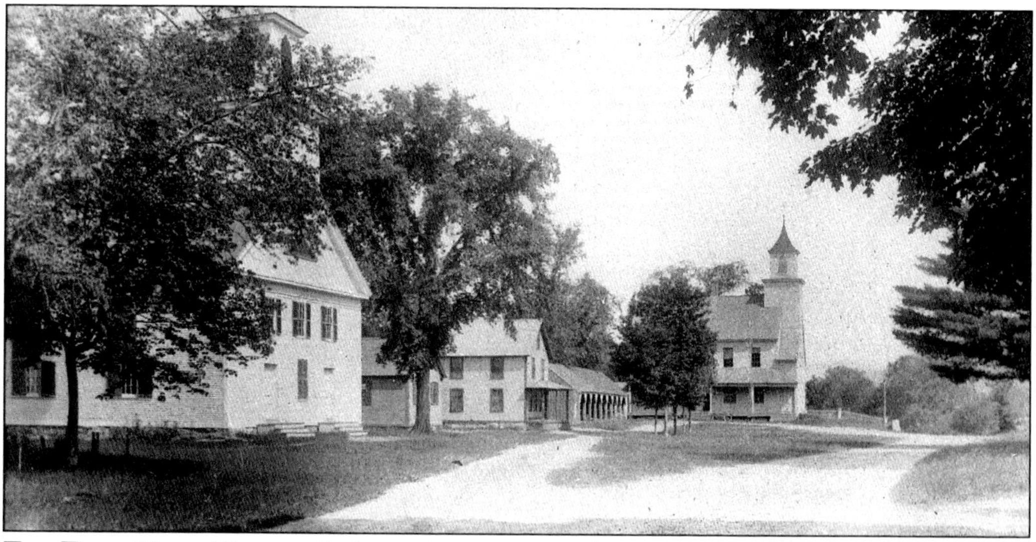

The Town Hall. The meetinghouse began its transformation into Surry Town Hall in the 1830s. In 1835, a two-stage belfry was added—a square base atop the east porch, surmounted by belfry proper with louvered lancet openings. Dr. John Thomson of Albany, New York, (see Reed Tavern, page 42) had commissioned a 30-inch bell to honor the village of his birth, and wished to have it installed by July 4, 1836, to celebrate the 60th jubilee of American independence. While the belfry was not ready to receive its 685-pound burden on the Fourth, its safe arrival in Surry was reason enough for a grateful and patriotic celebration. Interior renovations 20 years later completed the secularization of the building, as it added new uses such as village store, library, and gaol (British variation of "jail").

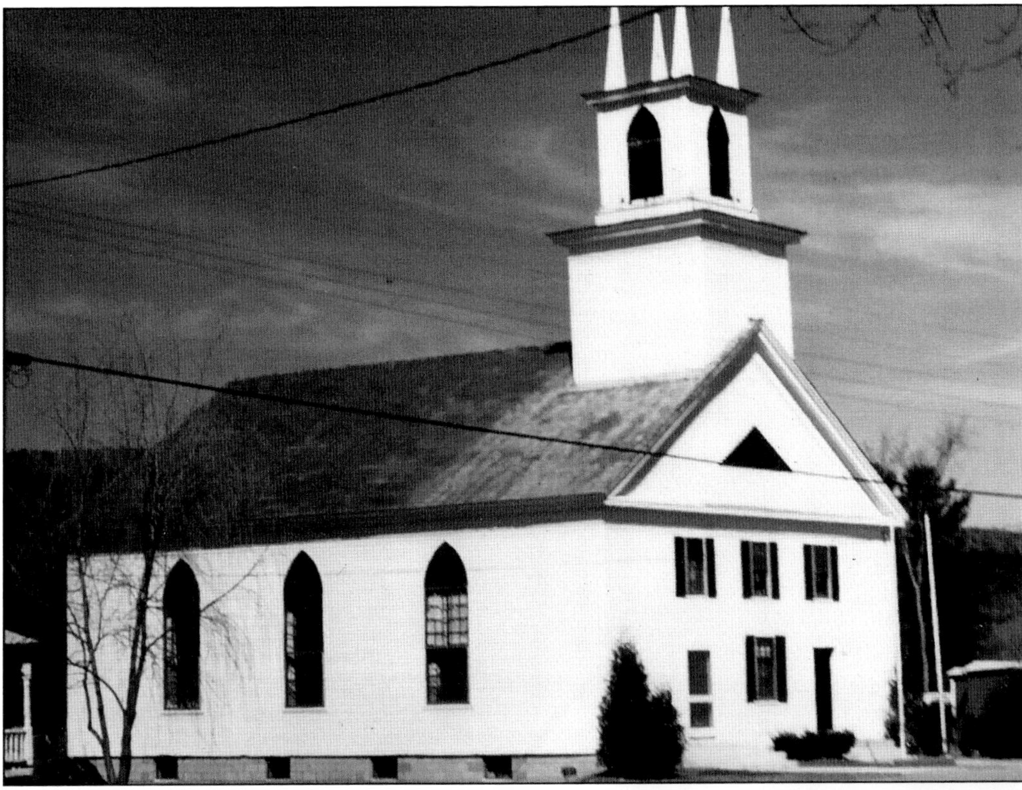

SURRY CONGREGATIONAL CHURCH ("CRANE'S CHURCH"). What permitted the meetinghouse to devolve into a municipal building was construction of a fine new Congregational church in the years 1838 to 1839. The effort was led by one Ichabod Crane, who provided both funds and labor to accomplish it. Like many early-19th-century churches in western New Hampshire, it employs Gothic Revival elements (lancet windows and belfry ventilators) on a Greek Revival base (pedimented gable facing the Great Road). The four-pinnacle steeple is less vulnerable to wind damage than a Wren-style spire.

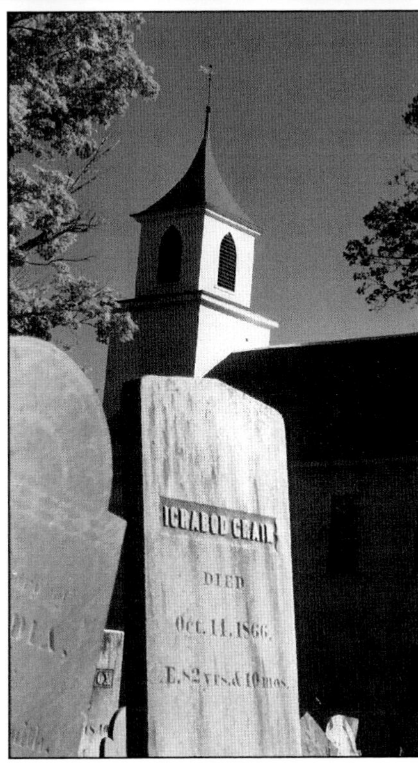

ICHABOD CRANE. Ichabod Crane (1784–1866), also spelled "Crain," was a farmer and lifelong resident of Surry. His father had moved here from Tolland, Connecticut, *c.* 1775, served in the Revolutionary War, returned to Surry, and raised a family of five, leaving the home farm to the eldest son, Ichabod. The latter had two marriages but no issue. An industrious and prospering farmer, Ichabod Crane invested in that which he fervently believed: congregational Christianity. Here is the resting place of Ichabod Crane, far from Sleepy Hollow, backdropped by the meetinghouse whose transformation he engineered.

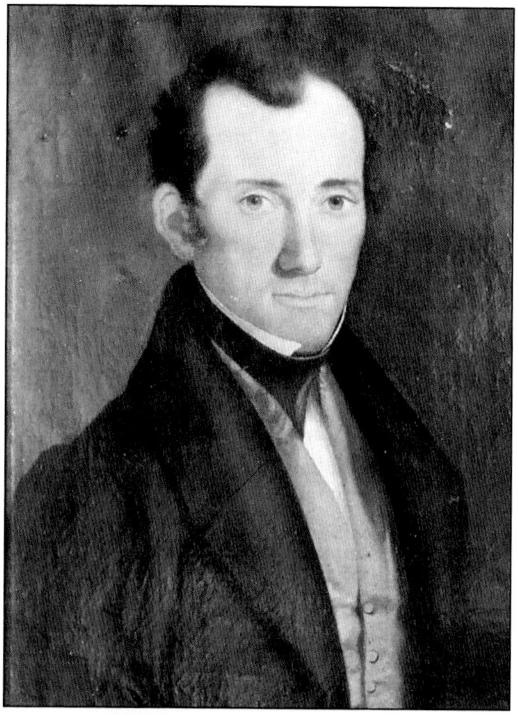

LOST AT THE ALAMO. Dr. Amos Pollard, born in 1803 in Westminster, Massachusetts, and reared in Surry (1808–*c.* 1828), had barely begun professional and married life when the lure of the frontier impelled him to travel to the Texas Territory to investigate land. He was swept up in the Texan struggle for independence from Mexico. He served as surgeon to the troops garrisoned at Mission San Antonio de Valero (known in American annals as the Alamo) and was one of the 180 men who died in its siege and capture (1836) by Mexican forces under Santa Anna. The Pollard portrait hangs to this day at the restored Alamo mission in San Antonio. (HSCC.)

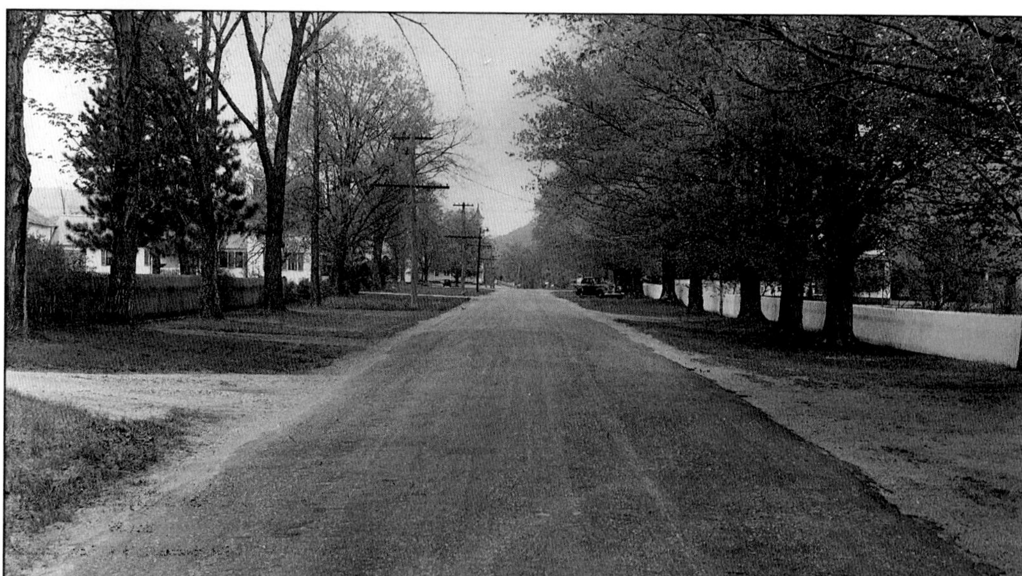

THE TURNPIKE. The Great Road that formed the primary axis of the town of Surry paralleled the Ashuelot River and Surry Mountain, conveying travelers north from Keene toward Alstead and Charlestown. At Charlestown's initiative, it was made an improved turnpike in 1804, and so operated through 1841. To operate as a stage road, it was widened to four rods (66 feet), straightened (as this 1930s image emphasizes), and enhanced by several taverns and hostelries, as later pictures demonstrate. Of note in this picture is Surry Town Hall at the left rear, with frontage fencing keeping livestock away from house yards, and a young elm tree victimized by Dutch elm disease. (HSCC.)

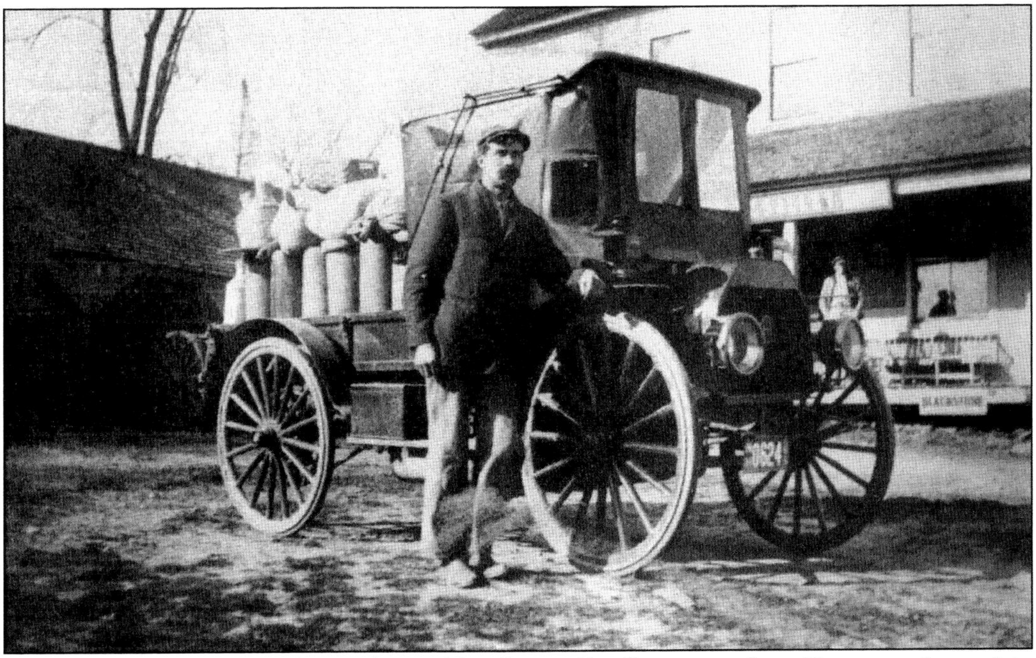

MILK DELIVERY, 1910. Sidney John Wilder drops off milk cans at the village store located in Surry Town Hall. The delivery truck has pneumatic tires, fenders, headlamps, running lights and running board, a gleaming radiator, and a state registration plate. Wilder lived and worked at the Holly Farm, near the old turnpike tollgate, before acquiring a farm of his own in Keene in 1920. He was one of nine children of Daniel Wilder, a Civil War veteran.

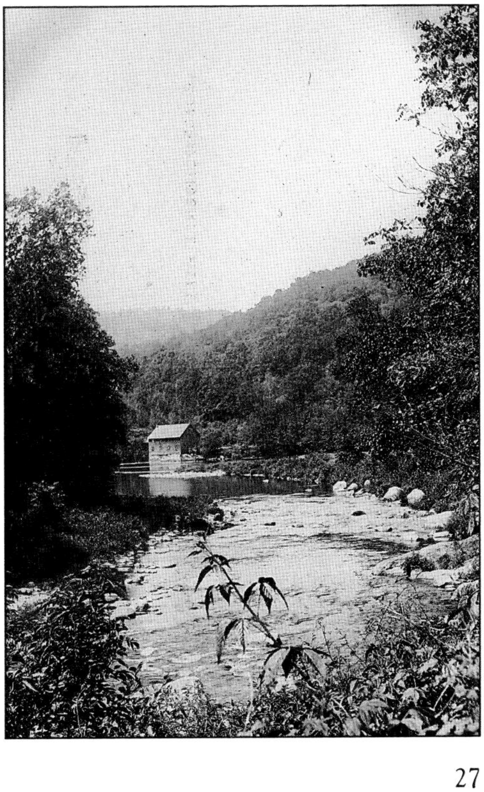

SCRIPTURE'S MILL. The Ashuelot descends more than 1,200 feet over its 50-mile course, but other towns had benefit of its principal falls for waterpower, notably Gilsum, Keene, and Swanzey. Surry's best site, where the river rushes down to the valley floodplain, supported a sawmill and gristmill throughout the 19th century. Built by Chaney and continued by Baxter, the mills passed to Harrison Scripture in 1865, who operated them for 35 years, upgrading with new applications in 1880, leaving his name associated with the site for living memory.

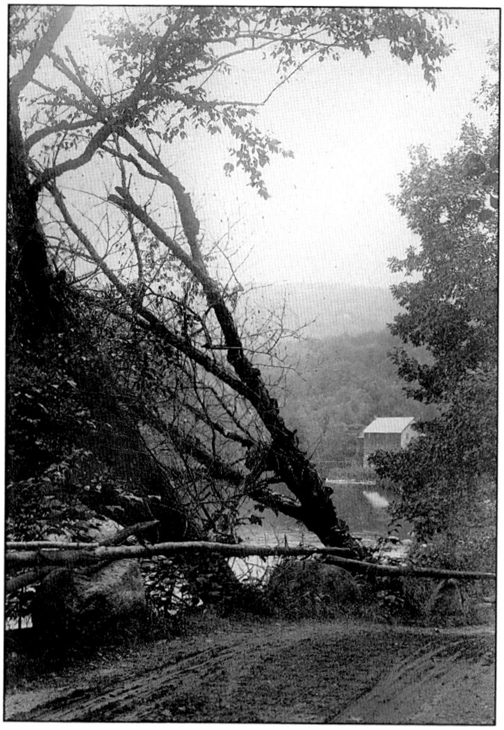

The Mill. Few images of the preindustrial world (that is, driven by natural energy, rather than combustion engines) evoke the romance of a water-powered mill. Photographer James E. Harvey frames the scene for us from a "scoot road" to the mill, with the simplest of guardrails to keep horse and human safe from the river's edge.

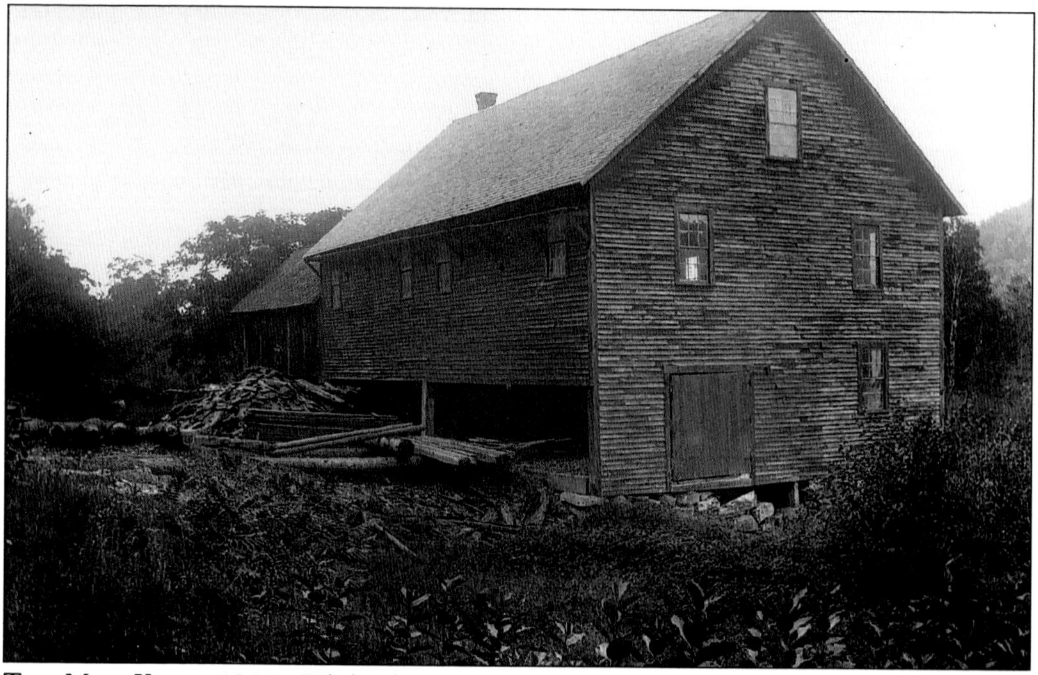

The Mill Yard, 1900. While the river provided motive power for actual sawmilling, considerable heavy labor was corollary to the operation. Raw sawlogs needed to be muscled about the yard prior to milling; finished timbers, staves, and slats needed to be removed from the mill and stored or readied for transportation. Here is the "inbox" and "outbox" of Scripture's "new" mill of 1880.

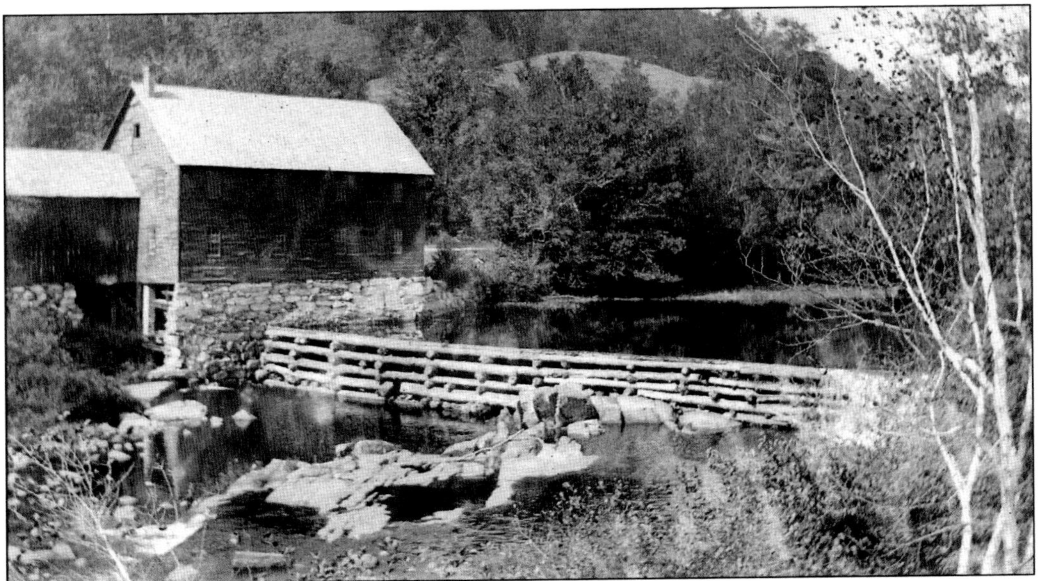

THE MILLDAM. Millers usually improved the fall by reinforcing, if not raising, the crest so that a dependable head of water was stored above the wheel in all seasons. These two beautiful pictures show the "sweat equity" that lay behind this vital community infrastructure. The dam is of log cribbing, with rock rubble anchoring the tie logs, whose butt ends face downstream. The dry-laid mill foundation is of quarried granite. A mill had to withstand not merely winter snows, like every homestead, but also the incessant structural reverberations caused by the wheel driving the application saws or stones. The worst hazards were floods and ice. The first might send the wheel amok or lift the building from its vulnerable perch; the second imperiled the foundations.

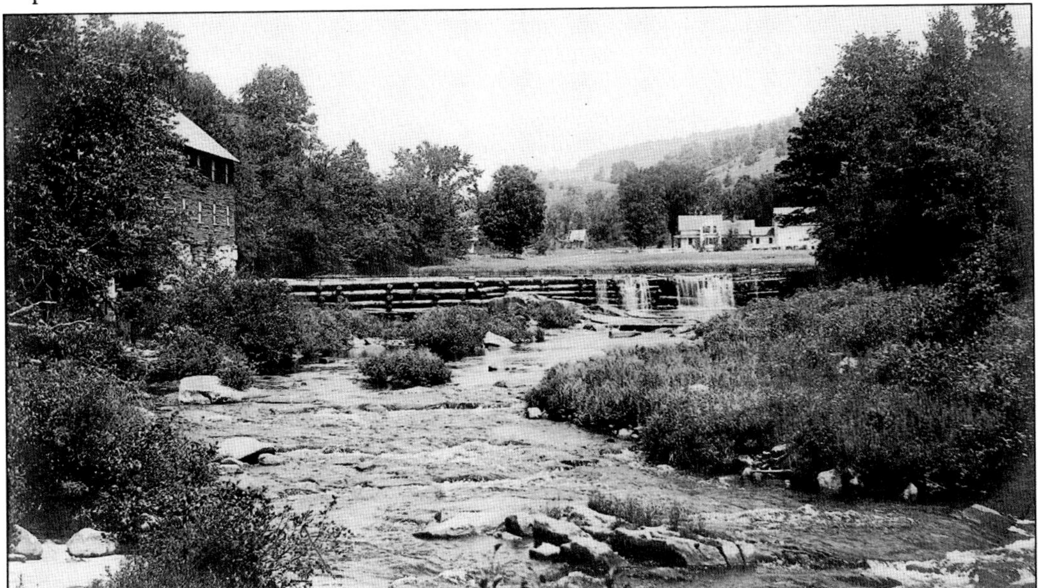

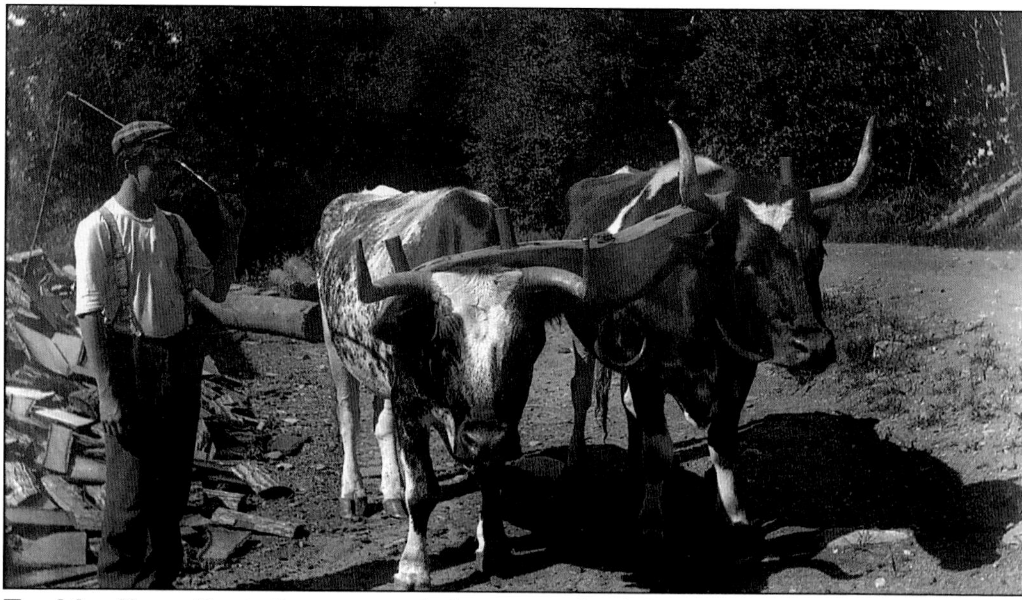

The Mill Yard. Harrie Scripture tends the oxen at his father's mill *c.* 1900. Notice the heap of hardwood waste behind the young drover and the larger logs beyond. Harrie Scripture farmed on family land into the 1930s, when he moved to Keene.

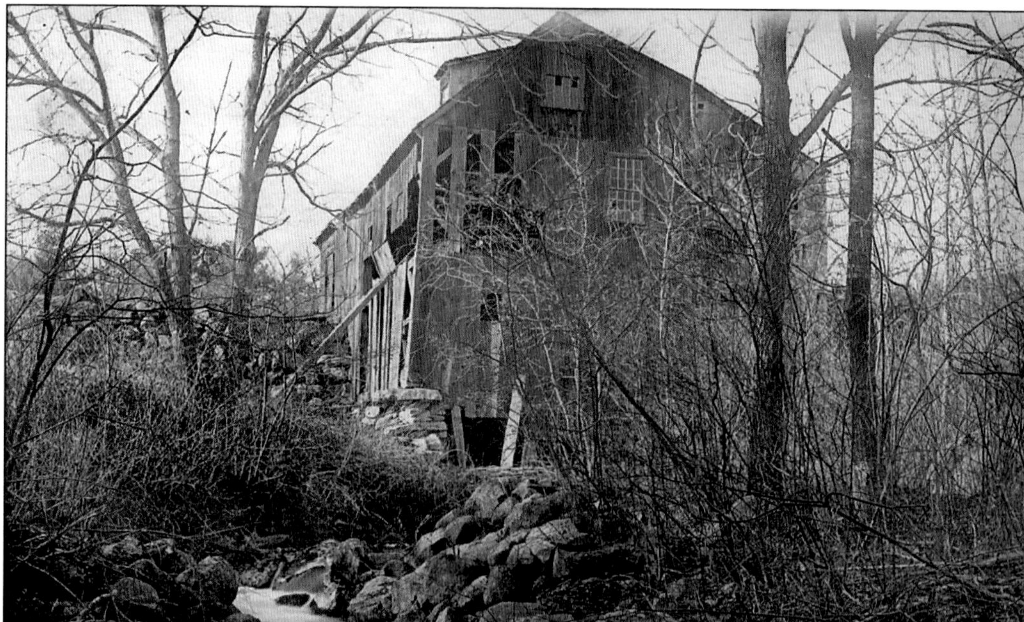

Better Days. Harrison Scripture fared well as a miller. To the original up-and-down saw of 1841 he added lathes and turning blades for fancier work when he rebuilt the mill in 1880. His business success earned him public trust for service as selectman, board of health officer, and state representative. Scripture's Mill fell to the hard winter of 1922, undermined by ice and crushed under snow load. Today nothing remains of the work performed at this site except for the timbers of many Surry homes, bearing the telltale stroke of an up-and-down saw, and the spindles, newels, and porch posts of the fancier equipment. (HSCC.)

THE SHINGLE MILL. Another woodworking operation useful to preindustrial communities is the shingle mill, in which logs are riven, rather than hewn or sawn, to make tapered shakes for roofing and, in other climes, siding. Pictured is that at Hollis Harvey's farm. On the right is a trestle to convey logs into the mill.

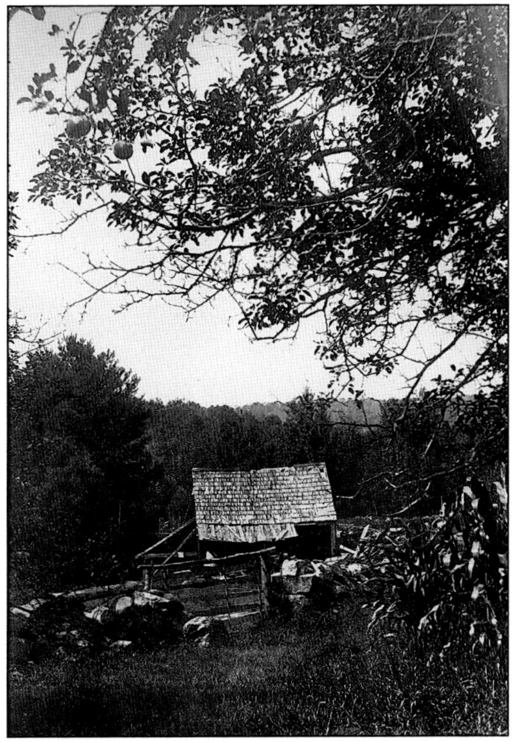

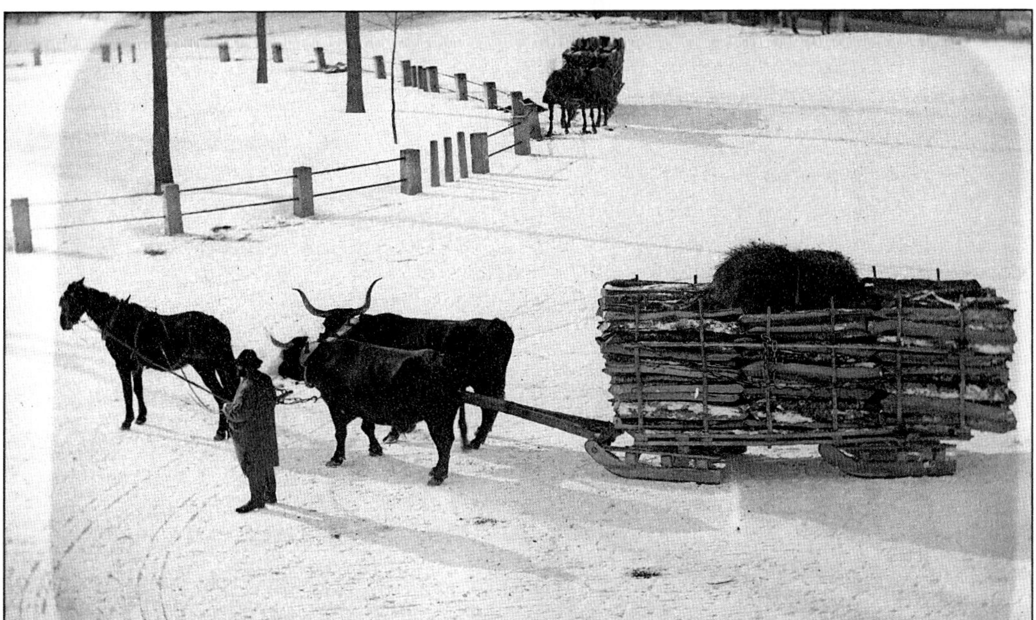

THE MASONIAN SKIDDER. Elijah B. Mason (1826–1908) has sledded a load of cordwood to market in Keene's Central Square. Kingsbury calls him the "last of the 19th-century yeomen" who carried on the trade, wearing a logo blue frock and cowhide boots. He worked at freelance logging with his brother Peter Mason, both men noted for short stature and unusual strength. Has he placed a lead horse in the same traces as two oxen?

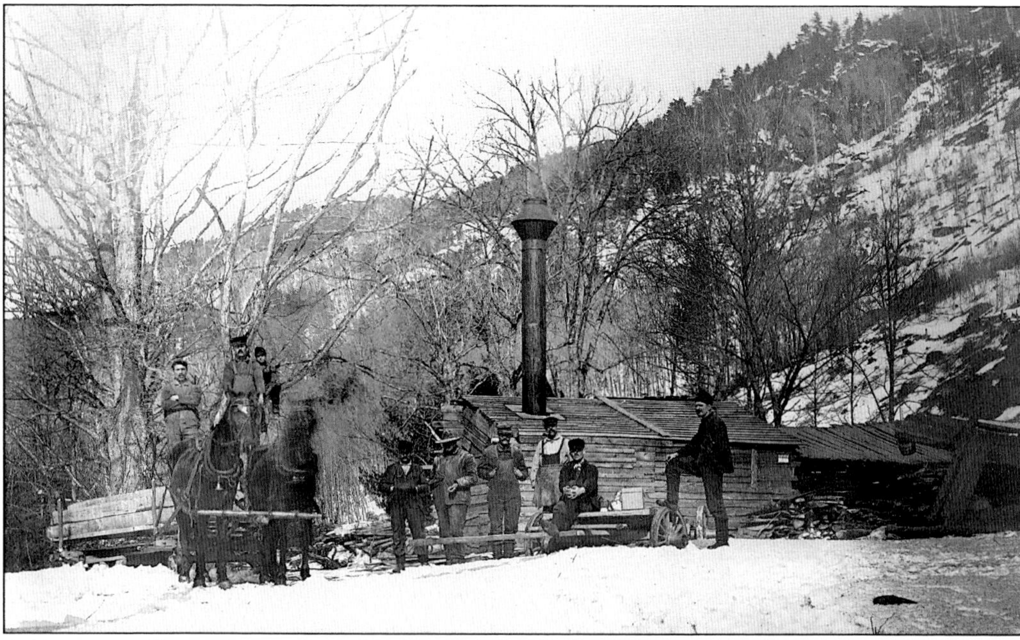

A Portable Steam Mill. Steam engines defined the industrial revolution, providing for the first time in human history an alternative to nature's energy (water, wind, thermal, animal). They found ready application in mines and transportation. Here is a steam mill at work on timber cut off Surry Mountain near Lily Pond Brook. The rusting hulks of such isolated mills can still be found today. (HSCC.)

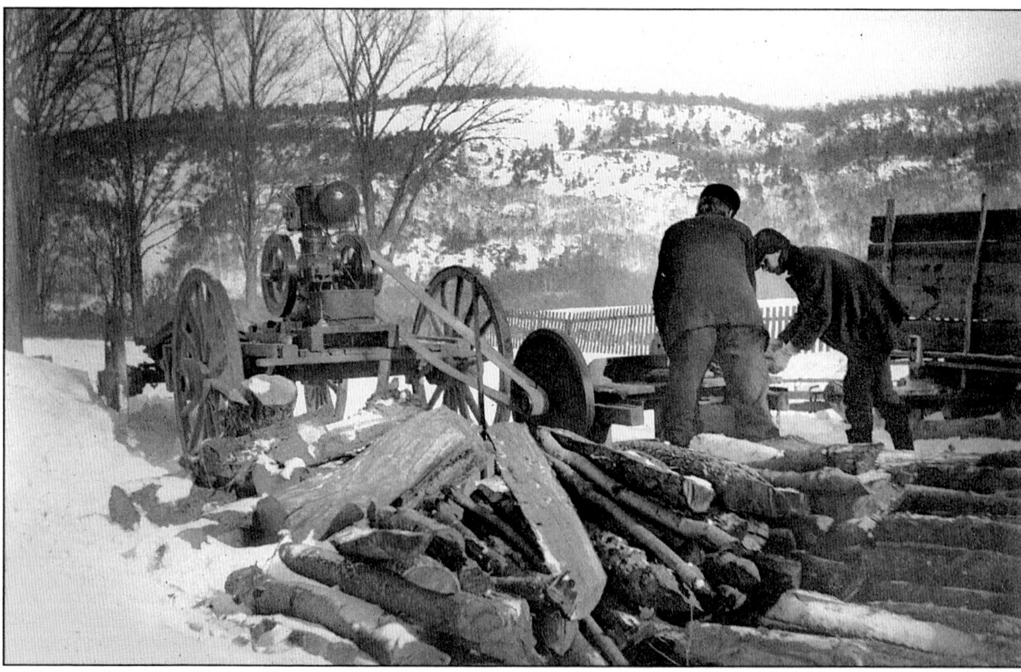

A "One-Lunger." Another application of internal combustion engines was to provide power for bucking up sawlogs into stove wood. This single-stroke engine put out one unit of work for every unit of input fuel and air, with the gratifying "lub-dub" rhythm of a heartbeat.

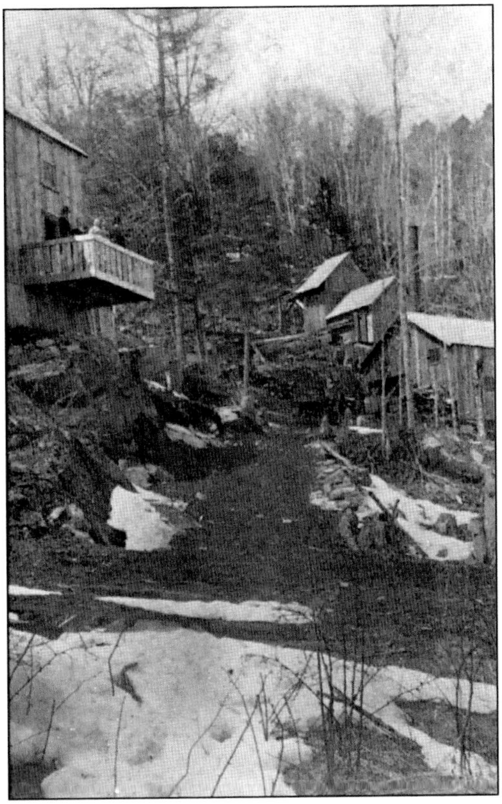

A Gold Mine. Surry Mountain was believed to have deposits of gold, silver, and other valuable minerals. The most ambitious attempt at extraction was that of the Granite State Gold and Silver Mining Company, incorporated in 1880. Infrastructure (access road, boardinghouse, and such) was built and a shaft sunk to 65 feet in 1881, and then to 80 feet in 1882. Some quantities of lead, copper, gold, and silver were smelted out, but never enough to sustain operations. Mining rights were sold in 1887 to pay deferred taxes, and these workmen of 1880 lost their jobs.

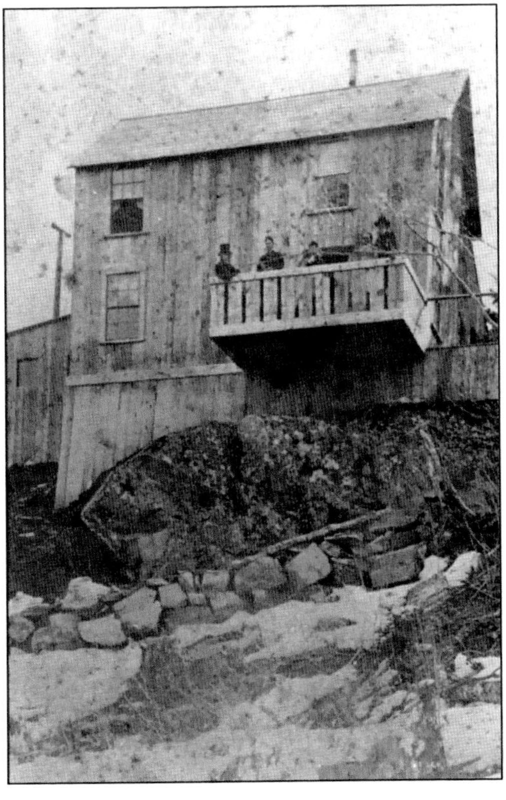

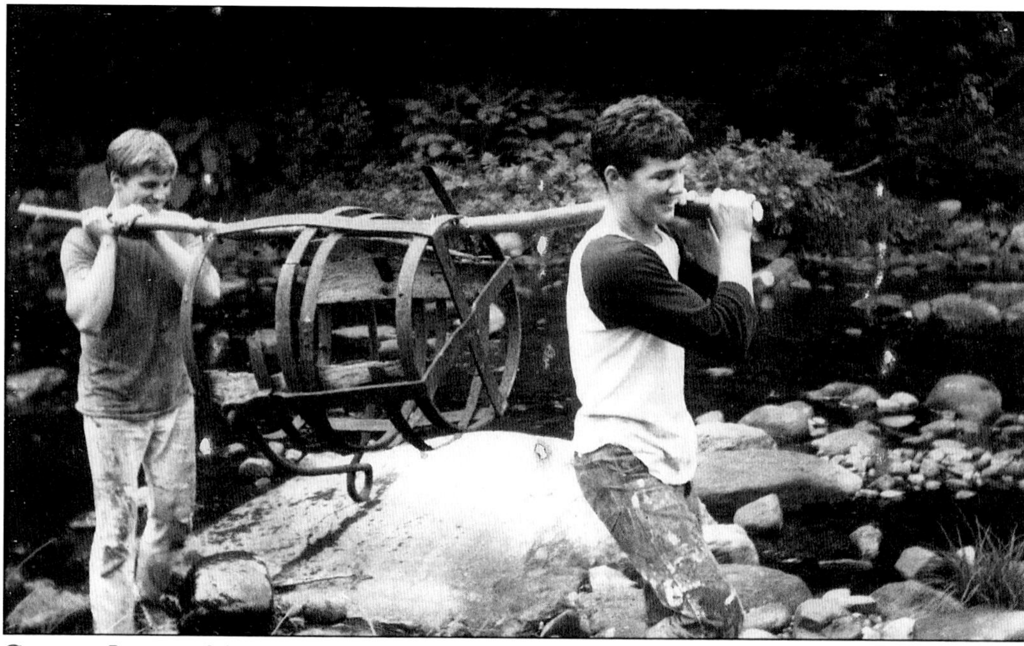

Glitter Litter. Mining operations often produce slag heaps, fouled streams, and other unpleasant byproducts. Since Surry mines never reached commercial scale, such aftereffects were negligible. However, a heavy-duty dredge bucket from the goldmine shaft was left behind, whose discovery led to this salvage effort in 1972 by Tad Lacey and Brian Tremblay. The oaken slats had rotted down to stubs, but the iron frame with wrought rivets can be revisited at the Historical Society of Cheshire County.

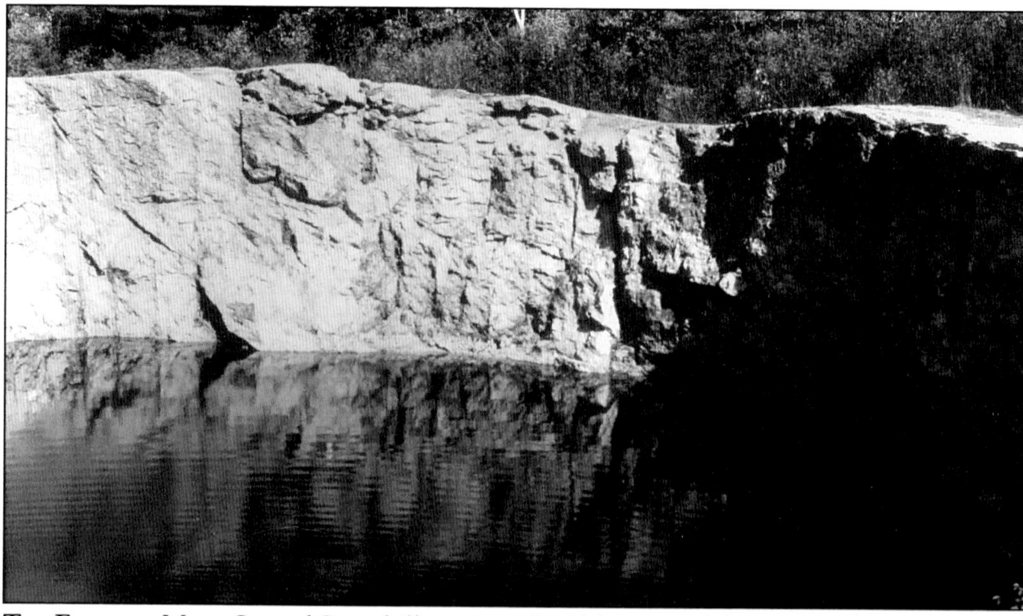

The Feldspar Mine. Several Surry hills were explored for mineral deposits, with resultant small mines still in evidence. Here, filled with water, is the quarry site of a feldspar mine on Carpenter Hill. A common constituent of granite and gneiss, feldspar was used in the manufacture of porcelain and glass. Other mines were located on Mine Ledge and Surry Mountain.

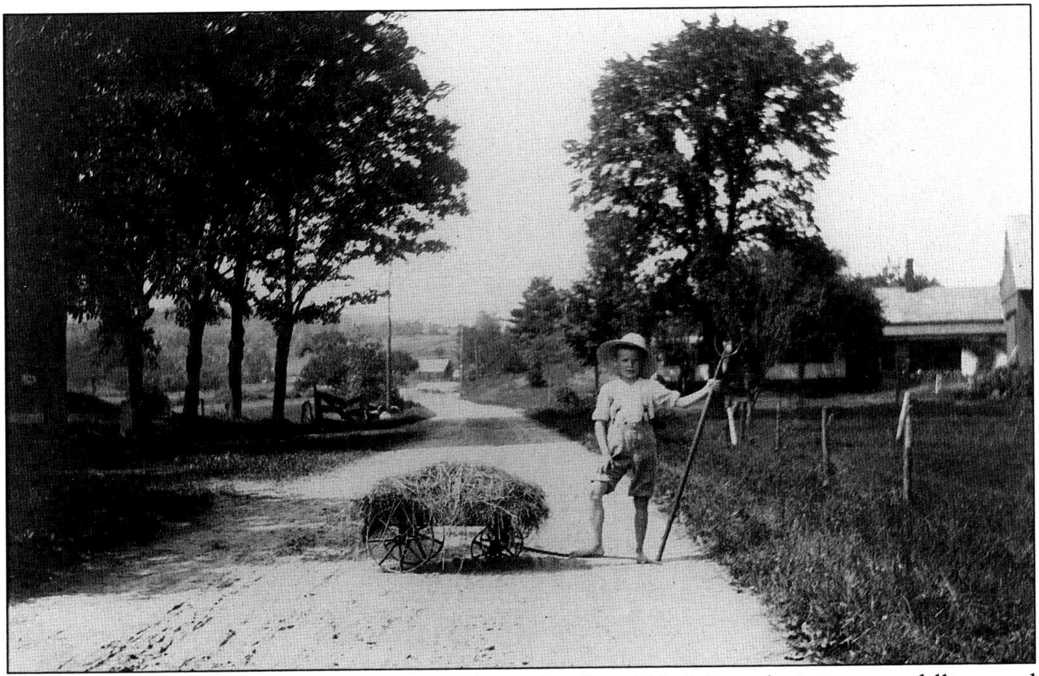

A Surry Swain. Not all of preindustrial life was hardscrabble labor of mining, tree felling, and subsistence agriculture. Play and sport were also present. Consider this rustic Neptune, trident hayfork cocked at a rakish angle, signaling a successful harvest being borne to port in his trusty vessel. The year is c. 1900.

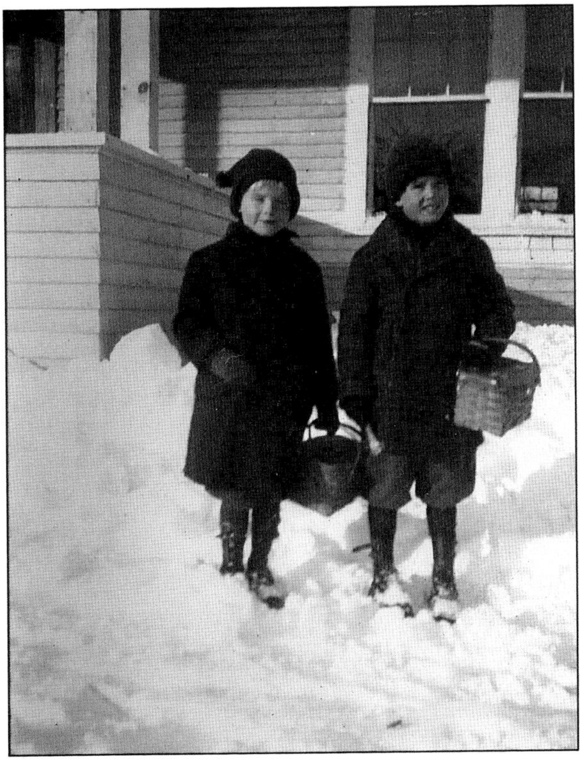

School Lunch? Two young members of the Stillings household set out for school on a sunny day following a snowstorm in 1915. Fred and Vint Stillings are well garbed, from boots to pullover caps and mittens. One wonders what is in those smart rattan baskets: bread and cheese? an apple from the cold cellar? or pencils, ruler, and lessons prepared the evening before?

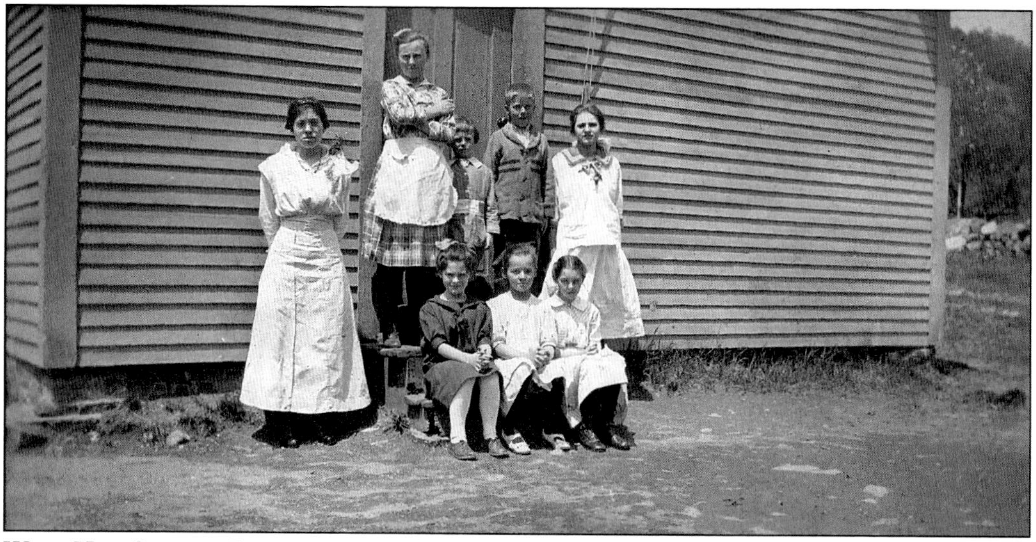

West Hill School, June 1917. World War I was grinding toward finality an ocean away, but lessons went on in the rural school districts of America. The seven pupils of West Hill School pose with their teacher in what is no doubt their respective finest for an end-of-year portrait. Identities are unknown.

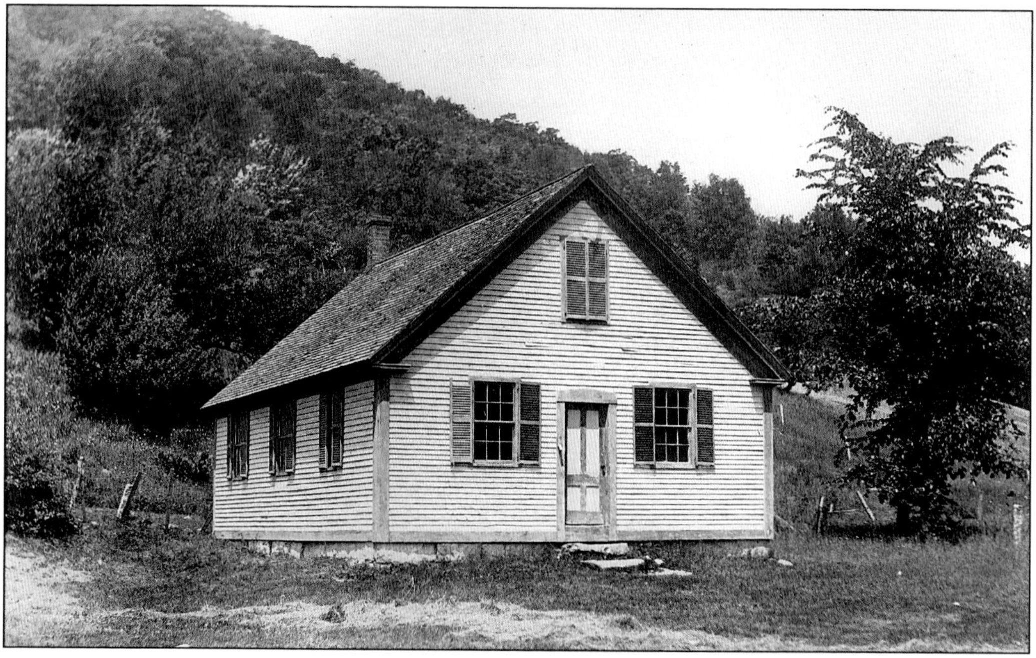

North End School. This modest district school building at Shaw's Corner, long since converted to private residence, once accommodated 56 pupils of all ages (1849). Perhaps its most distinguished occupant was Lewis B. Monroe, who taught here in 1840. The success of his *Monroe Reader* led him to found a School of Elocution in Boston, whence came Emerson College.

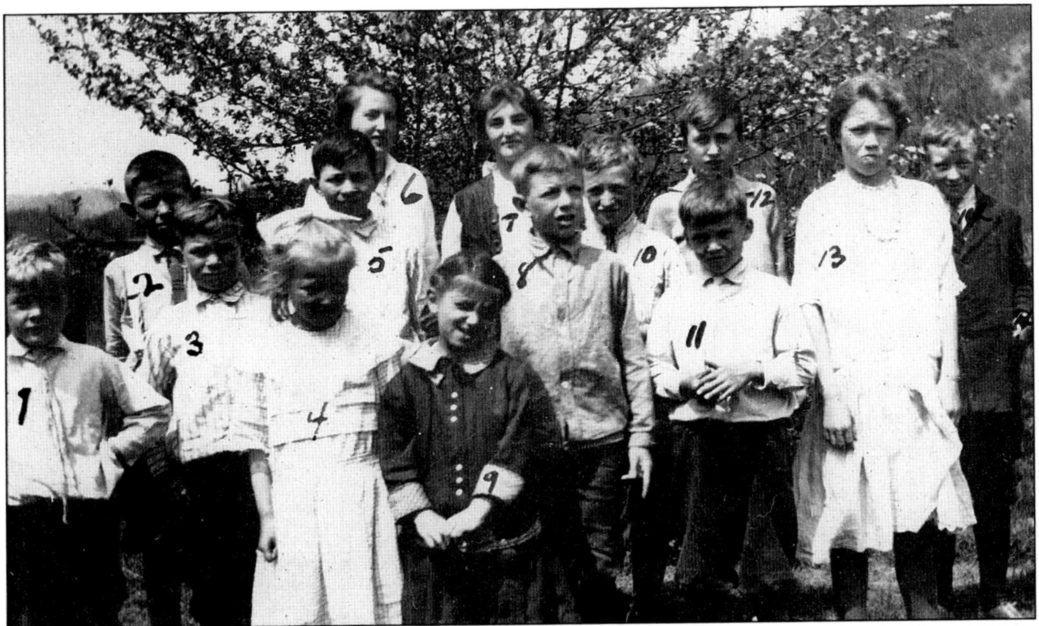

North End Scholars, 1915. Miss Merriam's pupils are identified in this family photograph: 1-Fred Stillings, 2-Alwyn Hodgkins, 3-Uno Lamminen, 4-Jettie Grout, 5-Evan Wilder, 6-teacher Miss Merriam, 7-Fern Goer, 8-Clifton Chambers, 9-Fern Buntlin, 10-John Grout, 11-Vint Stillings, 12-Francis Wilder, 13-Aimi Lamminen, and 14-Jessie Grout.

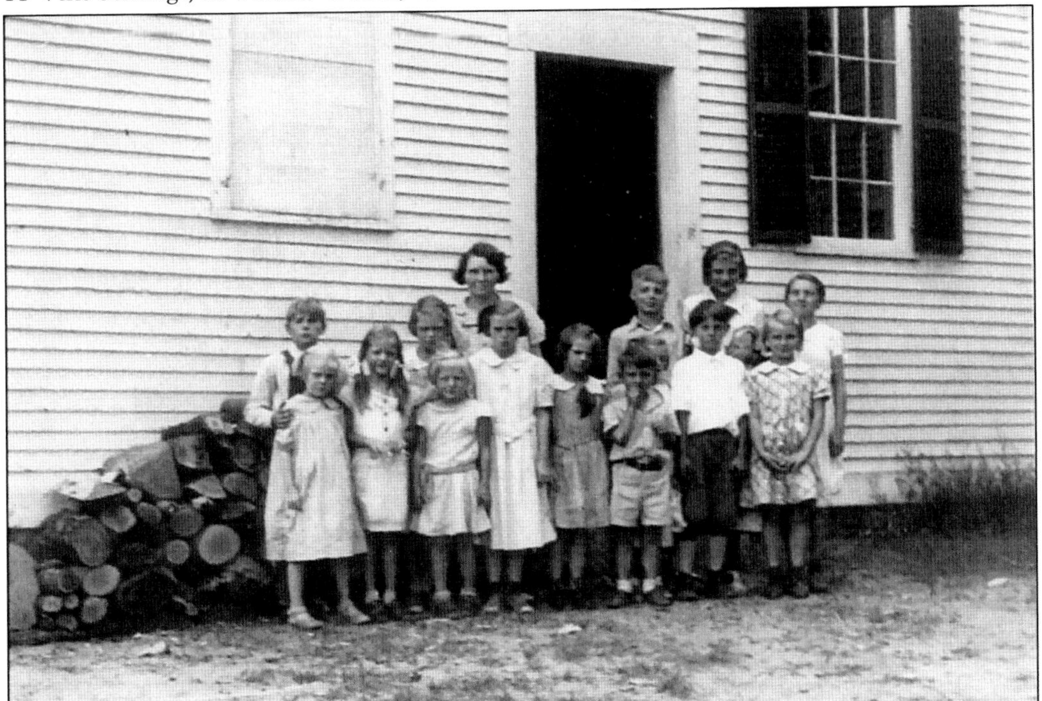

Village Center Scholars, 1930s. Identifications are incomplete, but Hugh Clark, Constance Young (Blewett), and Beulah Clark (Smith) are known to be in this photograph, along with teacher Ruth Connors.

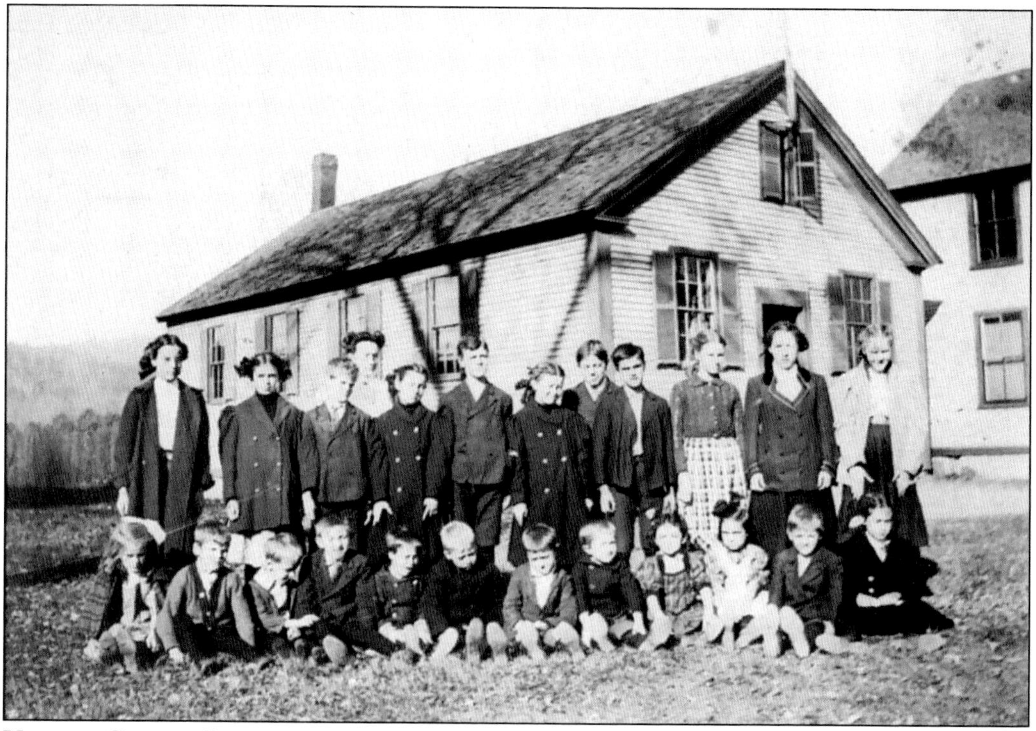

VILLAGE CENTER SCHOLARS, 1908. Twenty-three students pose calmly with their teacher, Alice Matthews, before their 1830 schoolhouse on a cool, sunny day in 1908. Mounted above the attic gable window is a flagpole. The flag was eventually lowered as the last class graduated, but the building enjoys an afterlife as private home on Route 12A. (HSCC.)

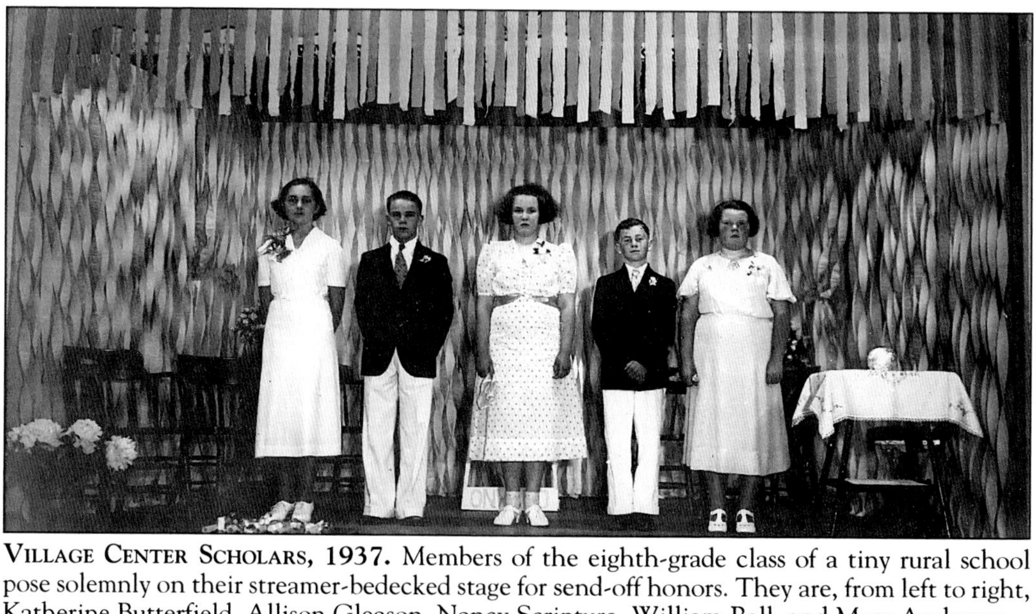

VILLAGE CENTER SCHOLARS, 1937. Members of the eighth-grade class of a tiny rural school pose solemnly on their streamer-bedecked stage for send-off honors. They are, from left to right, Katherine Butterfield, Allison Gleason, Nancy Scripture, William Ball, and Mary Anderson.

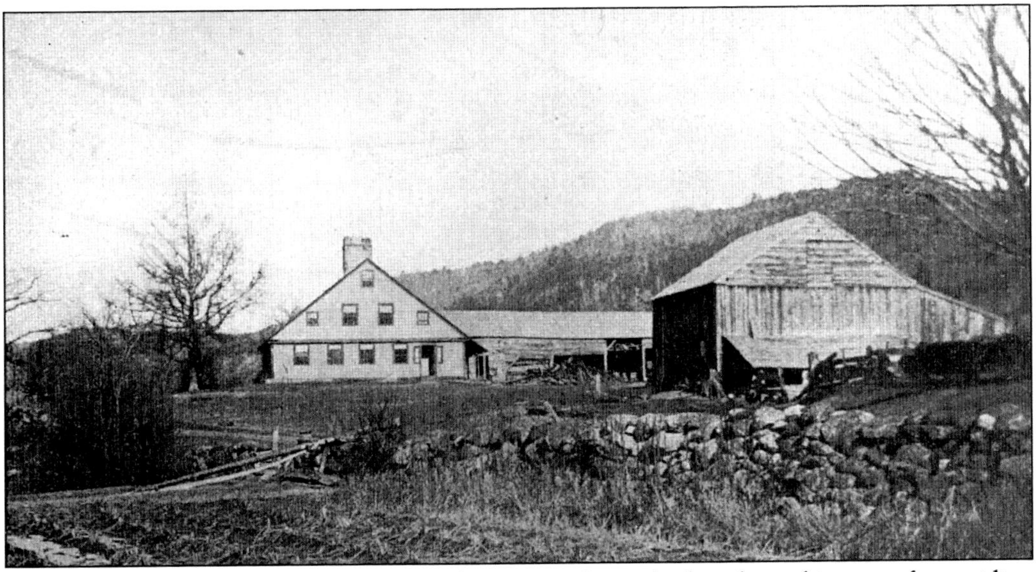

The Hayward Tavern. As a turnpike town, Surry had a long history of providing accommodation to wayfarers, whether gentlemen in stagecoaches or drovers herding animals to Brighton market. The first tavern license was issued in 1765 to Peter Hayward, who had just built this substantial center-chimney Cape with Indian shutters. There were more than 50 other public house licensees in Surry through 1850, at which point the newly completed Cheshire Railroad undermined the local hospitality trade.

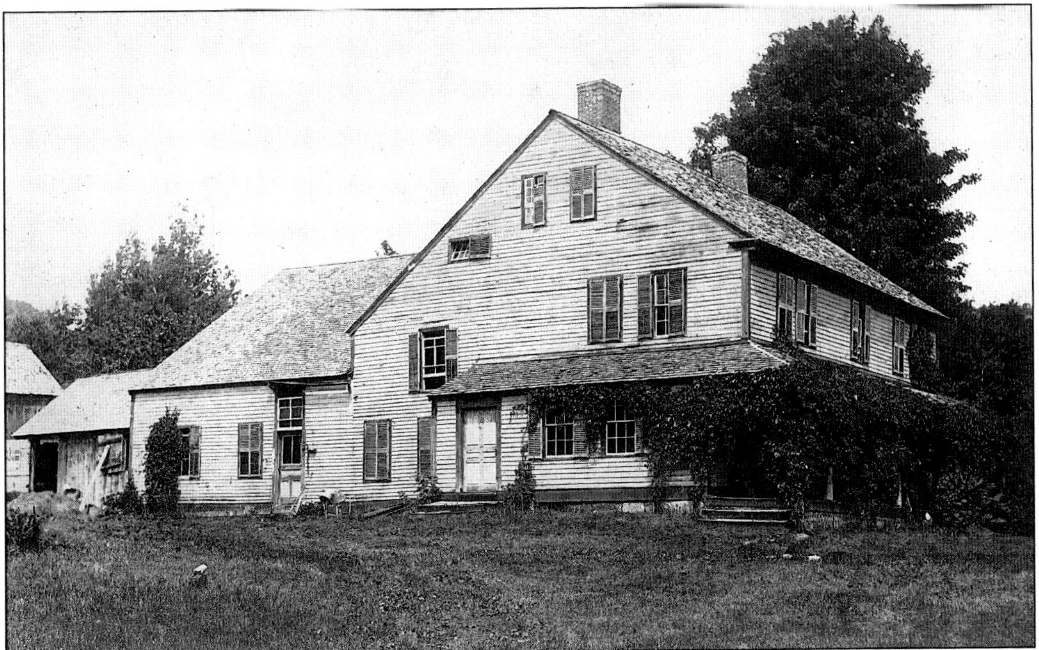

The Holbrook Tavern. The Holbrook Tavern operated at the north end of town from 1793 to 1860, earning appreciation for keeping supplemental teams of oxen and horses readied to assist in hauling heavy loads up the Alstead hills beyond (a practice that gave Trapelo Road in Waltham, Massachusetts, its name).

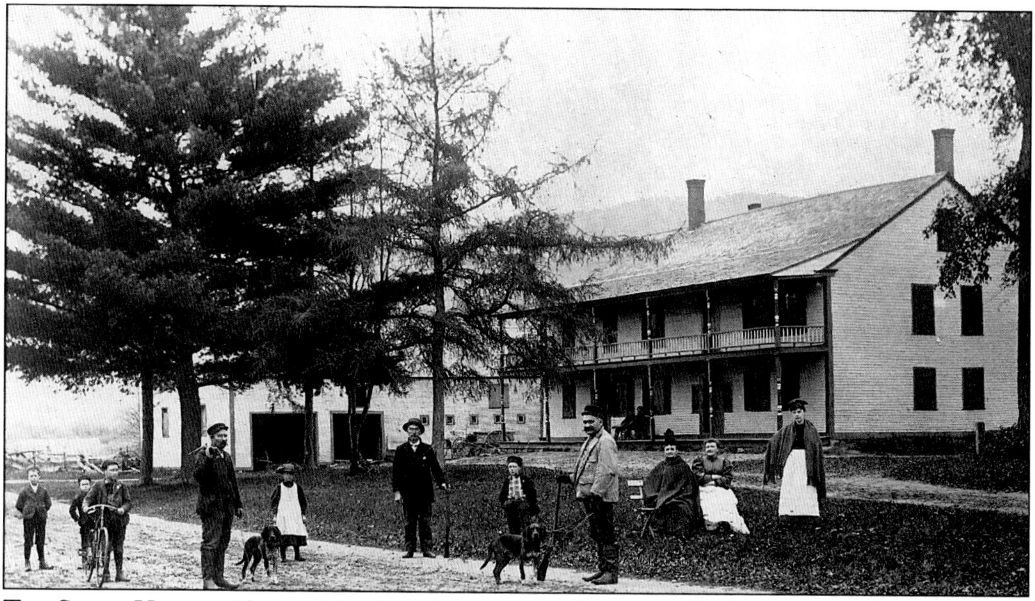

The Surry Village Hotel. This hotel was operated successfully for its first half century, less so for the second half. The Robinsons made a decent livelihood running it from 1793 to 1845, and their successor, Elijah Holbrook, used it as a springboard to the Cheshire House, Keene's premier hostelry. Once the railroad bypassed Surry of the patronage of wayfarers, the business was sold from one aspiring hotelier to another, until a 1907 fire destroyed all its buildings. Here, visiting huntsmen with hounds intrigue village schoolboys and staff alike.

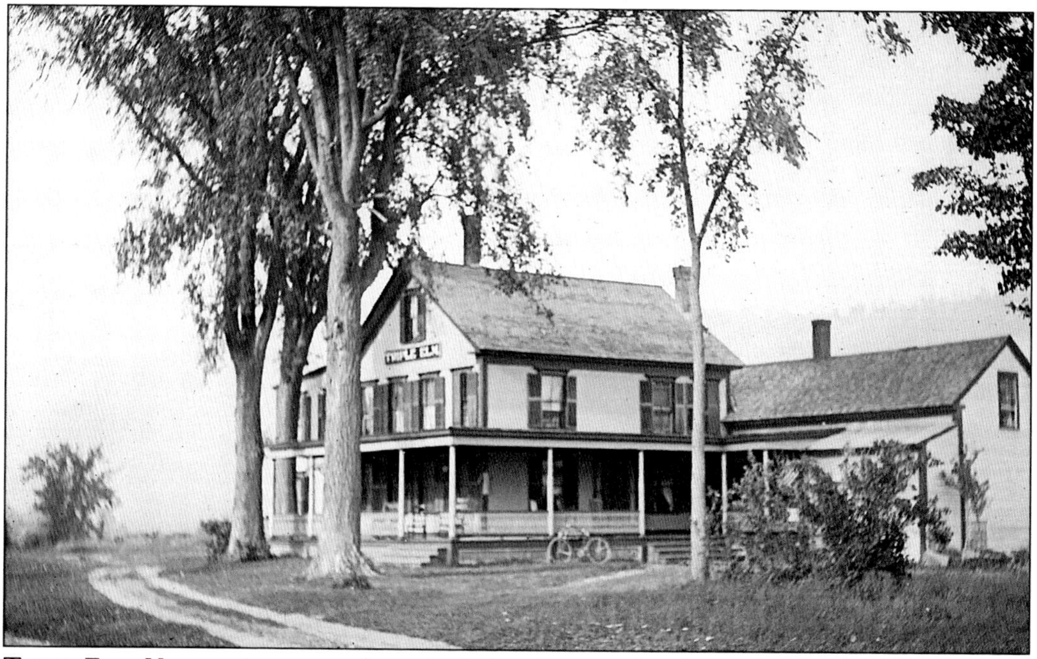

Triple Elm. Hope springs eternal, particularly when one has location. This home, diagonally opposite the town hall–village store and abutting the Village Hotel site, was opened by newcomer Erich Hans Raabe two years after the loss of the former. Triple Elm survived for five years and then turned into another village store under new ownership in 1920.

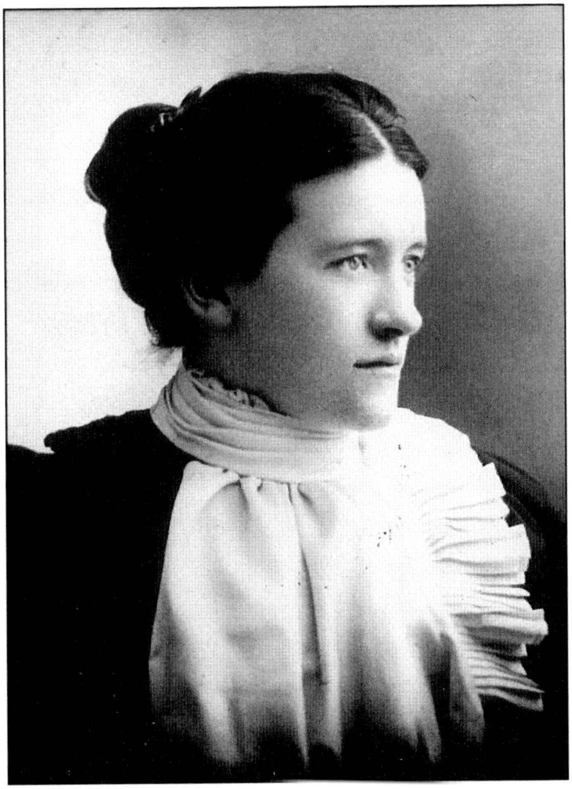

A NEWCOMER. Refugees from the potato famine in Ireland flooded American shores from 1845 onward. While many famously worked at laying rail during the boom years of railroad construction, others found opportunity in trade and commerce. Thomas Jefferson Kelly came to Surry from Connecticut in 1918 and operated Triple Elm as a general store in the 1920s. His wife, Rose Moran Kelly, the mother of his seven children, is seen here in her wedding portrait. She died in 1917 at age 41.

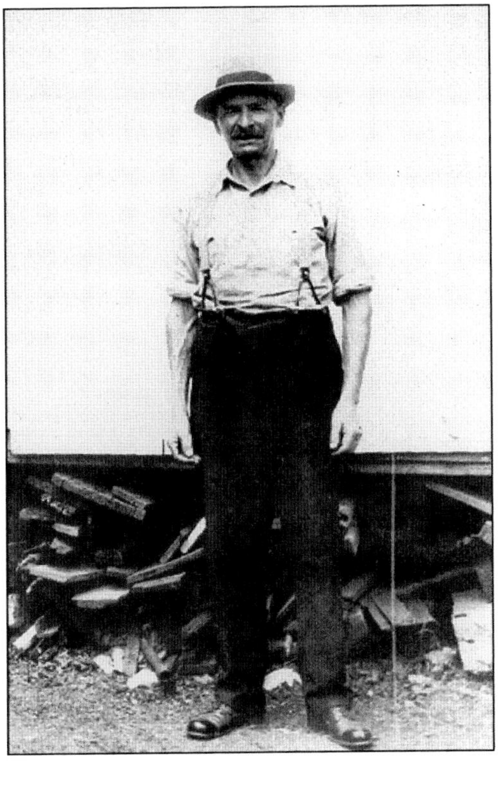

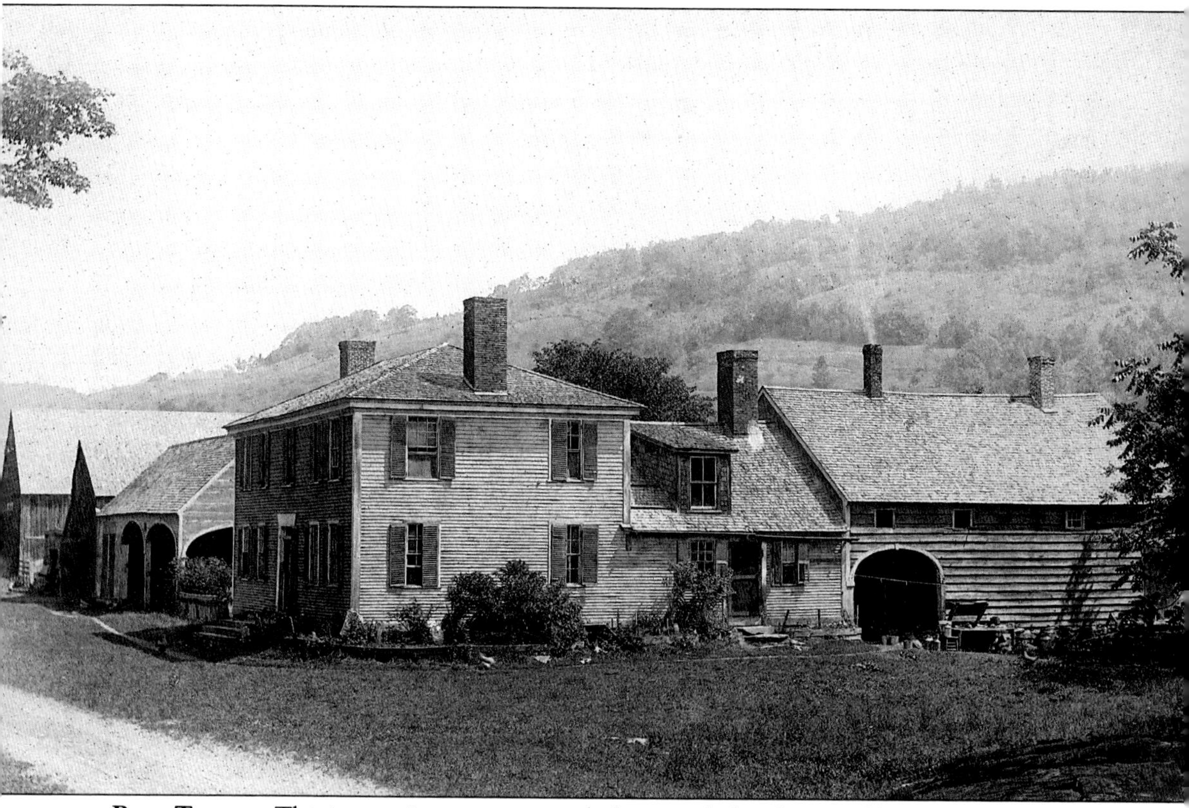

REED TAVERN. This impressive structure might be regarded as the crucible of Surry philanthropy. It was home to families of accomplishment who gave back to the town of their respective youth. Like the Holbrook Tavern, it exemplifies the unique New England style of "big house, little house, back house, barn," with especially fine carriage sheds enhancing this complex. The oldest section is the south-facing Cape-style ell with massive chimney (and added dormer). This was the childhood home of Dr. John Thomson, practitioner of a system of alternative medicine employing roots and herbs that was first developed by his father Samuel Thomson. The success of the Thomsonian system enabled him to commission the casting of a bell for installation in his home village on the 60th anniversary of American independence. It has hung in the town hall belfry since 1836. The hip-roofed Federal section of the house was built by Judge Elijah Knight in 1819. Knight served with distinction in the Revolutionary War, practiced law capably in Surry and in Vermont, kept inn, operated the first post office here for several years, and then moved to Keene, where he continued innkeeping until his death in 1842. Nathan Reed bought the property in 1864 and operated it as both tavern and post office. Despite losing his selectman's position over sympathy for the Confederacy during the Civil War, his kinfolk (nephews Charles and Gideon) remembered their birthplace with generous gifts creating the Reed Free Library. Gideon Reed, a diamond and pearl appraiser for Tiffany & Company, became Surry's first millionaire. Reed Tavern later became home to Ernest and Victoria Ball, whose beneficence is recognized in chapter 5.

THE REED FREE LIBRARY. C. Wharton Wilcox (1834–1919) was one of the five founding trustees of the Reed Free Library, along with George K. Harvey, Persis E. Harvey, Nancy A. Reed, and Dr. William H. Porter. This magnificent portrait shows the Emersonian New American: yeoman craftsman by day (he was a carriage maker), reader by evening, citizen by commitment. The library opened in town hall in 1881 with 757 volumes devoted to agriculture, history, mechanics, biography, and "useful" sciences. The freestanding brick library building was erected in 1932.

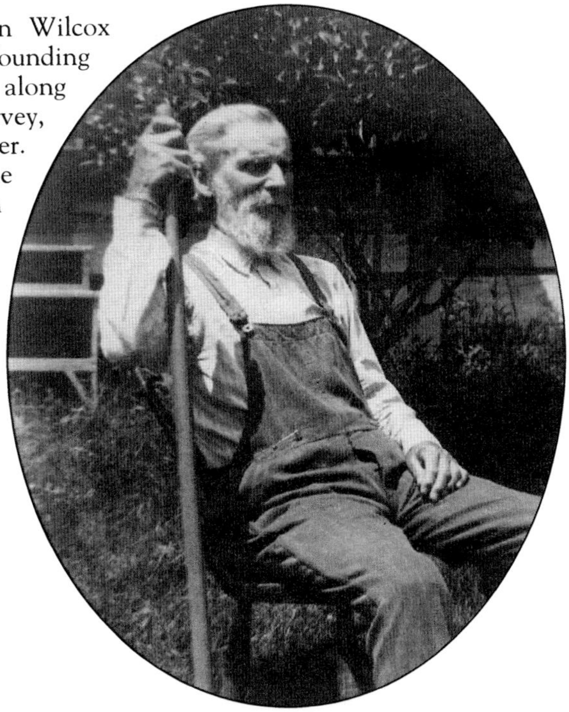

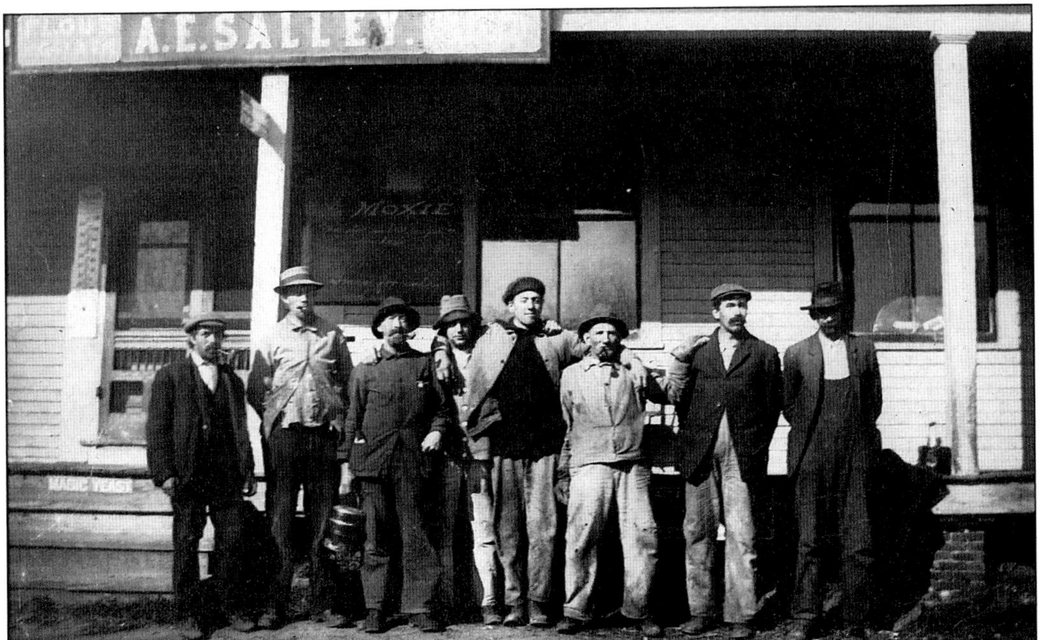

BOYS AT THE STORE, C. 1913. Here is a collection of Surry notables, all of whom are working for the state of New Hampshire on road maintenance, backdropped by Surry Town Hall in the guise of the general store, in this case, A.E. Salley's, selling flour, grain, Magic yeast, Moxie, and sundry other crowd pleasers. The "boys" are, from left to right, Fred Richardson, Anders Anderson, Herbert Webster, George Conley, Alba Wilder, Allen Green, Sidney Wilder, and Hollis Harvey. Salley, born in Kansas, operated the store from 1913 to 1918.

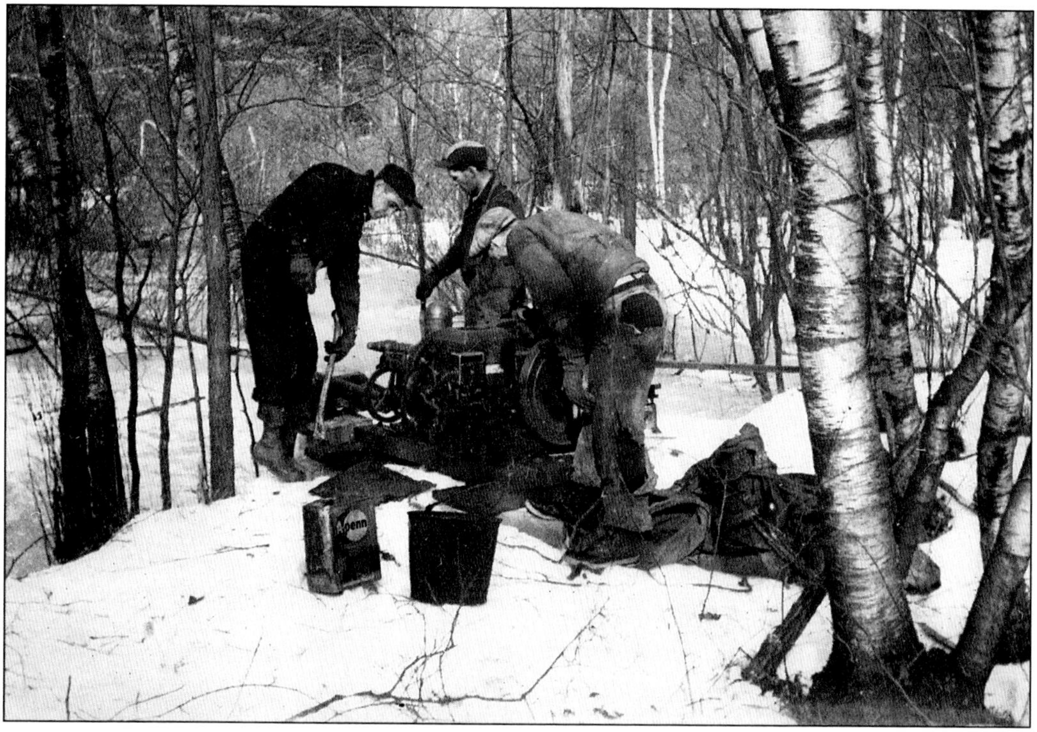

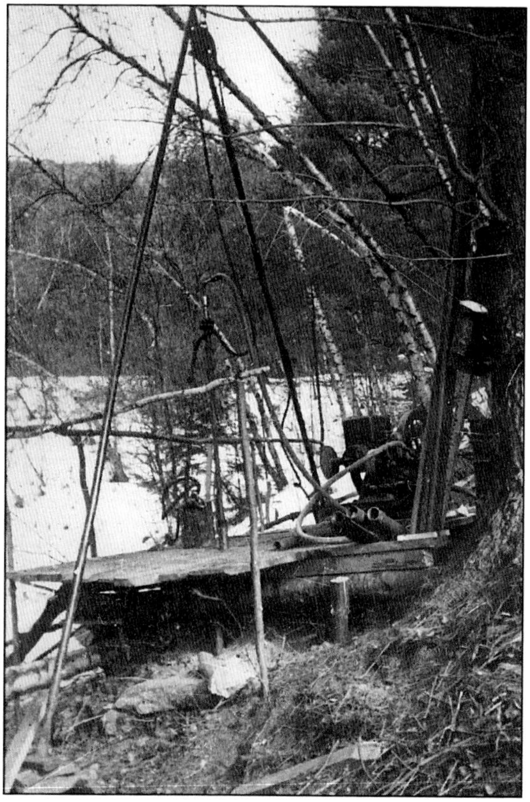

The Ice Harvest. Winter presents its own opportunities in the north country. Where skis, snowboards, ice fishing, and snowmobiling may predominate today, in earlier times it was the season to harvest ice, skid boulders to the wall, track game and set traps, buck up stove wood, and, at last, place taps for sugaring. Here at Green's Pond, Fred, Vint, and William Stillings fuss over their ice-cutting machine (above) and proudly document their pond-side winch for lifting out block (below).

CORN! Hollis and Minnie Harvey flaunt their prairie-quality cornstalks in this 1910 photograph. That such growth could be achieved in New England a generation before manufactured fertilizers denotes the tilth, fertility, and general soil health we have forfeited since 1900.

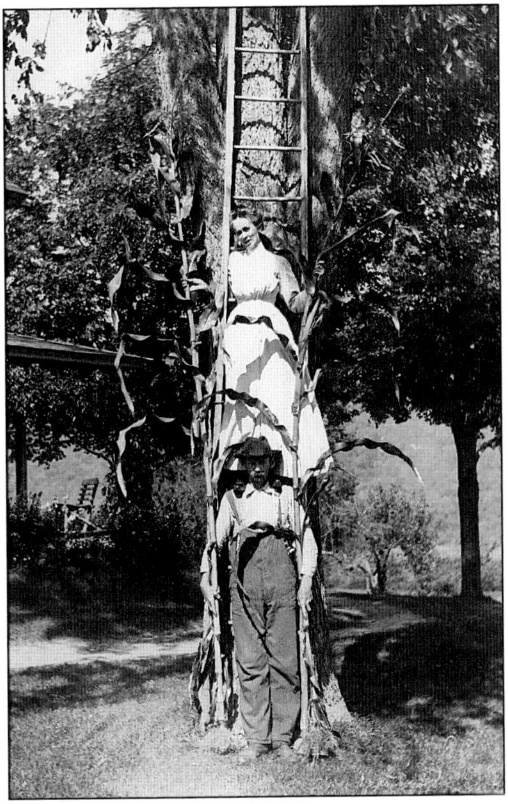

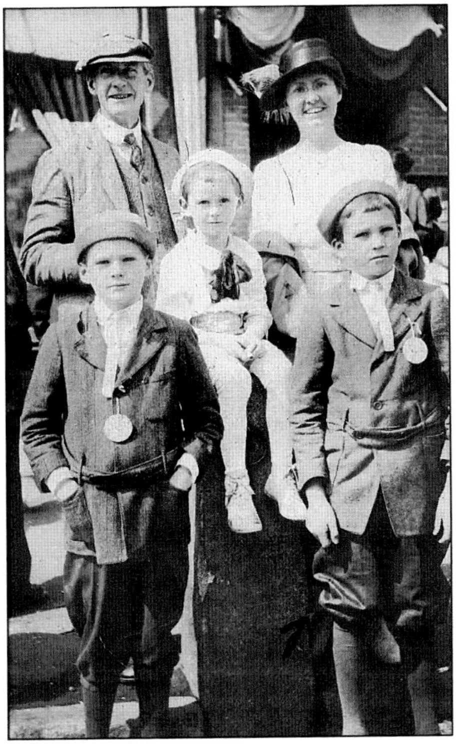

THE CHAMPION CORN GROWER, 1919. The annual competition sponsored by the New Hampshire Boys and Girls Club elicited a winner in Hollis Vinton Stillings, shown in the right front in this photograph taken at North Conway. The fertile floodplain off the Dort Road bested the yield of any other corn patch in the state.

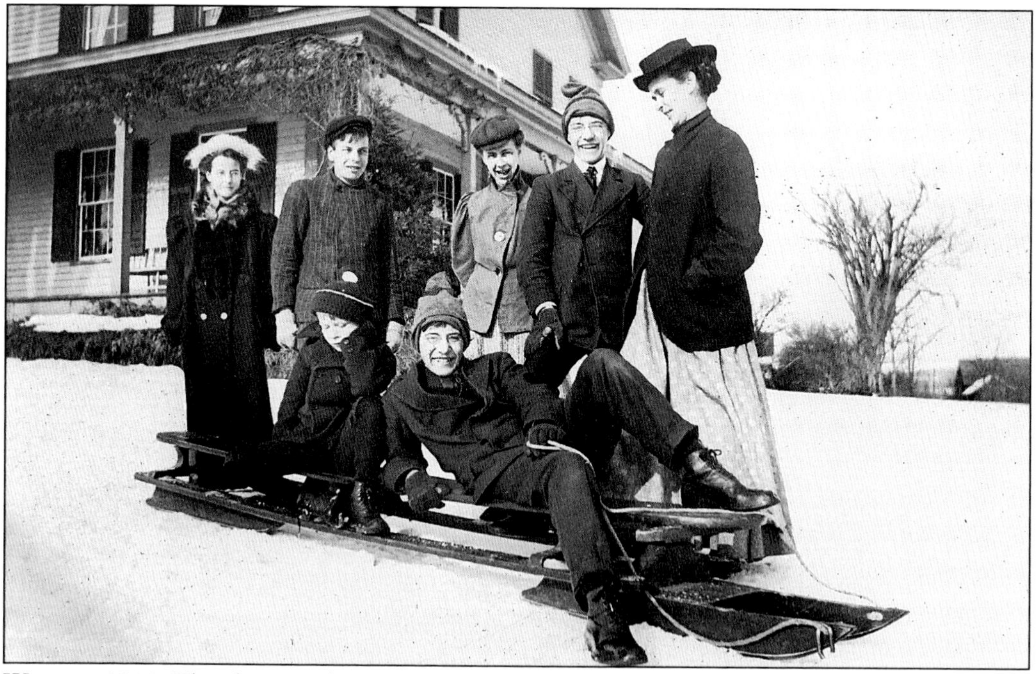

Winter, 1910. The photographer captures his extended family in a moment of wintertime play at the Hollis Harvey farm before "the lights went out" in Europe. Seated are George K. Harvey II and Robert W. Harvey. Standing, from left to right, are Margaret Porter (French), Henry Porter Jr., Elizabeth Britton, Shirley W. Harvey (twin brother to Robert), and Minnie Harvey.

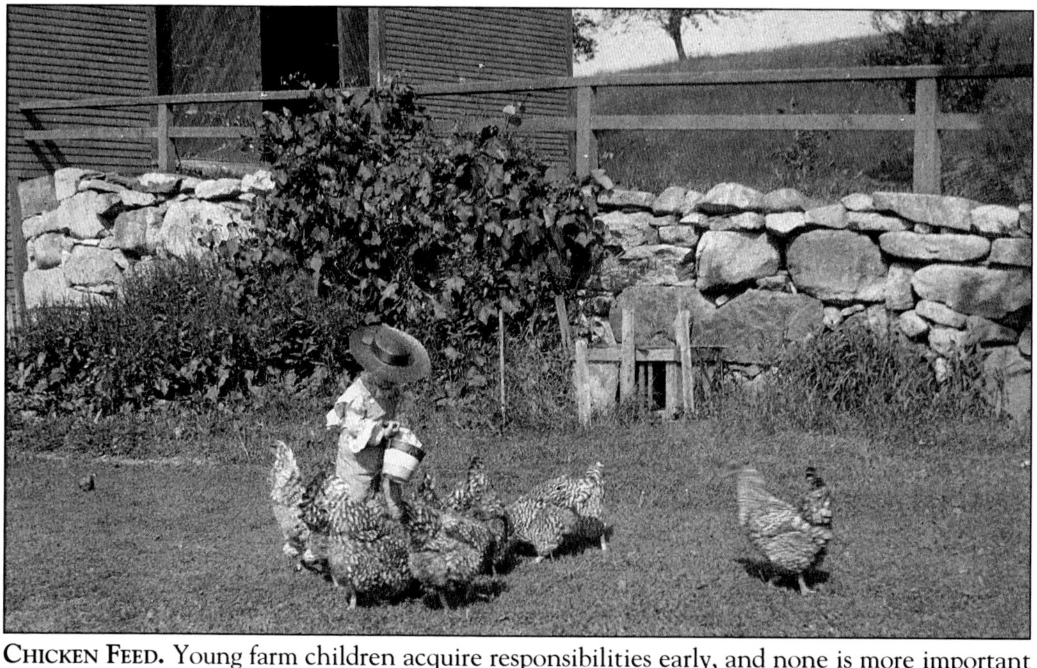

Chicken Feed. Young farm children acquire responsibilities early, and none is more important than the dependence of quasi-domesticated living creatures on the reliable provision of food and water. Here a youthful Harvey takes the first step toward such chicken-and-egg issues.

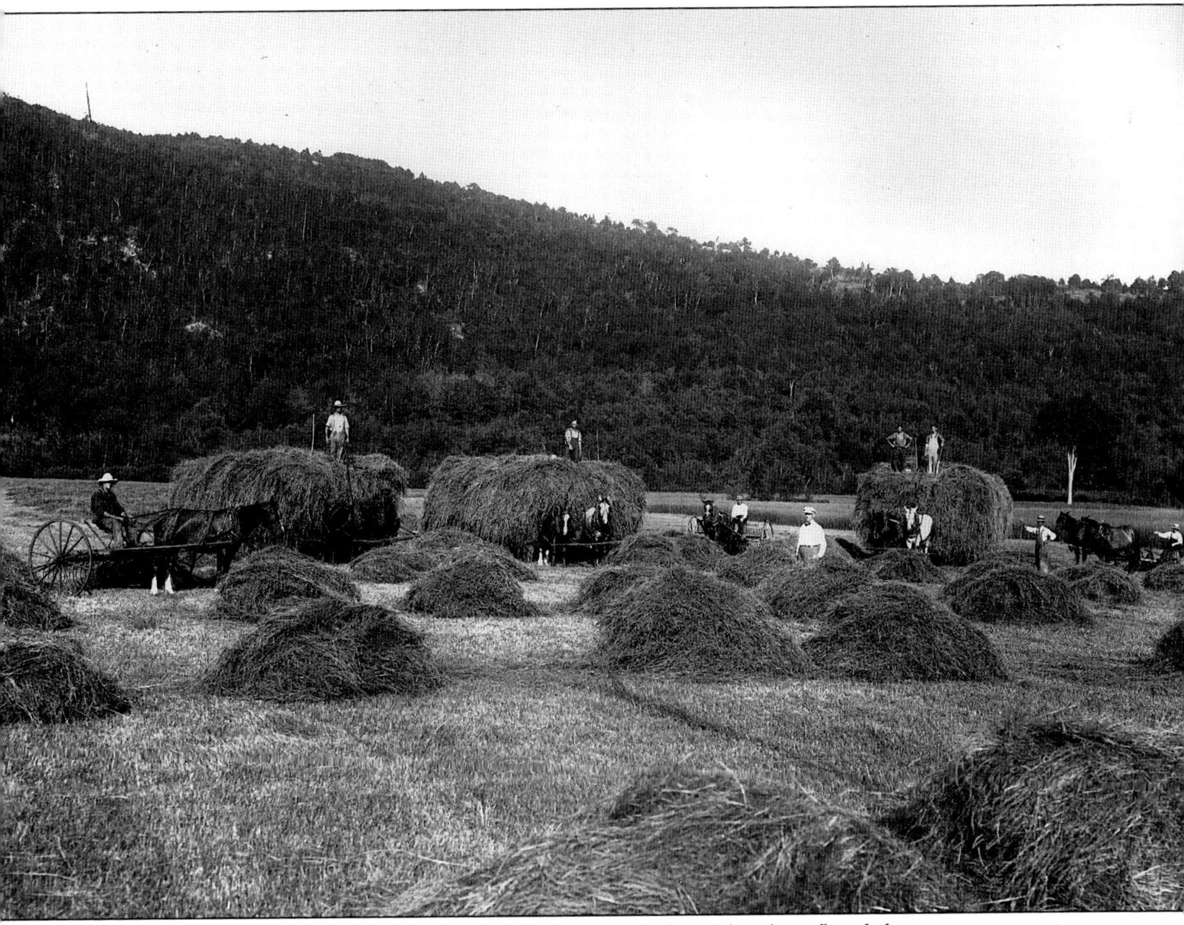

HAYING AT KELLER FARM. Cutting hay on the rich Ashuelot floodplain was a major undertaking. This *c.* 1900 photograph shows nine men, nine horses, and the proprietor engaged in this critical task on the Keller farm. Working, from left to right, are George Gillis on rake, Barnard Carey and Harry Knight on hay wagon, Ray Gates on rake, proprietor Jasper Keller standing in foreground, two unidentified men on hay wagon, Will Gates standing with fork, and Frank Ellis on tedder.

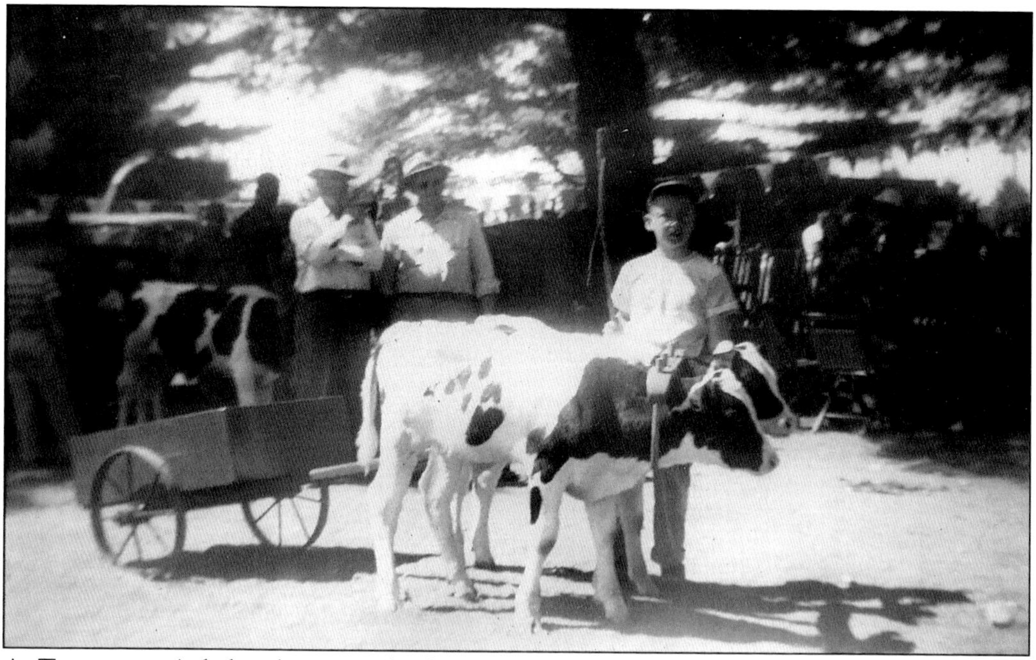

A Teamster. A lad is learning the basics of droving with his young team. His name is Roger Wilbur, and his age is nine. The team is unidentified. But Wilbur skills are being bequeathed seamlessly to the next generation (see chapter 5).

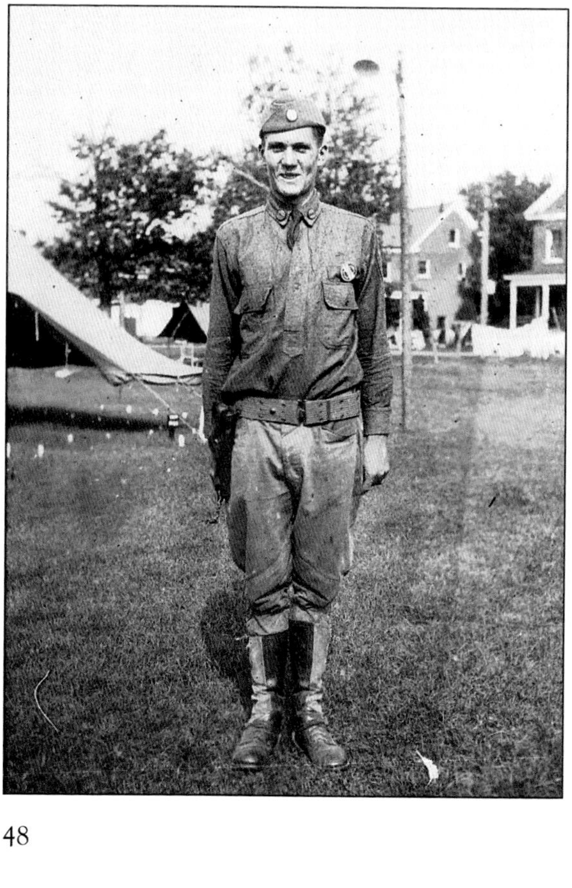

The Enlistee. Hollis Vinton Stillings, whom we met earlier as a schoolchild, has been swept into national life in the period following the end of World War I. He stands proudly in uniform at an unidentified bivouac site in New Hampshire.

Three

HOMESTEADS

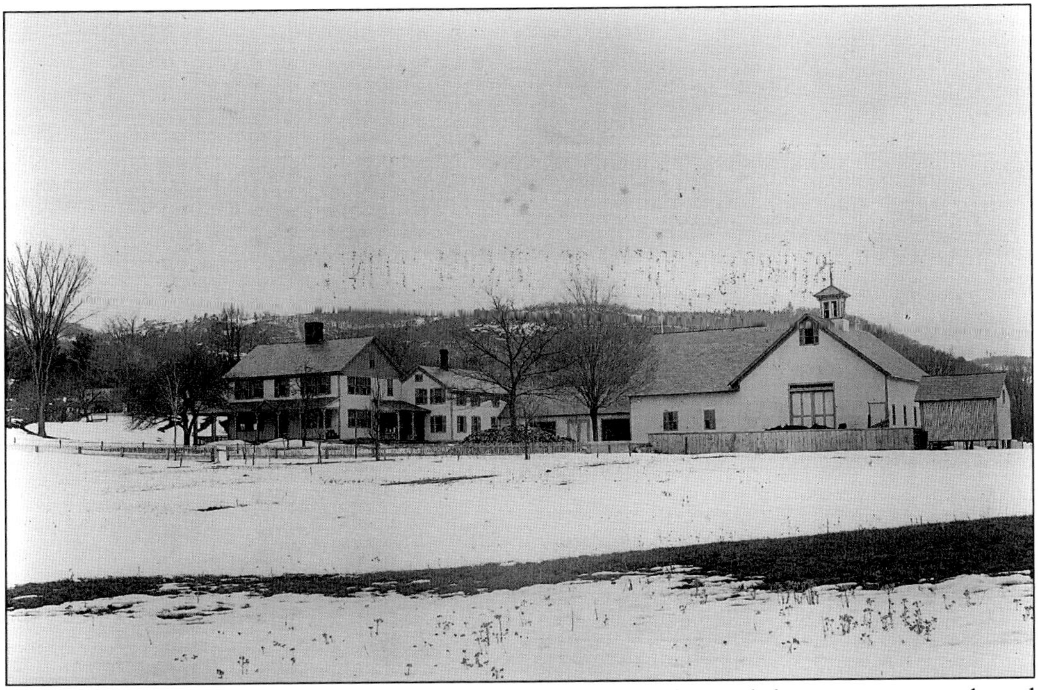

HOLLY FARM. Human settlement of the New England landscape left its imprint in cleared fields, stone fences, cart paths, and roadways. Then came the "built environment"—primarily homesteads, but also public spaces such as church, meetinghouse, and bridges. This chapter shows how Surry forefathers defined "home" at the start of the 20th century. Most of the photographs are James E. Harvey's, supplemented by a few from private collections. What they reveal is a world closer to the 18th century than the 21st. The vernacular New England farmhouse predominates, taking the form of "big house, little house, back house, barn." This was an elastic design that expanded with the family and the farm yet enabled a component of unassailable respectability to face "the street," and the wider public beyond. The "run-on" house was a practical solution to the New England winter: one could tend cows and other barnyard animals, raise water from the well, and retrieve root crops from the cellar, all more or less sheltered from the elements. Shown here is an exemplar of the type, Holly Farm. It takes its name from Hollis Wilcox, prominent member of the family who built and occupied it for more than a century. This is where "Holly" lived.

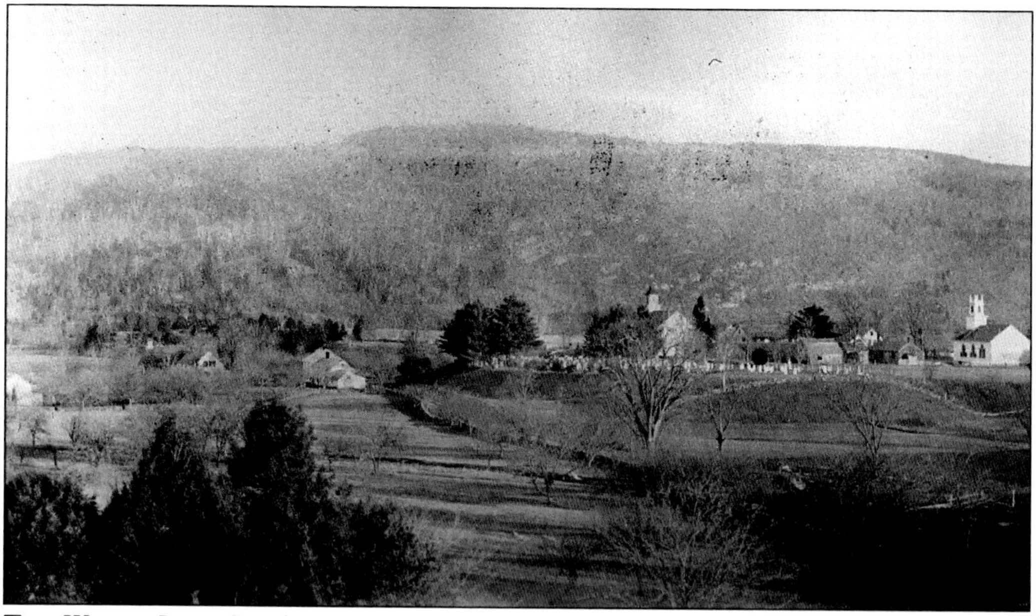

The Wrack Line. Beachcombers know this term as the line where high tides normally peak, leaving behind a defining scrim of seaweed. This picture shows Surry village (right) flanked by lower properties that will never reappear. The Edward Britton farm, and others, fell within the high-water mark of the flood-control zone. After appropriate proceedings (see chapter 4), houses were removed and the land has returned to a natural state (subject to once-a-generation flooding). (HSCC.)

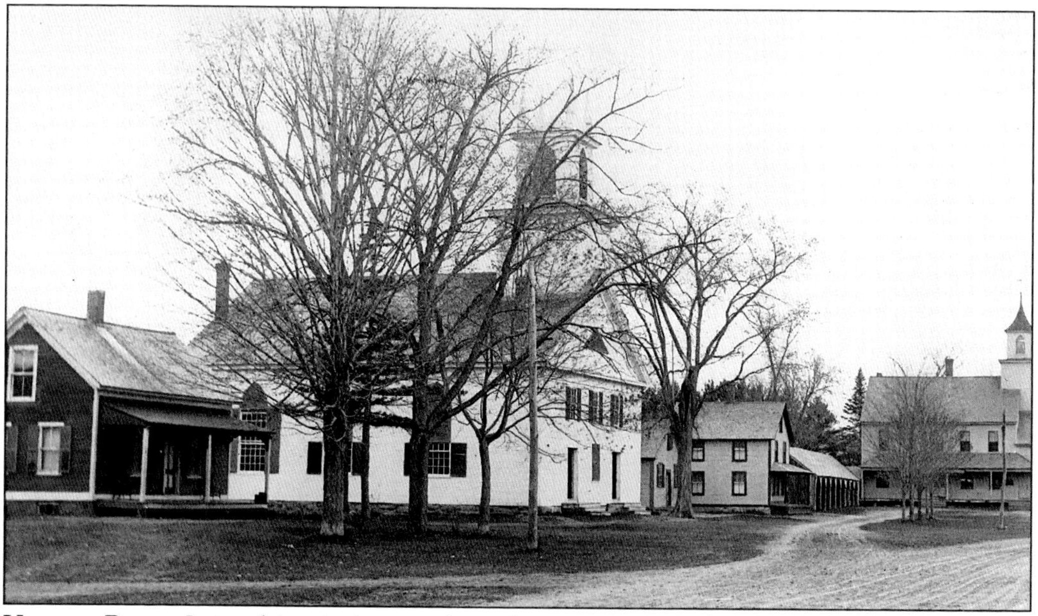

Village Road. It is a historical irony that what was a "turnpike"—a straightened, drained, "improved" road that users would pay fees to use for its advantages—should have devolved into Village Road, with a cul-de-sac at both ends. This fine photograph shows the landmark structures, along with the village school, a home on the site of the former blacksmith shop, and the horse sheds that served the meetinghouse. (HSCC.)

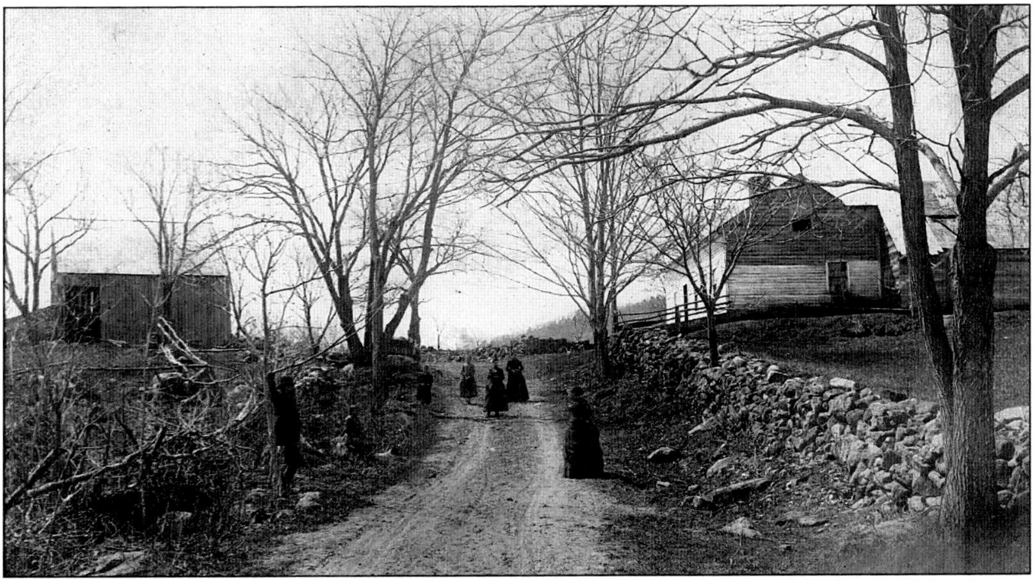

THE KENNY FARM. Four women, two children, and a bearded man in bowler hat and frock coat array themselves before their homestead on Cottage Street (Pond Road). It appears to be a warm day in an early, dry spring—neither mud nor leaf litter is visible. Notice the close-grazed pasture on the right, the mark of sheep or goats. Whitewashing of the house is a work in progress, on pause at the gable end for a season. Both house and barn remain occupied homes into the 21st century.

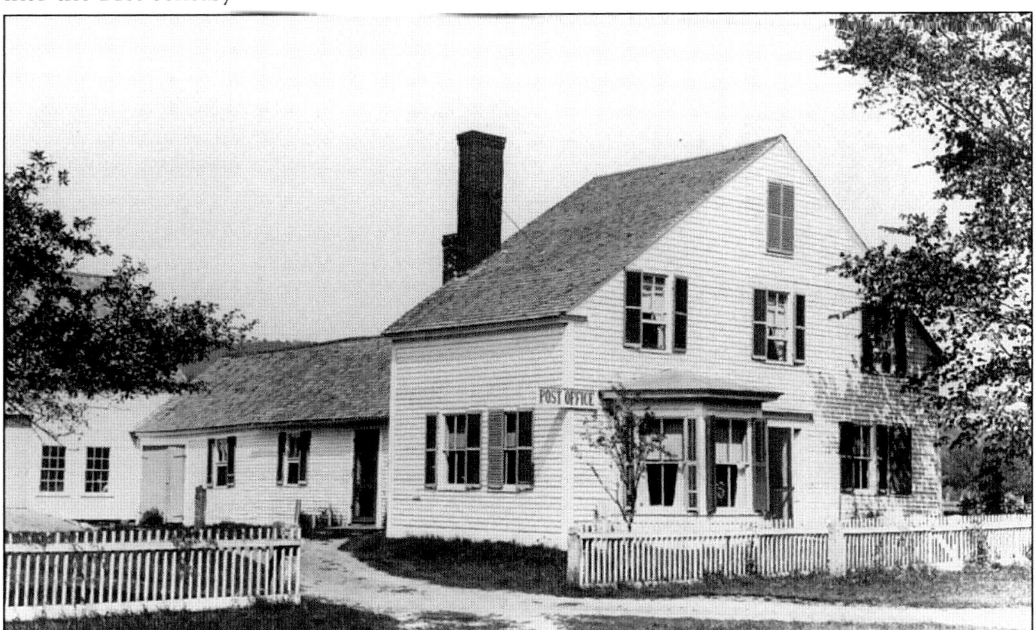

THE POST OFFICE. Reed Tavern, as noted, had been the first post office in Surry, but it was north of the northernmost section of Wilcoxville, scarcely accessible to the many who lived in the older village centers. In 1901, this fine "run-on" farmstead in the village center got the contract to disburse U.S. mail. Judging by the chimneys, it was a summer kitchen that fulfilled the new federal role.

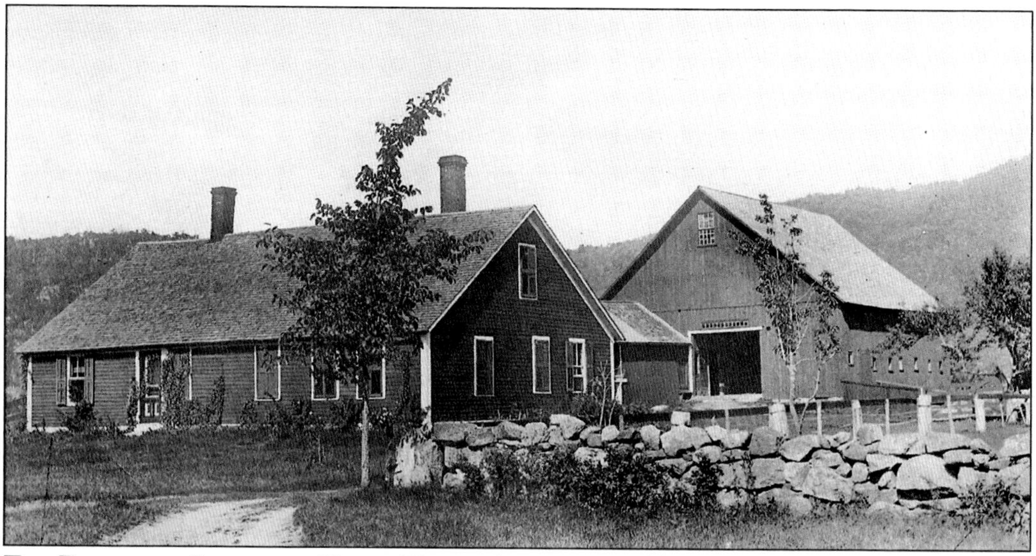

THE BROCKWAY-CARPENTER HOME. The settlement-period look to this home is authentic (it was second or third after the Hayward Tavern), but in fact it was rebuilt in 1805 following a fire. A 16-foot extension in 1826 converted it to a sometime duplex. Families besides the original Brockways who called this home were Robinsons, Blakes, Wilburs, and Brittons. The nearby town whipping post was pitched by vandals into its very deep (35-foot) well. The house served as post office from 1936 to 1959 under Arthur Carpenter and his daughter Isabel Young. (HSCC.)

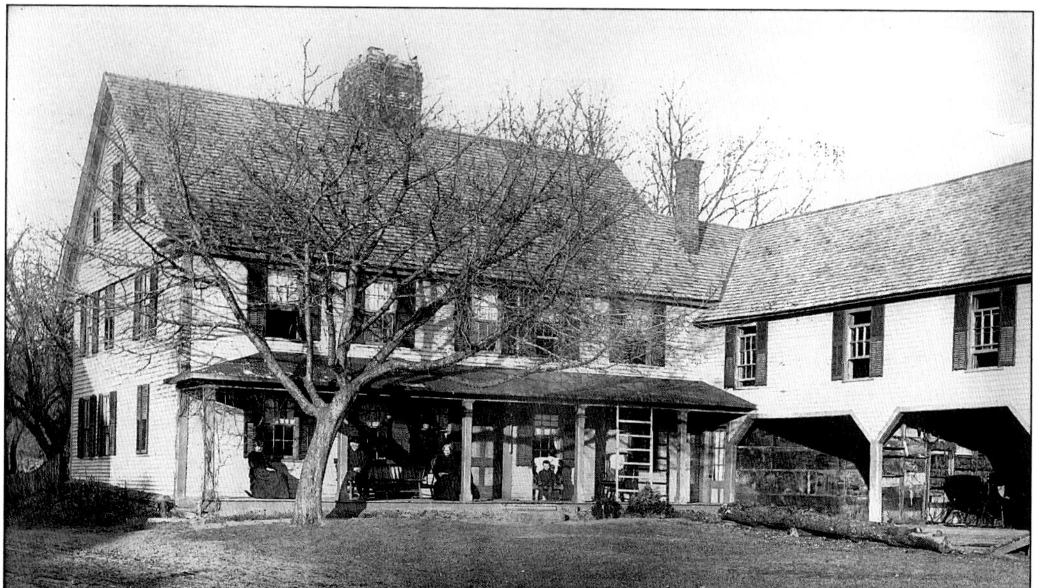

THE ELLIS HOMESTEAD. While American emissaries (Adams, Franklin, Jay) negotiated for peace and independence in Paris in the 1780s, kin of Peter Hayward were building this expansive homestead around a massive central chimney on the Great Road. When it passed into the Field and Ellis family in the 19th century, an ell was added (1878), with carriage sheds below and a dance floor above. As befits a farm possessing a cider mill from the outset, the yard tree is an apple. (HSCC.)

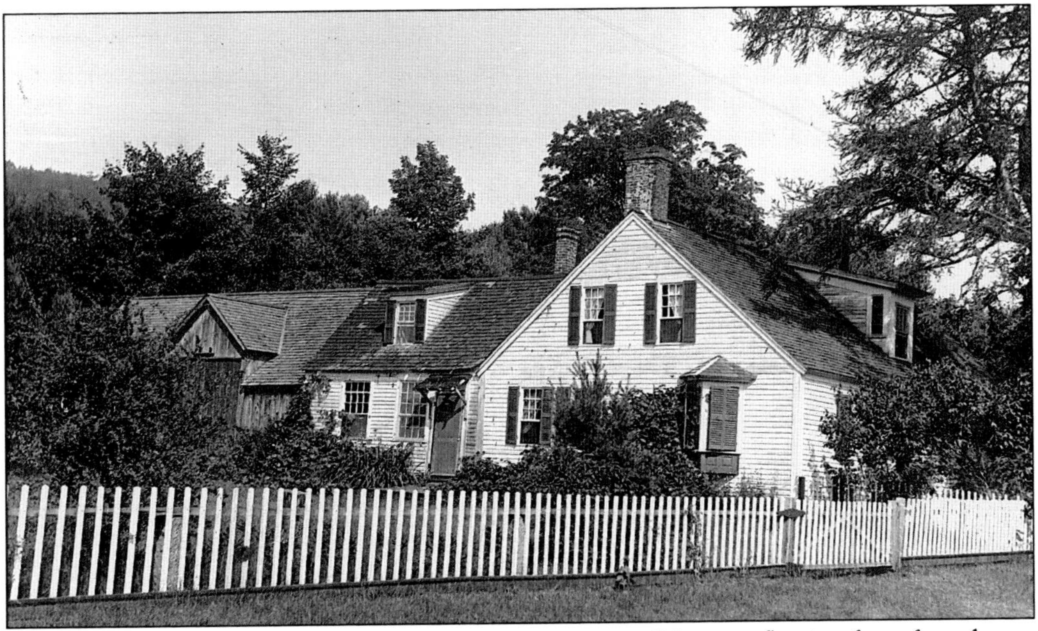

The Tollgate House. This is another of Surry's "run-on" houses, flowing from front house back through diminishing spaces to animal quarters in a connected barn. Begun in 1815, most of the house is probably the work of Levi Brooks (1782–1853), a reputable local carpenter and wheelwright. As tollhouse on the turnpike, it features one-of-a-kind windows in the corner bay and front dormer to facilitate the monitoring of traffic. (HSCC.)

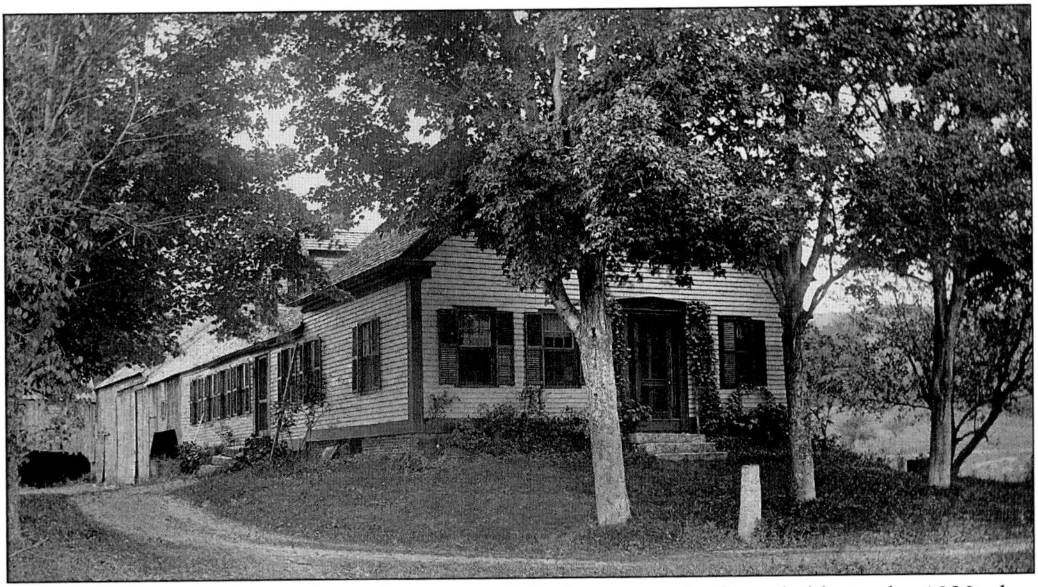

The Porter House. The older ell portion of the house was built probably in the 1830s, but the acquirer of 1852 (H. Randall) turned the ell 90 degrees, and added a reconstructed home taken from a nearby site. Dr. William H. Porter bought the property in 1865 and raised his family of four there, eventually passing the home to daughter Kate Porter (see page 15). Besides attending the ill and injured, Dr. Porter served his adoptive town wholeheartedly, including terms as town clerk, postmaster, treasurer, and state representative.

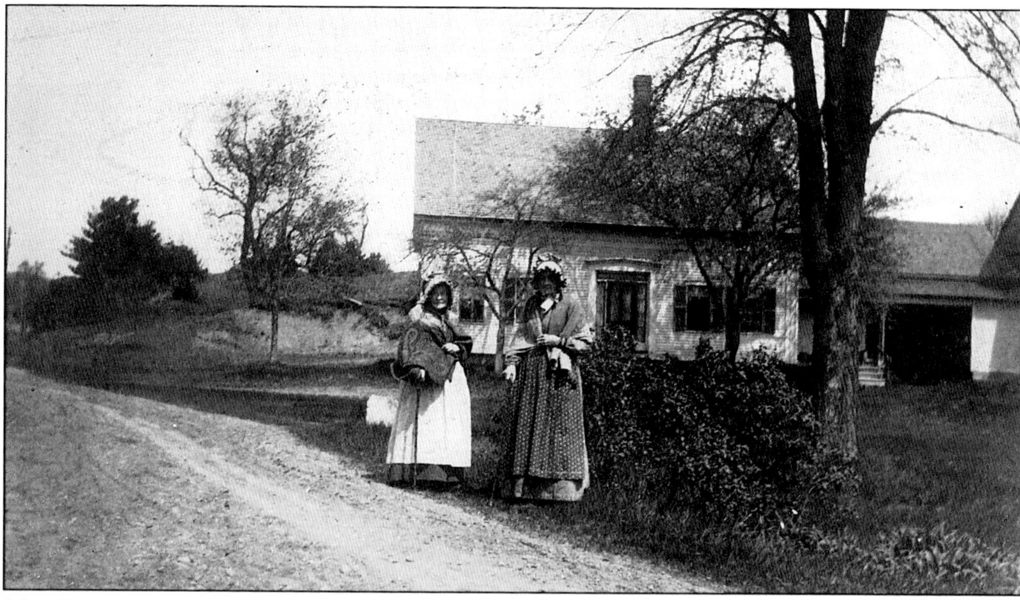

MRS. PORTER AT 80, MRS. BRITTON AT 90. World War I is under way at the time of this 1915 picture, but there is not a hint of the 20th century in the photograph—not a utility or convenience in sight, including rural free delivery (RFD). Mrs. Britton, who lived next door, named one of her daughters after soprano Jennie Lind, the "Swedish Nightingale" of mid-century.

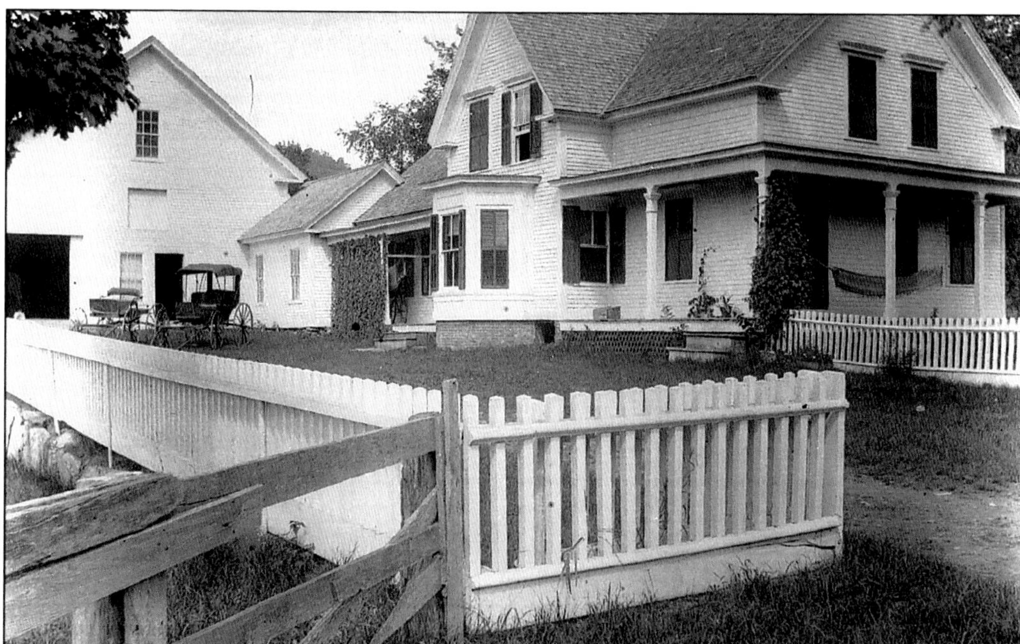

THE SCRIPTURE HOMESTEAD. Another "run-on" farmhouse, this was where the Scripture sawyers made their home. Apart from sulky and phaeton in the barnyard, who would date this picture as Victorian? In fact, the queen died in 1901, the very year this home burned to the ground. Gone are the Greek Revival front, the wraparound porch with hammock, the cross-gable with bay window, the morning-glorified side porch.

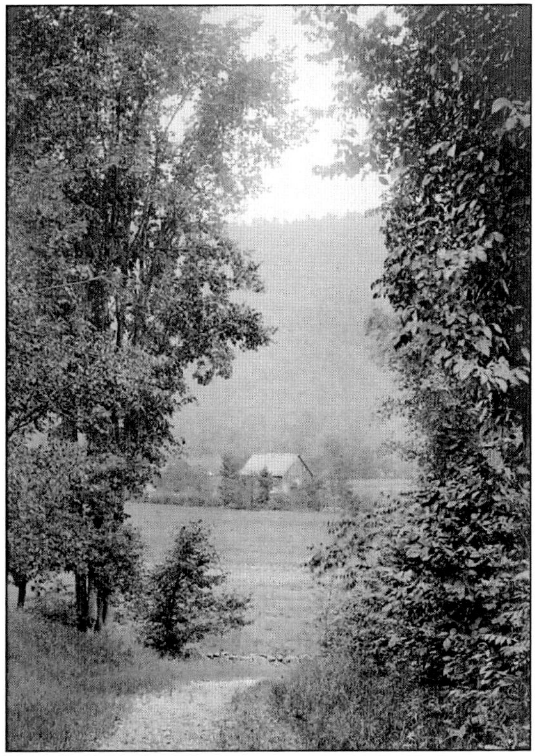

Summer and Winter on the Dort Road. James E. Harvey's artistic eye was so taken by the elegant natural framing that he returned in winter to capture a scene taken in summer. We are glad he did. A gently descending cart path bordered by stone fence turns down onto rich floodplain farmland, set against the ever-present backdrop of Surry Mountain. The Dort farm, then owned by Victor Lamminen, was one of the 15 "takings" for construction of the Surry Mountain Dam.

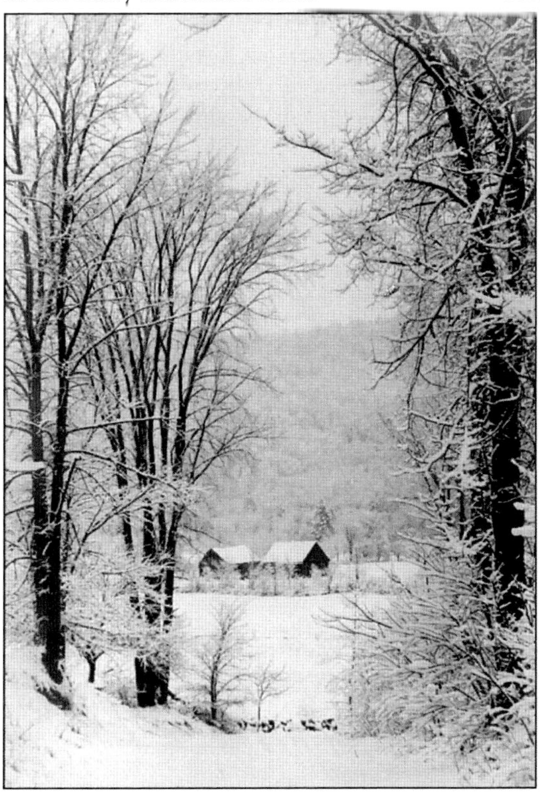

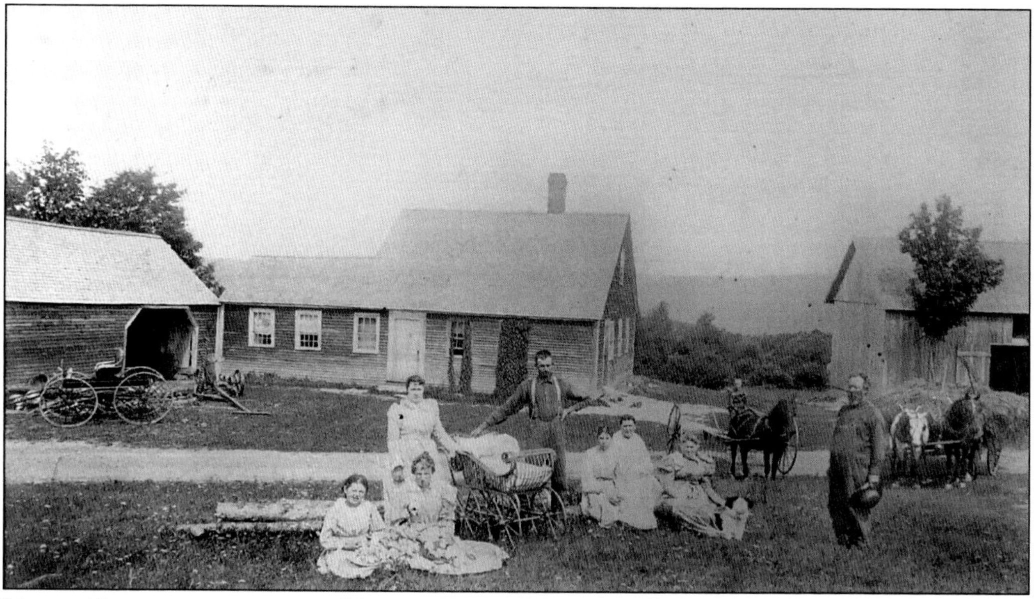

THREE GENERATIONS ON THE WILBUR FARM. Alonzo Wilbur, his son Clifford Wilbur, and their spouses and children pause to accommodate the visiting photographer. The photograph antedates 1917, when the house had a porch and other improvements added. Wicker baby carriage, hay rake, hay team, and free-range chickens flesh out this Old Walpole Road hill farm at the beginning of the 20th century.

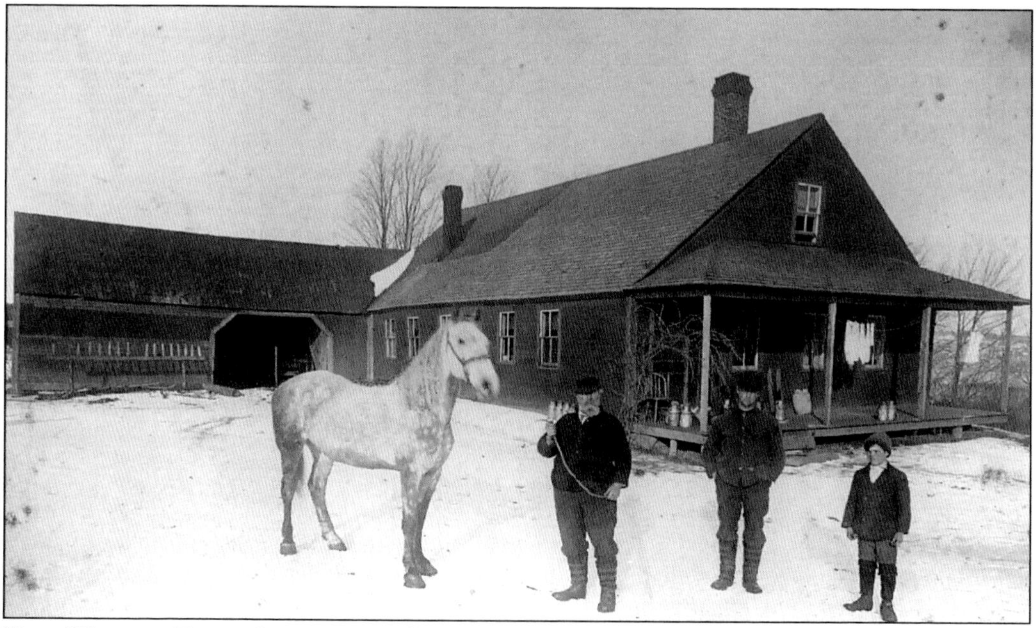

THE WILBUR FARM IMPROVED. The Wilburs—Alonzo, Clifford, and the latter's son Denman—meet the camera's gaze with equanimity in front of their improved homestead c. 1919. Notice the knee-length leather boots on each. The new porch provides an auxiliary laundry line. The homestead burned five years later, in 1924, but was promptly rebuilt on the existing foundation.

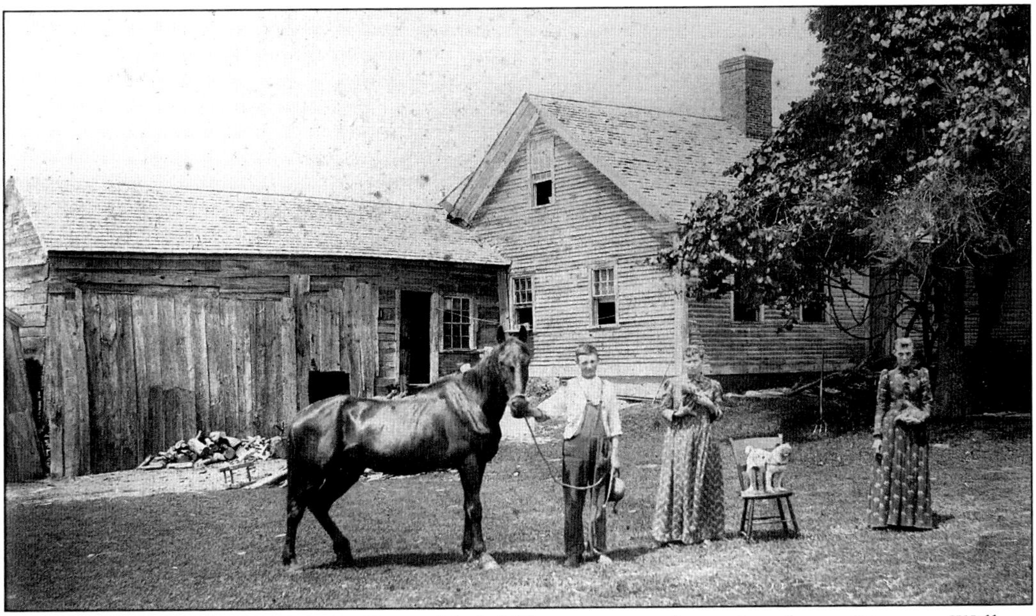

The White-Britton-Anderson Farm. Viola White, maternal grandmother to Denman Wilbur, is shown here *c.* 1900 with family at the White farmstead on Mine Ledge Road. A lapped-plank shed complements the center-chimney Cape, while a mature catalpa tree casts cool summer shade. Brittons lived in a house trailer at the foot of the road in winters during the 1940s so that their children could be availed of school transportation.

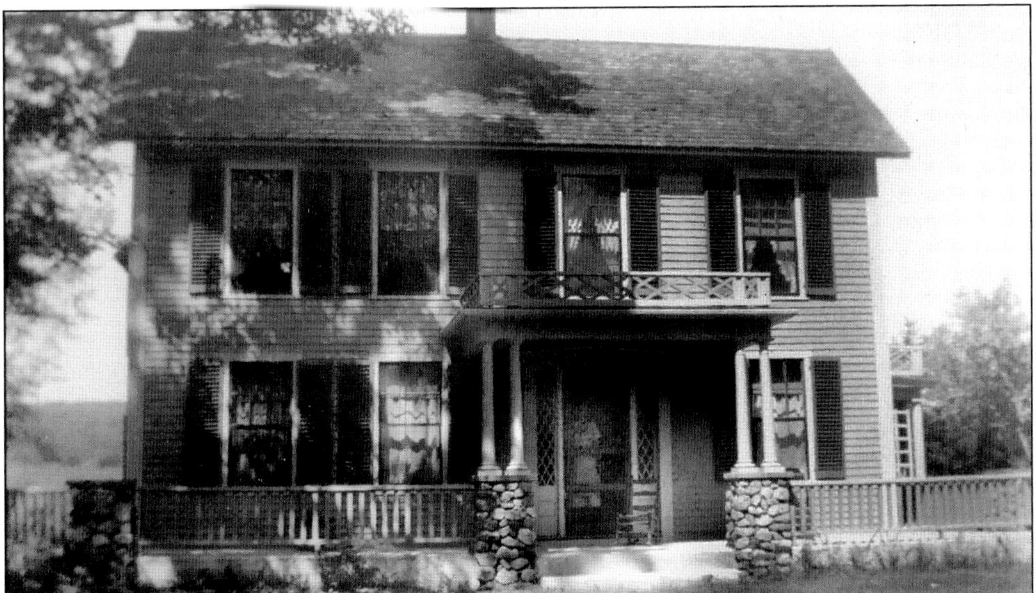

The Old Wilbur Home, 1933. First built in 1840 as a single-story home by Jonathan Field, this house has experienced multiple additions and changes over the decades, as hinted even by the front facade. Notice the asymmetrical window bays, the too-small "center" chimney, the large-sash windows, the neoclassic detail of pediment and portico intermixed with fieldstone pedestals and concrete piazza. A concerned occupant in white watches picture taking from the front hall.

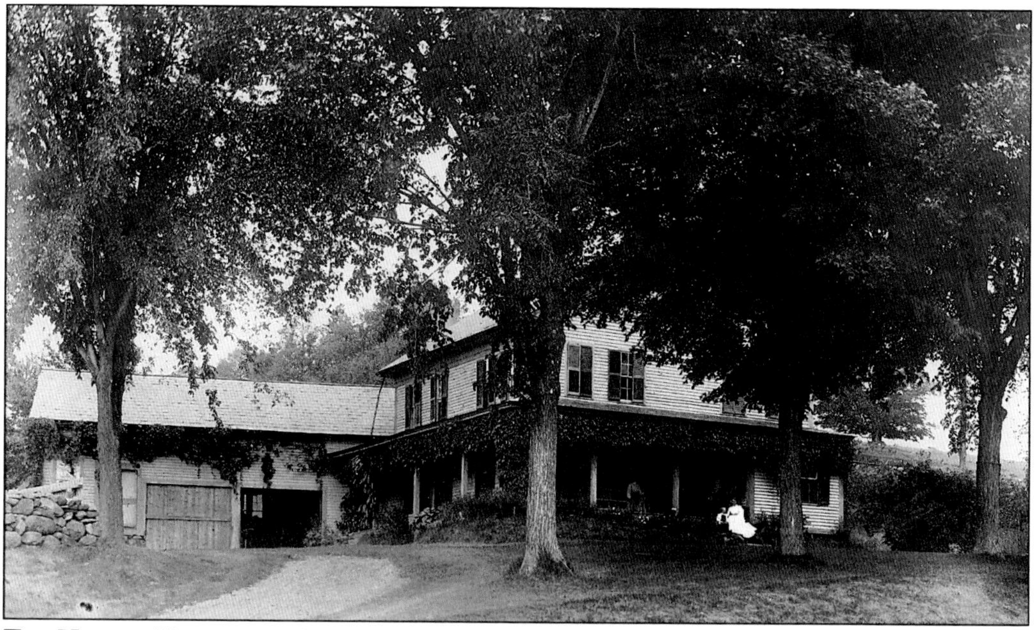

The Harvey Homestead. James E. Harvey photographed his many kin during return trips to Surry. We indulge the photographer with some family images. Here is the home farm, then occupied by his brother Hollis Harvey. A trailing vine shrouds the two-sided porch. A solid Surry citizen, Hollis Harvey held most principal offices and advocated strongly for state roads (see page 43). He chaired the first Surry History Committee. This home was used in New Hampshire television advertising throughout the 1990s.

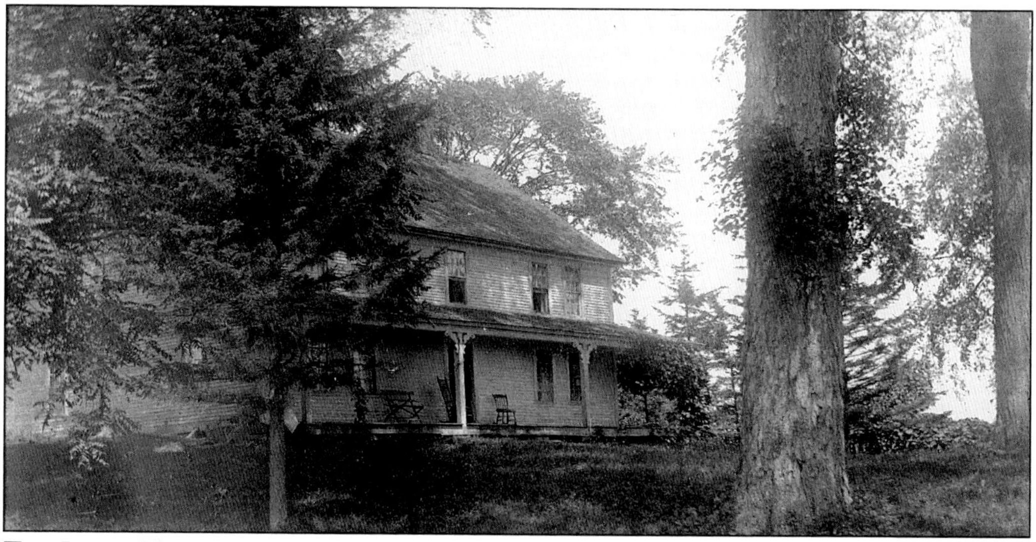

The Joslin Homestead, 1766–1928. Built by Capt. Thomas Harvey as a tavern a decade prior to the outbreak of the Revolution, this house was the second two-story structure in town. A smallpox epidemic struck several members of the family in 1801–1802, turning their home into Surry's *de facto* pesthouse. A yard marker denotes one young victim. Legends survive the house—Indians sleeping in the barn, rattlesnake in the henhouse—but none outweighs the fact of the 1928 fire that took the lives of Edward and sister Mary Joslin at ages 89 and 91, respectively.

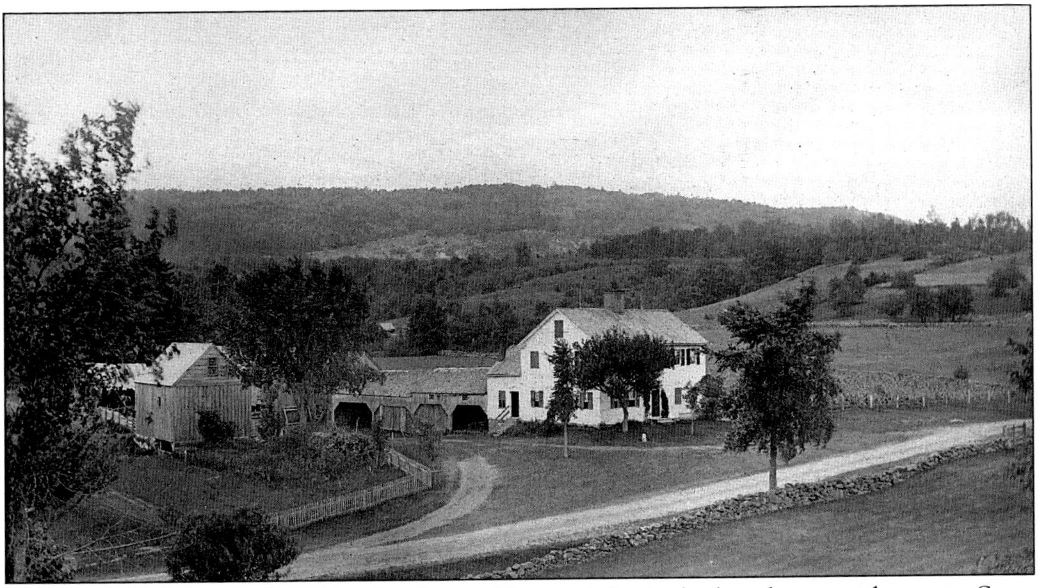

The Home. This was the farm that James Harvey inherited when he came home to Surry in 1919. Built by Rev. Perley Howe in 1812, it passed into Jonathan Harvey Jr.'s family in the 1840s. His daughter Persis, a schoolteacher and library trustee, occupied it throughout her life (1833–1901), passed it on to her brother George K. Harvey, and then to his son James Harvey. It is said that James Harvey introduced the radio to Surry (as well as photography) upon his return.

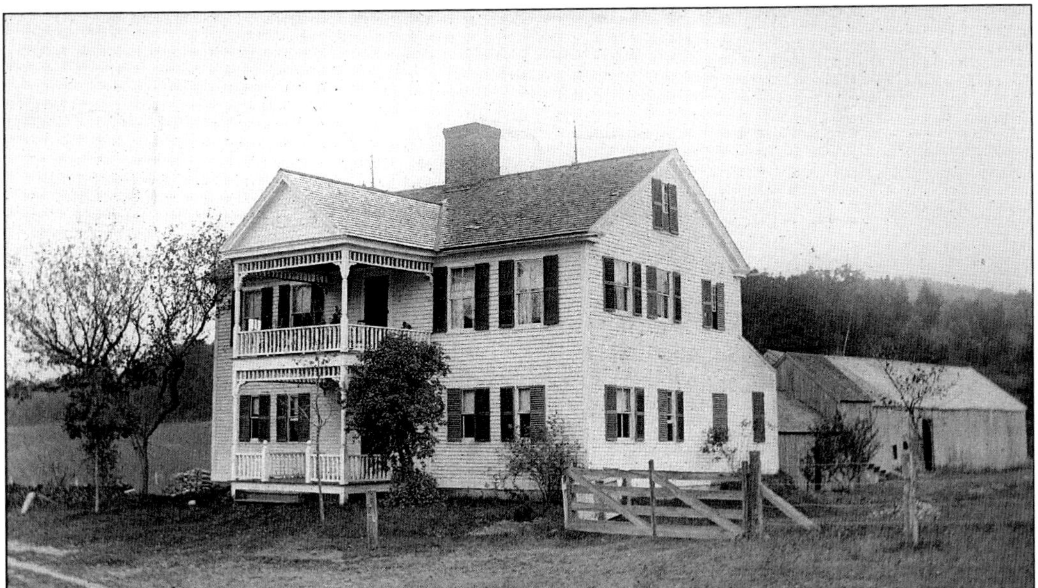

Antediluvian Harvey. James Harvey's twin sons, Shirley and Robert Harvey, inherited the house in the 1920s, added protective lightning rods, but ironically lost the house to an act of man, not God: it was one of 15 homesteads in the floodplain taken by the U.S. Army Corps of Engineers for flood-control purposes in the late 1930s (see page 72).

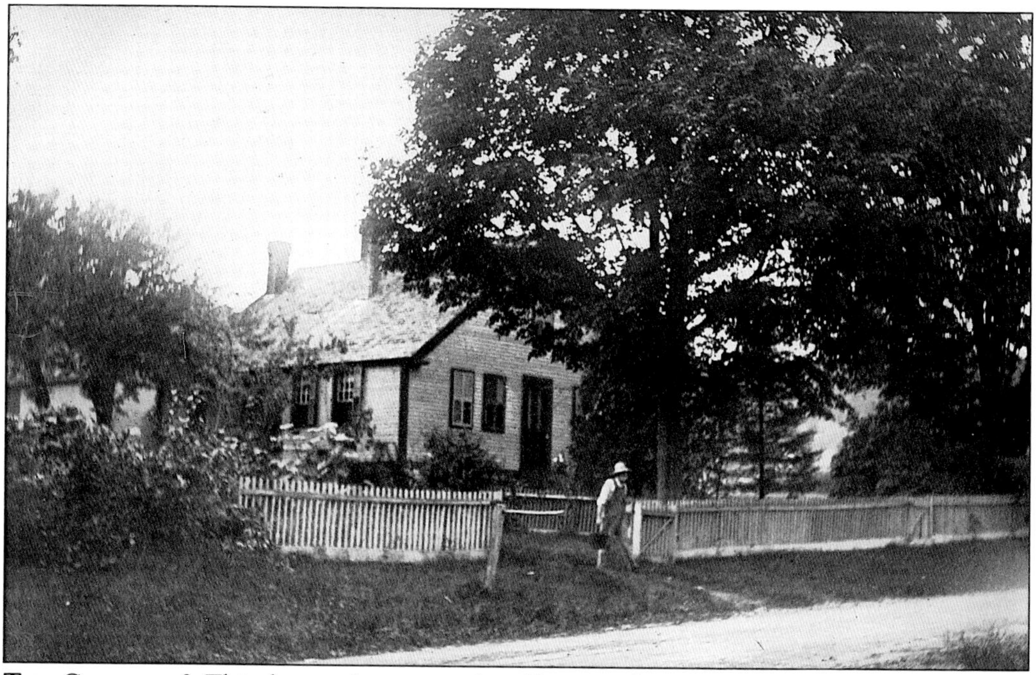

The Commuter? This farmer figure, another Harvey who remains unidentified, obligingly strides out his cart path early one morning looking quite like a suburbanite off to catch the tram for another workday in the metropolis. Our subject, however, carries a large wooden pail rather than a briefcase, and the gated picket fence signifies hog and goat protection, not aesthetics.

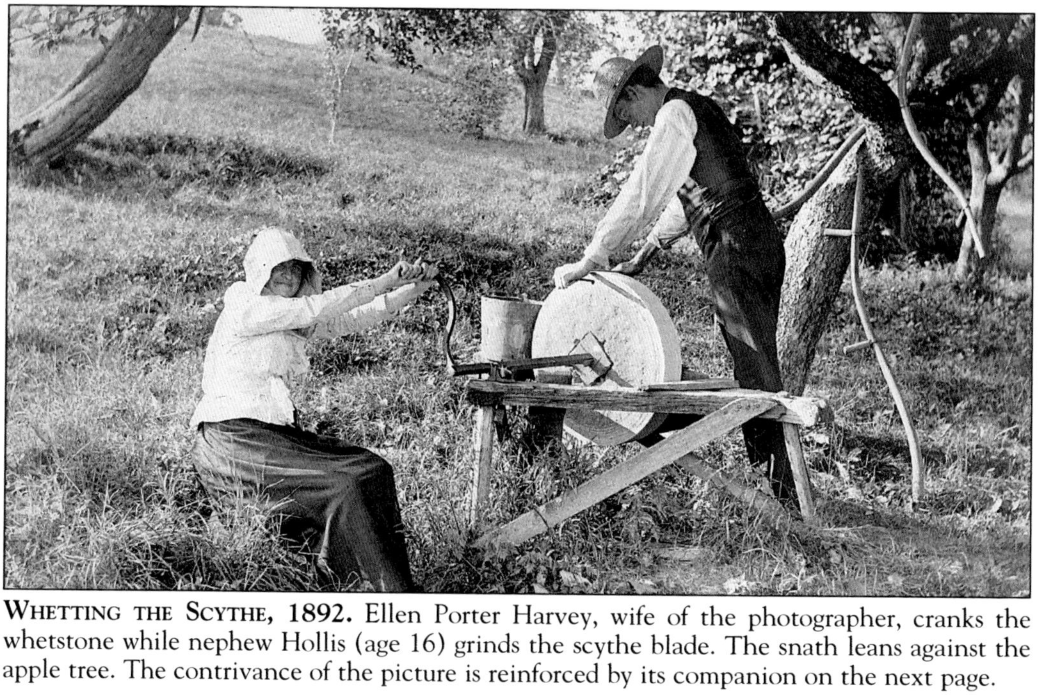

Whetting the Scythe, 1892. Ellen Porter Harvey, wife of the photographer, cranks the whetstone while nephew Hollis (age 16) grinds the scythe blade. The snath leans against the apple tree. The contrivance of the picture is reinforced by its companion on the next page.

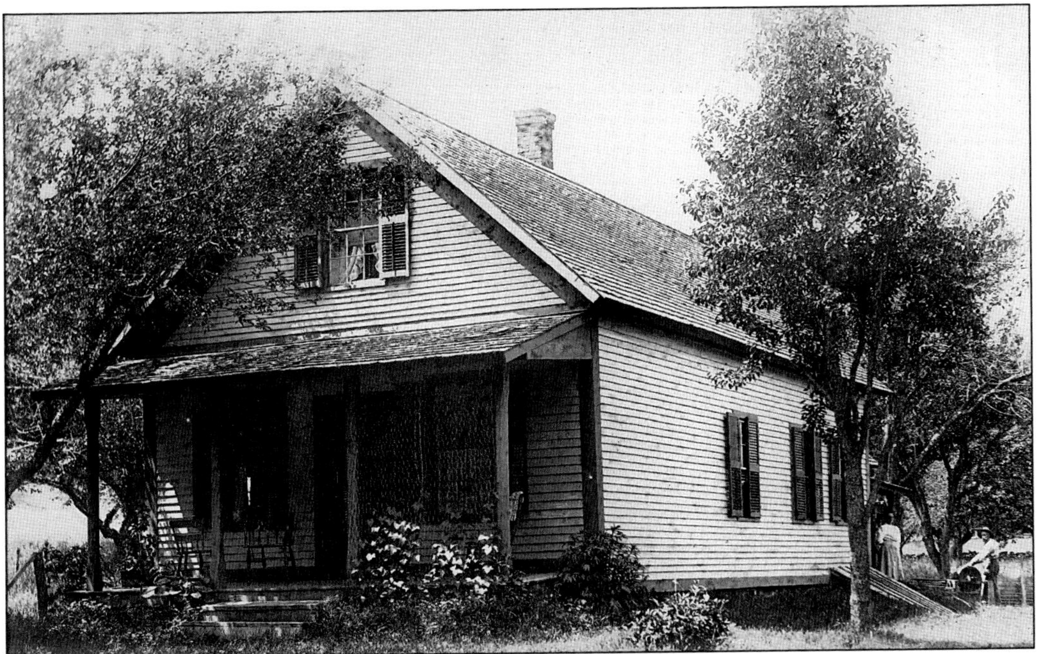

The Home and the Stone. The orchard lot where the previous picture was taken is clearly visible at the rear of this modest house, along with mounted whetstone and family participants. James F. Harvey obviously relished the rustic simplicities of Surry life, following his career in eastern cities.

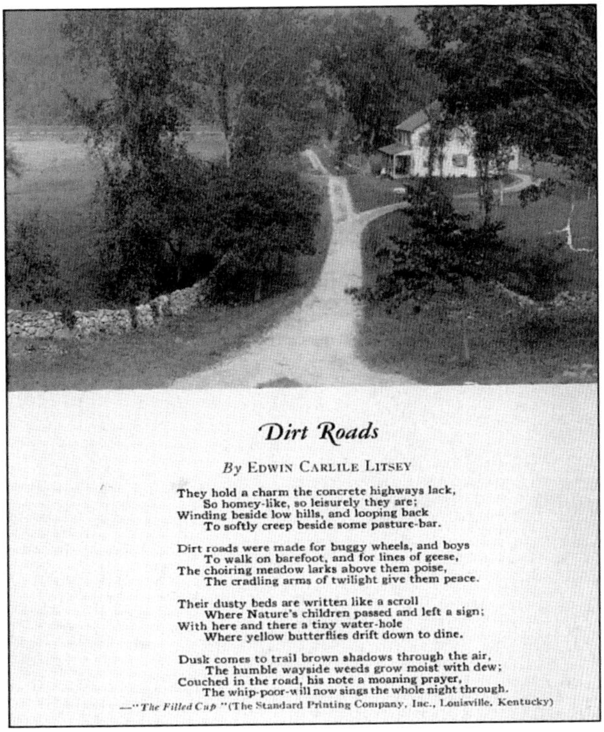

Dirt Roads

By Edwin Carlile Litsey

They hold a charm the concrete highways lack,
So homey-like, so leisurely they are;
Winding beside low hills, and looping back
To softly creep beside some pasture-bar.

Dirt roads were made for buggy wheels, and boys
To walk on barefoot, and for lines of geese,
The choiring meadow larks above them poise,
The cradling arms of twilight give them peace.

Their dusty beds are written like a scroll
Where Nature's children passed and left a sign;
With here and there a tiny water-hole
Where yellow butterflies drift down to dine.

Dusk comes to trail brown shadows through the air,
The humble wayside weeds grow moist with dew;
Couched in the road, his note a moaning prayer,
The whip-poor-will now sings the whole night through.

—"*The Filled Cup*" (The Standard Printing Company, Inc., Louisville, Kentucky)

"Dirt Roads." This expansive farmstead illustrated the cover (1936) of a regional periodical called *New Hampshire Troubadour*, paired with verse by E.C. Litsey extolling the charms of unpaved roadways. Owned by the Stillings family for much of the 20th century, the house featured two Rufus Porter–style wall murals. The barn straddles the line of the flood-storage zone, and its title is thereby divided between the current owner and the Army Corps of Engineers.

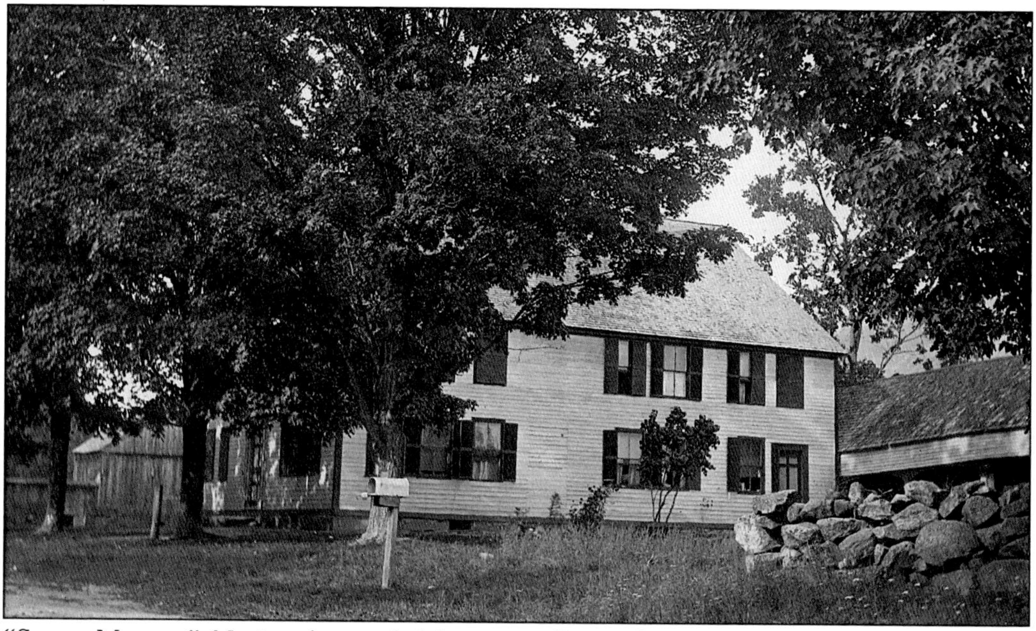

"Seven Maples." Notice the rural delivery mailbox—the only homestead in the Harvey portfolio so furnished. This substantial house retains Indian shutters in its earliest rooms and a "spring" dance floor from its tavern days. Its eponymous maples have shaded and "sugared" more than 15 owners over two centuries, including the Malcolm family, who occupied this house from the second decade of the 20th century to the 1950s.

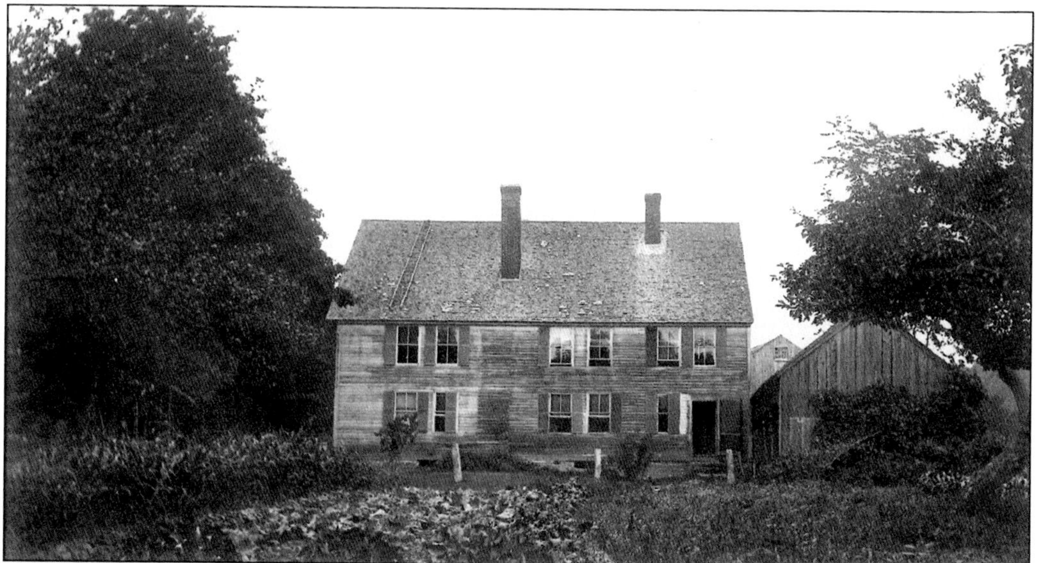

"Seven Maples," Later. This undated photograph from Floyd Britton's family album shows "Seven Maples" in less happy days. Until the automobile became a mass consumer item in the post–World War II era, such farmhouses had become too large for all but the most prolific and dedicated agricultural families and too remote to attract the growing middle classes interested in rural escapes from town and city. However, the Malcolms salvaged it and sold it in 1953 to the Kirks, who opened here the first antiques business in Surry—a sure mark of developing tourism. (HSCC.)

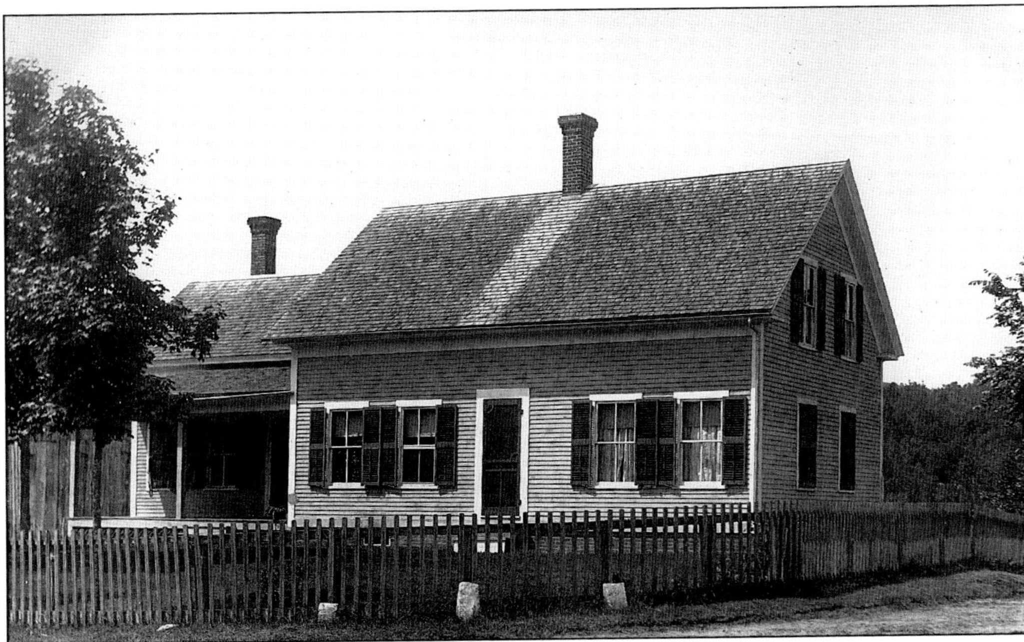

"Five Maples." Clapboards and trim are signature features of this village home, built in a restrained Greek Revival style. Historian Frank Kingsbury lists a tortuous chain of 19th-century titles, but an 1878 fire led to a complete rebuilding, as currently seen. The soft-spoken classicism is sustained in the eaves-line entablature and unadorned window heads. Two of the maples were hammock trees.

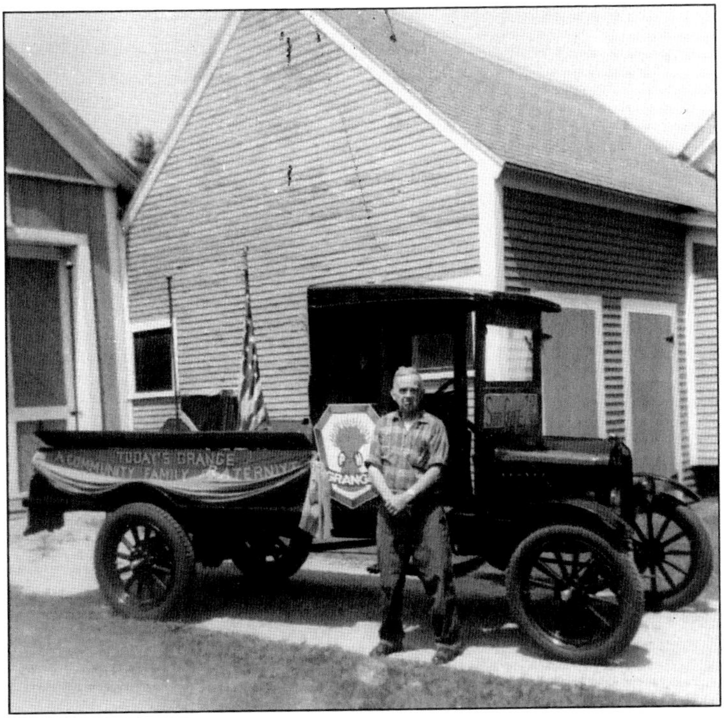

A Granger. Ralph Steele gladly accedes to a photograph before a truck, emblazoned with Grange proclamations ("Family, Community, Fraternity"), at "Five Maples." A family property, Conleys and Steeles occupied this home for nine decades, and Hattie Steele contributed mightily to its appearance by her love of gardening. The Surry Grange was organized in 1890 with 52 charter members, and no group did more to promote "industry, good-will and harmony," according to author Frank Kingsbury.

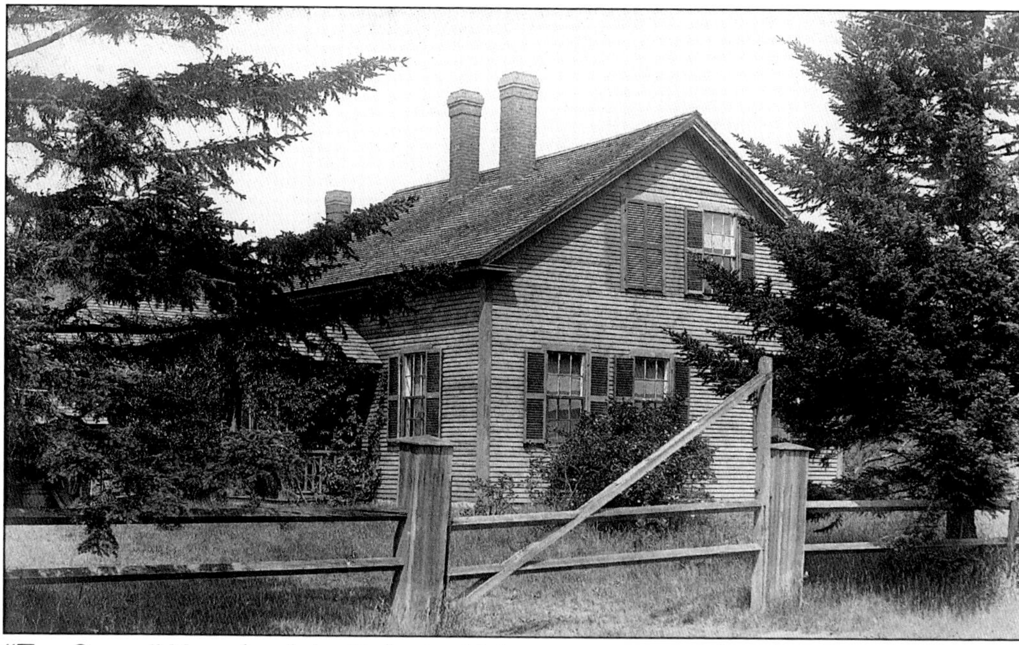

"THE CONES." Named such by Catherine Upham, a summer resident from Boston, this house has seen many owners, a move uphill, and a barn fire. Absent its fancy fence, it remains today on lower Village Road.

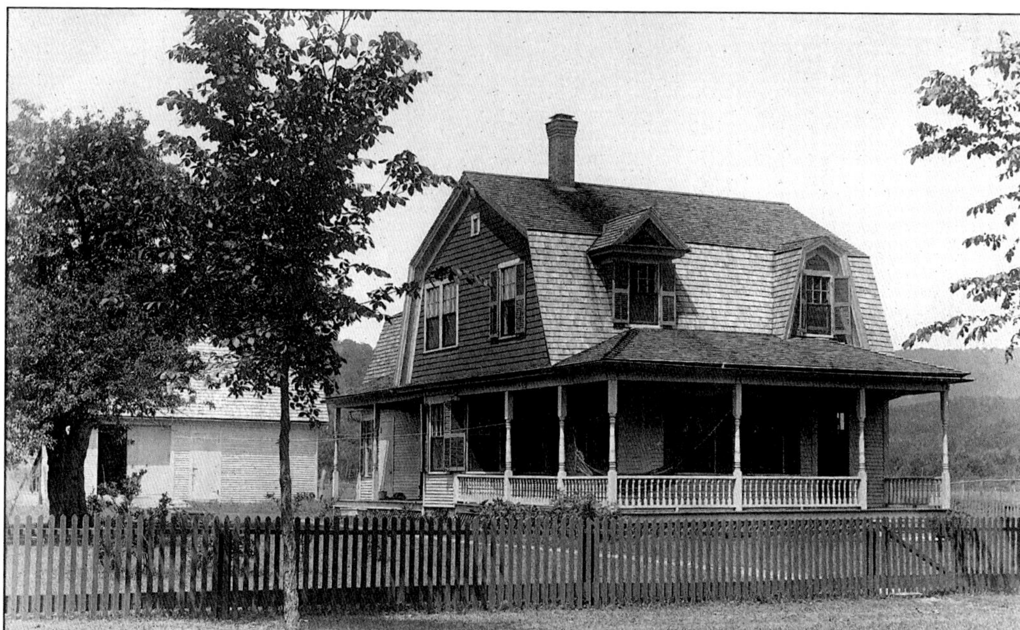

WRIGHT COTTAGE. One of two gambrel houses in the village, this unique structure was built by Mason A. Carpenter—a name to instill confidence in construction if ever there was one. The town entrusted Carpenter as state representative, selectman, treasurer, moderator, justice of the peace, and constable. His unmatched dormers emanate from the variability of late-Victorian design, as in the Colony Block in Keene. The house is most associated with Marietta Wright, a Carpenter descendant.

Four

FLOODS AND FEDERALISM

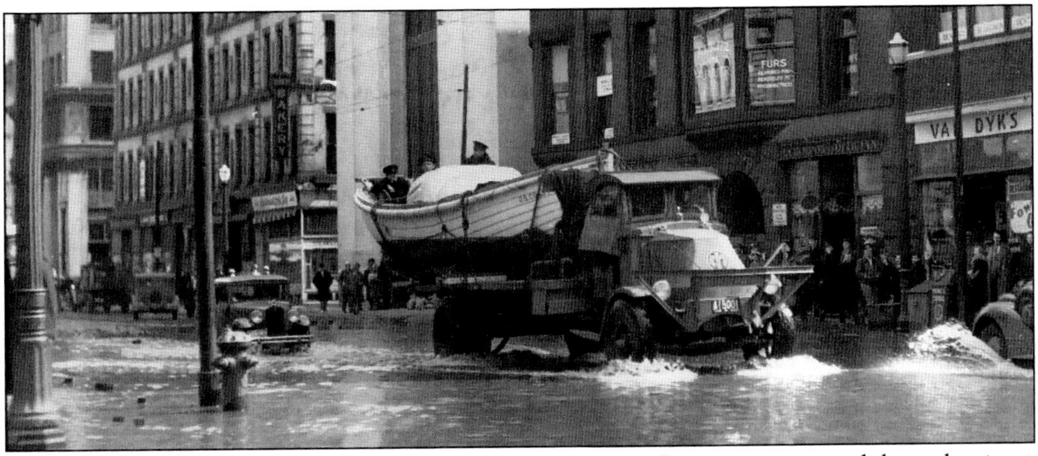

FLOOD! The principal cities on the lower Connecticut River were visited by calamitous flooding in 1936 and 1938. Many older homes still bear telltale waterlines on mantelpieces or wainscoting, and businesses suffered damaged basements, boilers, and the like, as here on State Street, Springfield, Massachusetts. Damage to Springfield, Connecticut's capital Hartford, and other cities ran in the millions of dollars. Congress responded by enacting the Flood Control Act of 1936, which supported construction of flood-control dams throughout the Connecticut River Basin. Surry was selected as one of the first sites, owing to its control of a 100-square-mile watershed of the Ashuelot River, a favorable topography and geology, a small population, and a key location upstream of Keene, the economic hub (long prone to flooding) of southwest New Hampshire. Following acquisition of 44 parcels (15 occupied) on Surry's floodplain, the Army Corps of Engineers constructed a dam beginning in August 1939. It went into operation in June 1942, becoming the third on line after the Knightville and Birch Hill dams in Massachusetts. The effect on Surry was to change it from a 19th-century agricultural town to a contemporary "exurb" of recreation and country residences. Establishment of a permanent 15-foot-deep pool (1962) and of a public recreation area attracted as many as 100,000 visitors per year to Surry Mountain Lake. The town benefited from contract work for the Army Corps and from annual compensation by southern New England states for the diminished tax base. With a 68-foot-high belt strap flashing a significant federal buckle across its riparian waistline, Surry was transformed. What follows, from the archives of the Army Corps of Engineers, is a pictorial history of the Surry Mountain Dam.

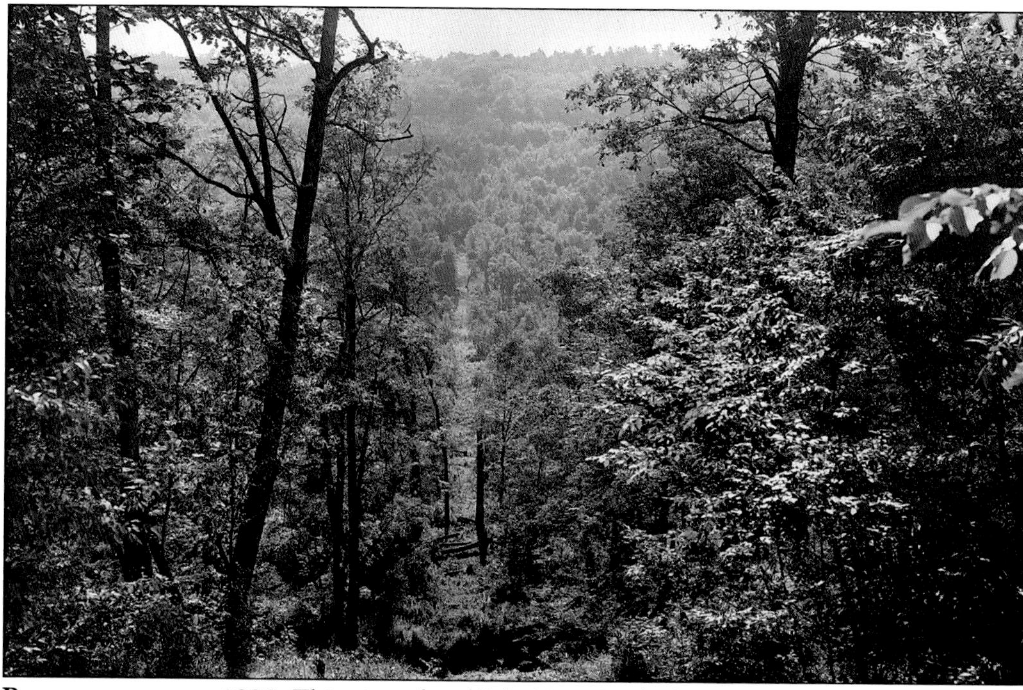

Preconstruction, 1939. This view, dated July 22, 1939, looks down a survey swath from the site of the future intake portal, on the west side of the dam-to-be, across the valley floor to the eventual eastern abutment. Deciduous trees predominate on the photographer's side of the scene; coniferous stands characterize the less-settled opposite "shore."

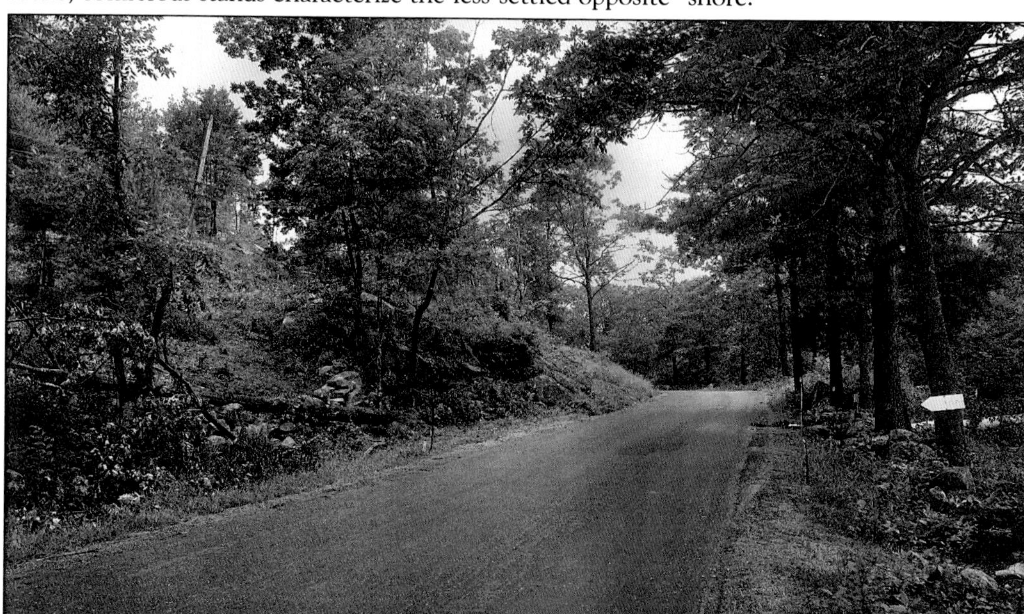

Preconstruction. The old Cheshire Turnpike, now a pastoral roadbed, is soon to be transformed into the spillway of a first-generation flood-control dam in the Connecticut River watershed. The view is upstream, and the swath on the left presages the spillway. The second tree on the right marks the approximate location of the tunnel outlet.

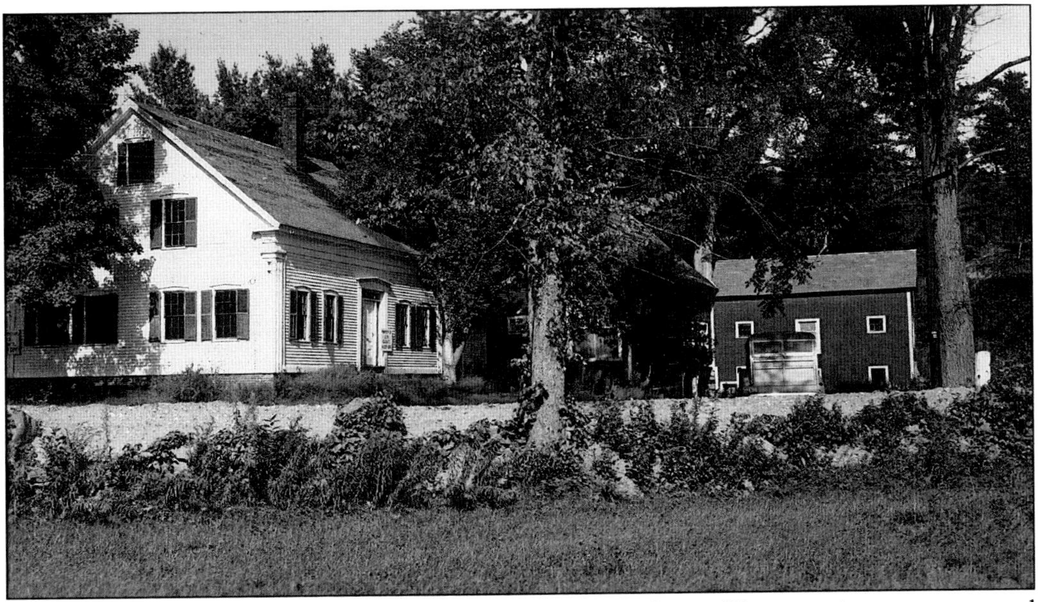

EMINENT DOMAIN AND THE COLLECTIVE GOOD, 1941. Some 15 properties were removed from the valley for use as flood storage. Appraisals were performed, acquisitions negotiated, and homesteads removed with varying degrees of finality. The following photographs, most from the files of the Army Corps of Engineers, record the lost world of antediluvian Surry. The William Sheldon farm was a substantial Revival house with 64 acres north of the village. Nature lovers who roam these old hayfields invariably come upon the huge foundation and, in midsummer, roses from Mrs. Sheldon's gardens still blooming beside the stream.

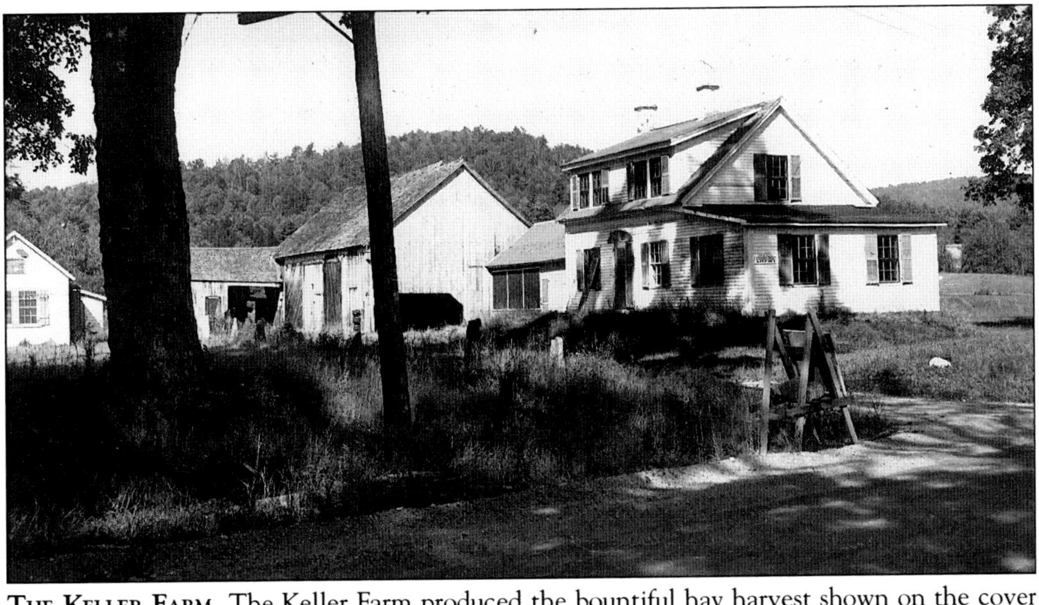

THE KELLER FARM. The Keller Farm produced the bountiful hay harvest shown on the cover of this book. J.N. Keller had been president of New England Tel & Tel during the decades of buying up local exchanges to create the regional Bell system. This was his chosen retirement farm. It was a traditional "run-on" farmstead, built around a very modest Cape.

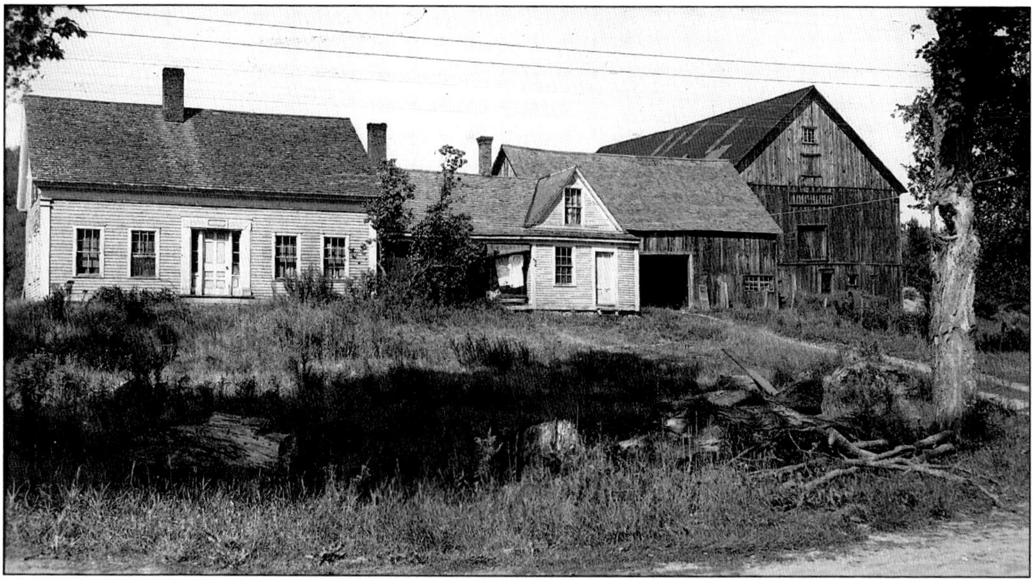

The Harry and Florence Knight Farm. This handsome farmhouse grew by stages. The ell chimney is largest, indicating the oldest section of the house. The off-center chimney on the main house suggests separate stages of construction. The house has classical revival features (corner pilasters with capital moldings, entablature, side and transom lights at the pilastered door) and, of course, connected back buildings. Harry Knight subsequently raised harness horses and cattle on a farm two miles south in Keene.

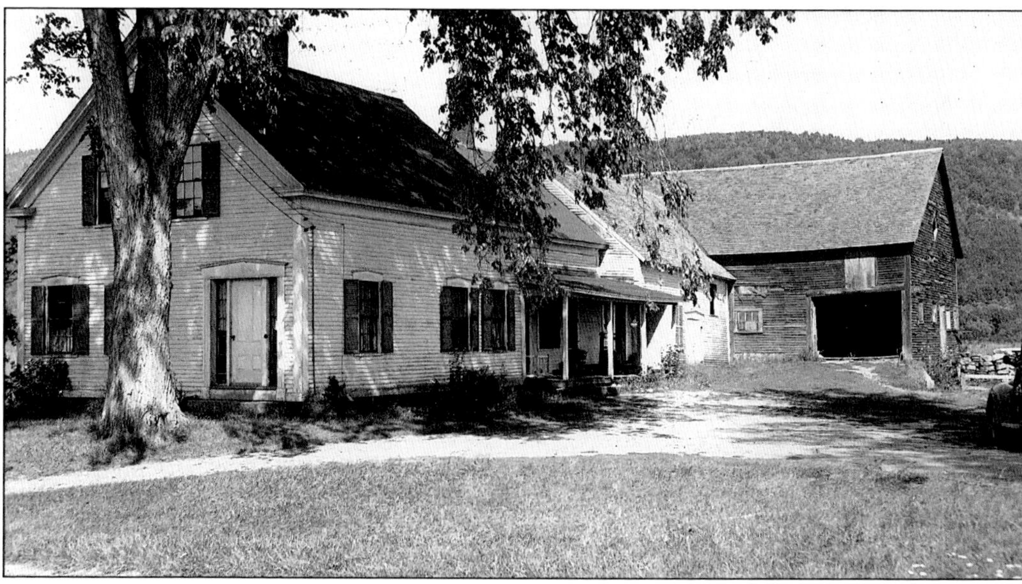

The Arthur Britton Farm. This beautiful Greek Revival farmhouse stood just north of the village, with 40-plus acres of fields extending to the river. Again a "run-on," with origins in the porch ell, the front house is a classic of its type: gable end forward, corner pilasters, off-center entry with side lights, and pedimented window and door heads. The barn, like the ell, originated probably *c.* 1800, as it was built in the English style, with the principal door in the long side. Lilacs still bloom in the dooryard that was.

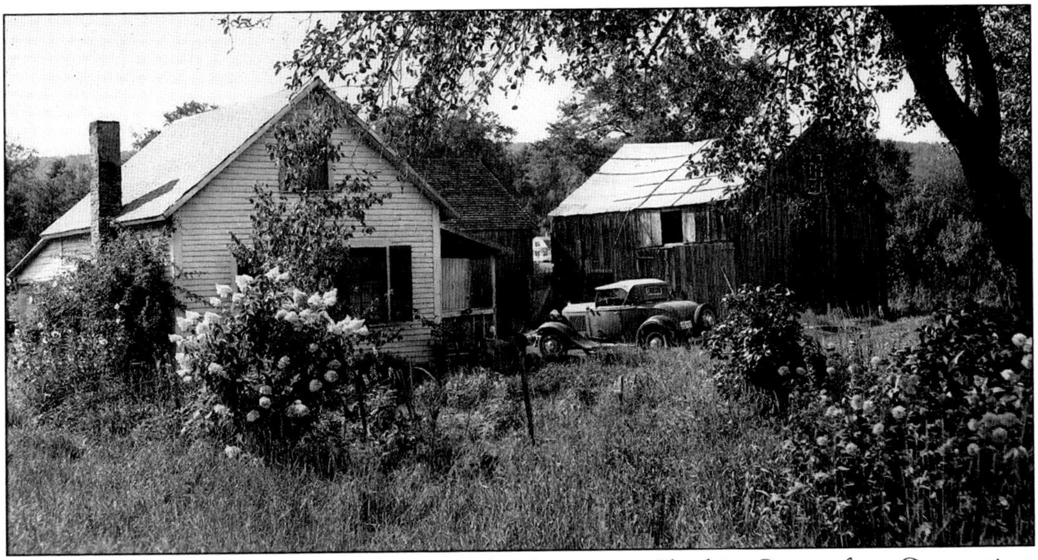

THE CATHERINE GRIGGS HOME. The Griggs family came to Cheshire County from Connecticut in the 1920s and farmed in Westmoreland and Surry. A serious fire destroyed the main part of the house, but widow Griggs managed to remain in the undamaged ell with a daughter and son-in-law until its purchase by the Army Corps of Engineers. Stone front steps still invite entry into a home that is no more.

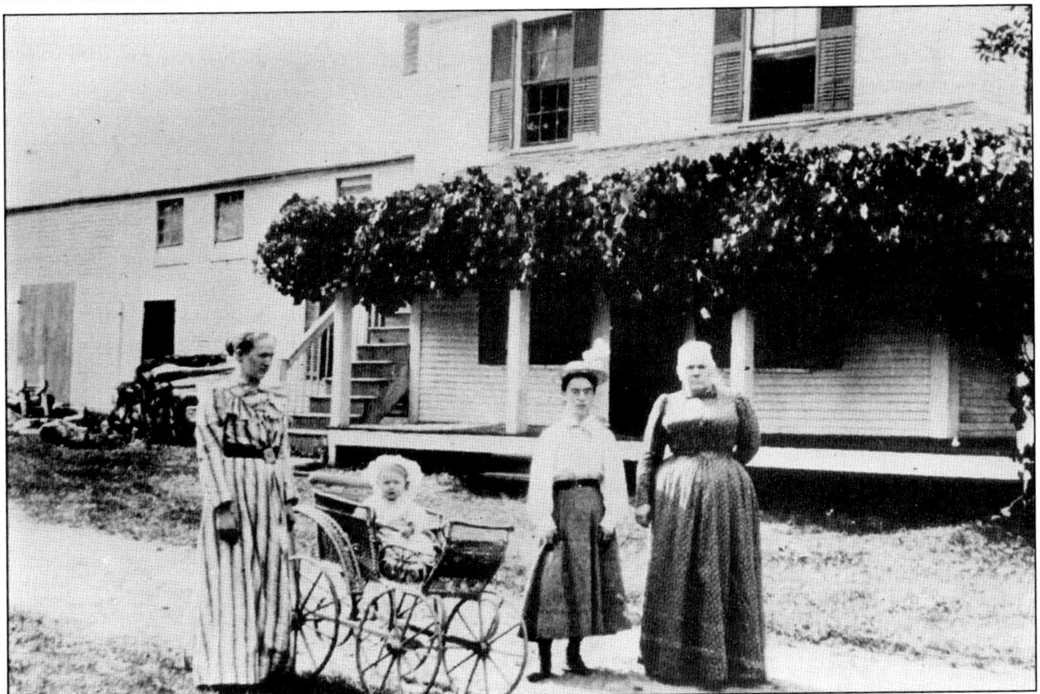

THE EDWARD BRITTON FARM. This two-and-a-half-story farmhouse with Greek Revival flourishes stood downhill from the village cemetery. Farmer Edward Britton's stone walls remain in place, brightened each spring by the flowering of bloodroot. This family photograph of 1900 shows his wife, Bertha; eldest son, Frank, in the wicker carriage; aunt Mary Allen; and his mother, Lucy Britton. Espaliered along the porch eave line is a Concord grapevine.

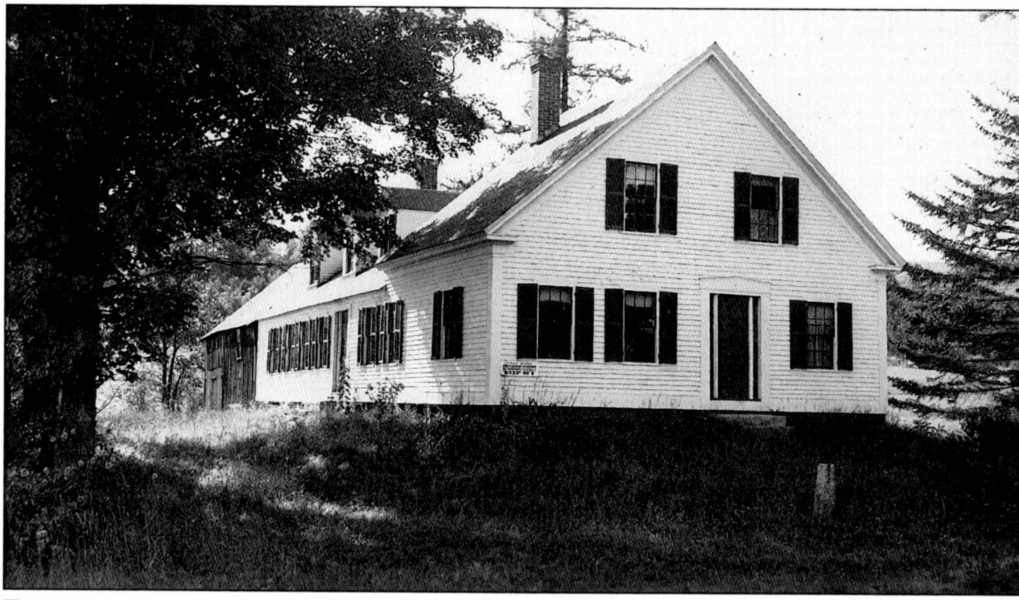

The Ellen Harvey House. James Harvey's own home fell to the dam, as well as that inherited by his sons. This unassuming Greek Revival, with the extraordinary bank of windows in the back house, belonged to his widow, Ellen (Porter) Harvey. Note the corner pilasters, the raking cornice of a very capacious second floor, and the off-center doorway with diminutive side lights and pedimented door head. The home of the sons, Robert and Shirley Harvey, is shown in chapter 3.

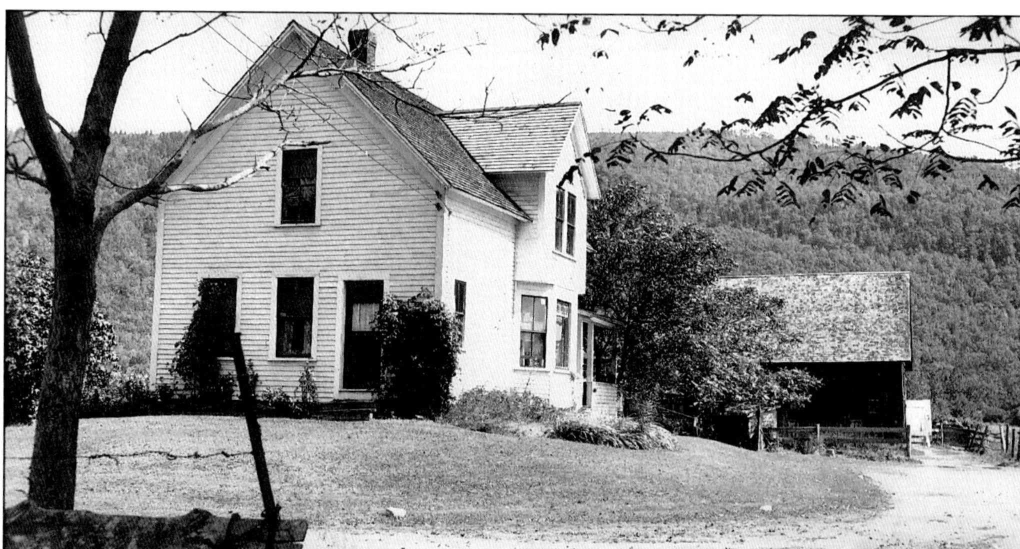

The Henry Porter House. This house clearly stood on a dry hummock, but its floodplain site on the Dort Road imperiled it once floodgates were shut. It is difficult to read architecturally, as its Revival origins have been eroded by many adaptations. However, the bay window addition, later surmounted by a cross-gable dormer, combined with foundation plantings, day-lily bed, and mountain ash (foreground), signal a beloved homestead. It survives today on the Crain Road.

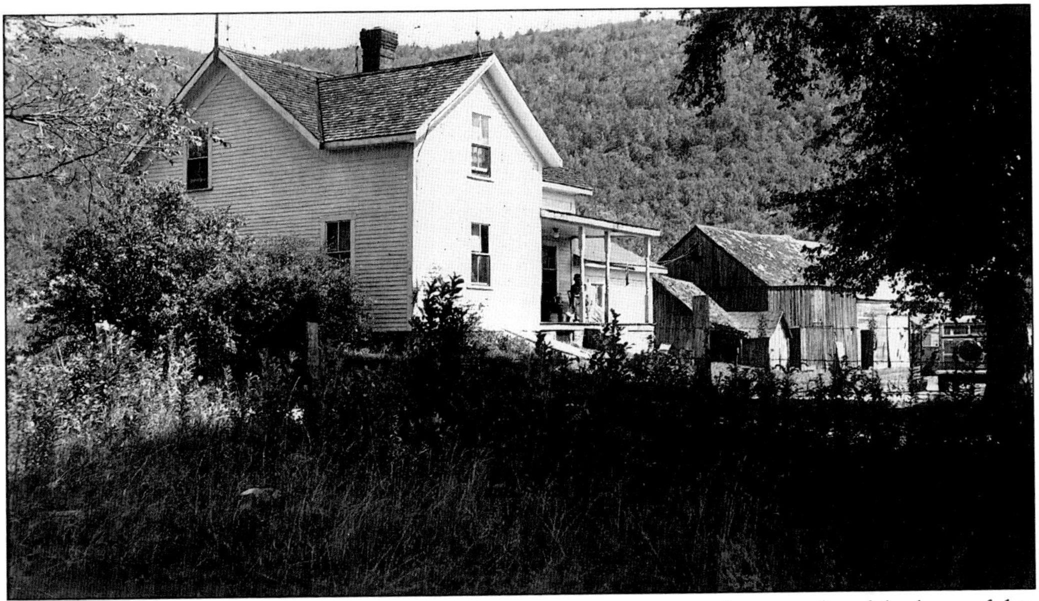

The Victor Lamminen Farm. James E. Harvey's winter-summer photographs of the barn of this extended structure east of the Dort Road appeared on page 55. Originally the Captain Dort farm, it was acquired by immigrant Victor Lamminen, following a not untypical exodus from Finland to Fitchburg, Massachusetts, and Marquette, Michigan (both having major Finnish settlements). How must he have reacted to the seizure of this farm by his adoptive government?

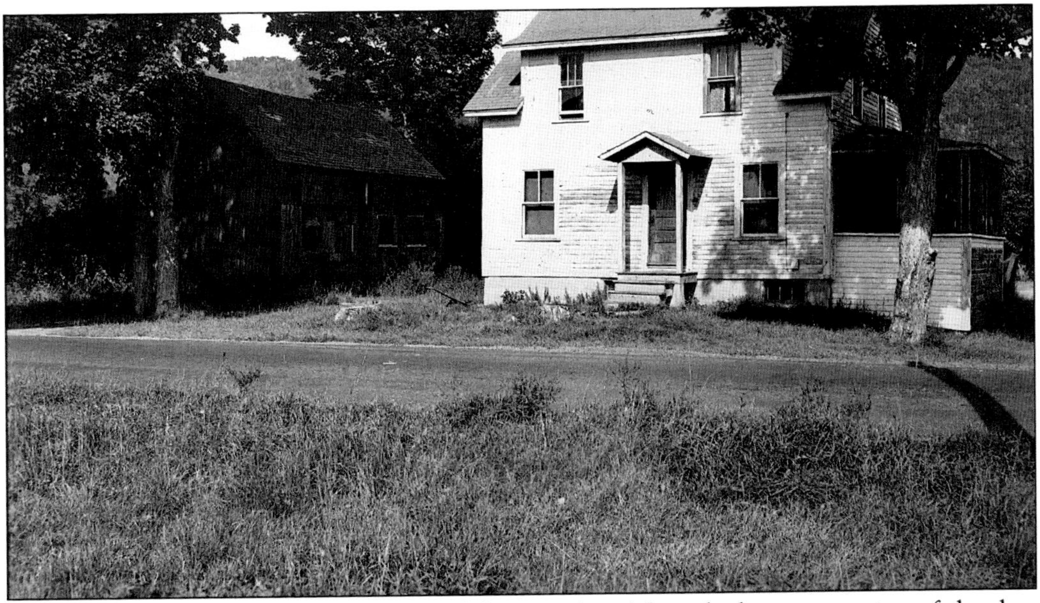

The William Kelly Farm. This house did not end its life with the construction of the dam but was removed to higher and dryer ground in 1942. It still functions as a home on the Crain Road. William Moran Kelly was the third child of Thomas and Rose (Moran) Kelly, village merchants of the 1920s (see page 41).

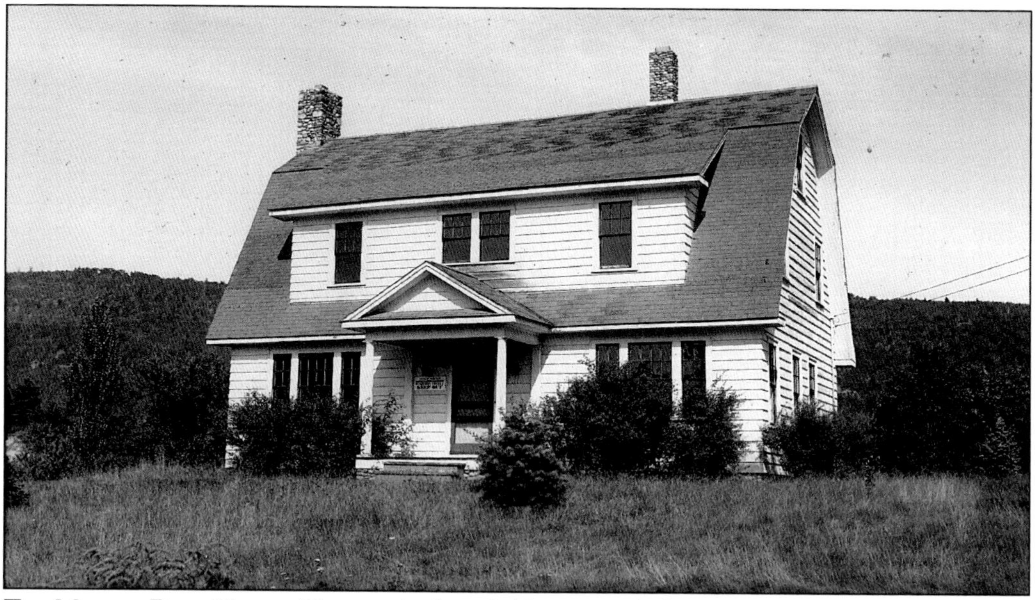

The Marion Bain House. This gambrel-roofed home, with distinctive rubble-stone chimneys, was saved and moved onto dry ground in the village center. The Bain clan originated in Scotland and arrived in Surry via Nova Scotia and Cambridge, Massachusetts.

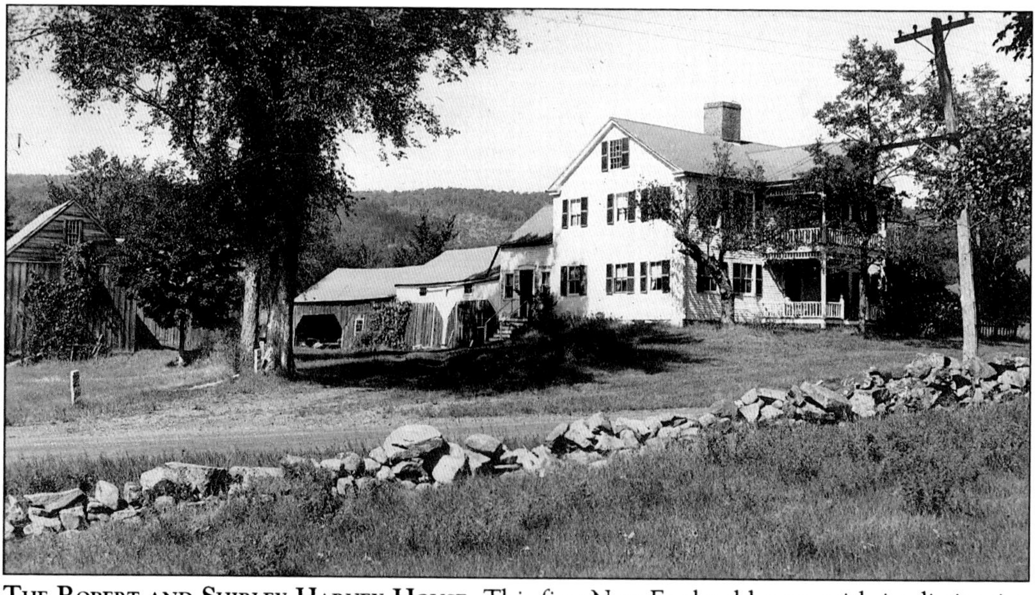

The Robert and Shirley Harvey House. This fine New England home, with its distinctive double-decker front porch (offering spectacular views, it is said) and "run-on" outbuildings, was removed in its entirety. As noted earlier, this was a family property of photographer James E. Harvey, by now belonging to his sons.

CLEAR-CUT. This view, printed in October 1939, shows the first steps to the redesign of the Ashuelot Valley floor at Surry. Forest growth has been removed, and stumps are being excavated, disclosing a classic meander of the river (perhaps a once or future oxbow). The scene faces the future east abutment.

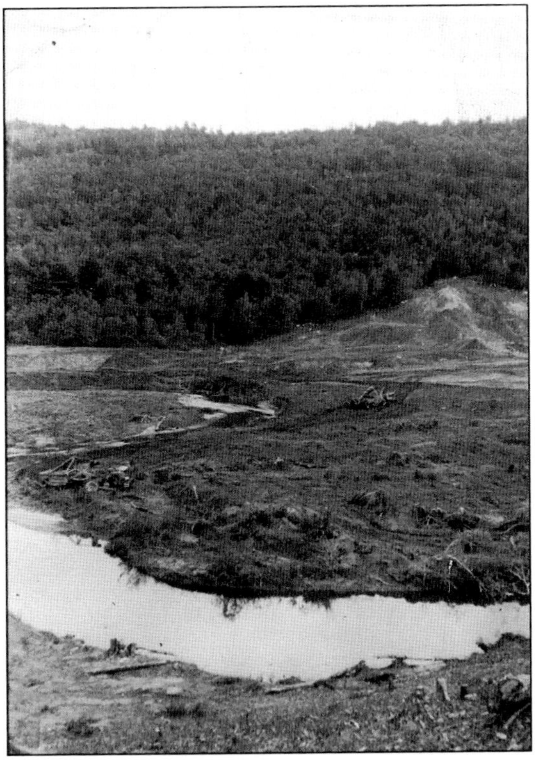

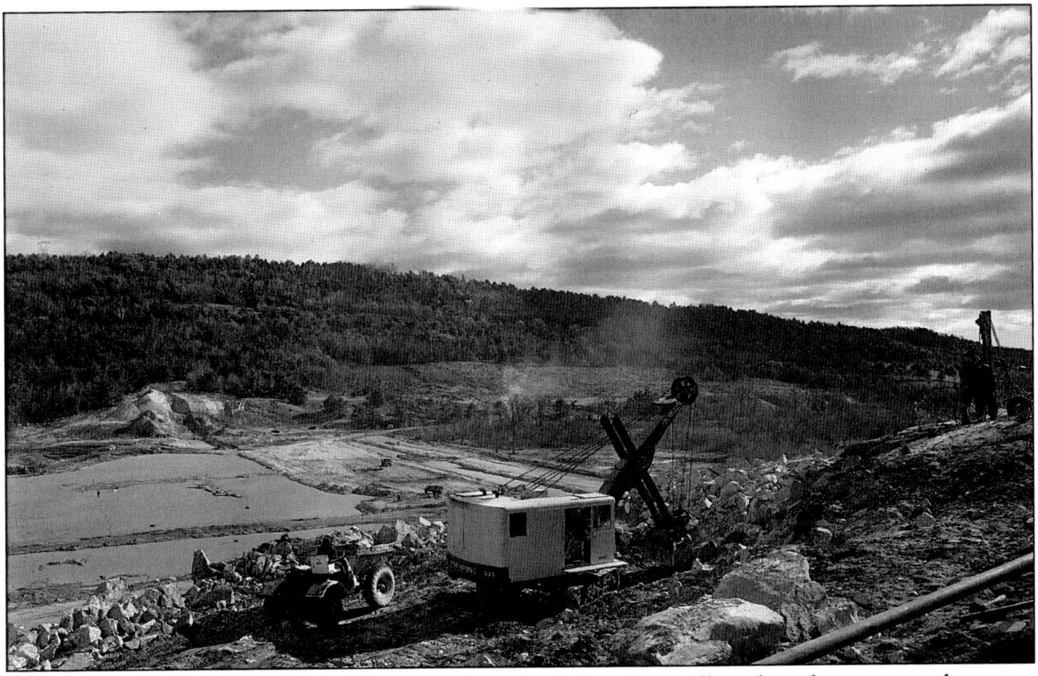

SITE WORK, NOVEMBER 1939. This view from the ledge that will anchor the western abutment shows progress made since August 1939: the site has been clear-cut, the valley floor scoured, and the river channeled. Dynamite borings are under way at the right, while the power shovel excavates the rubble.

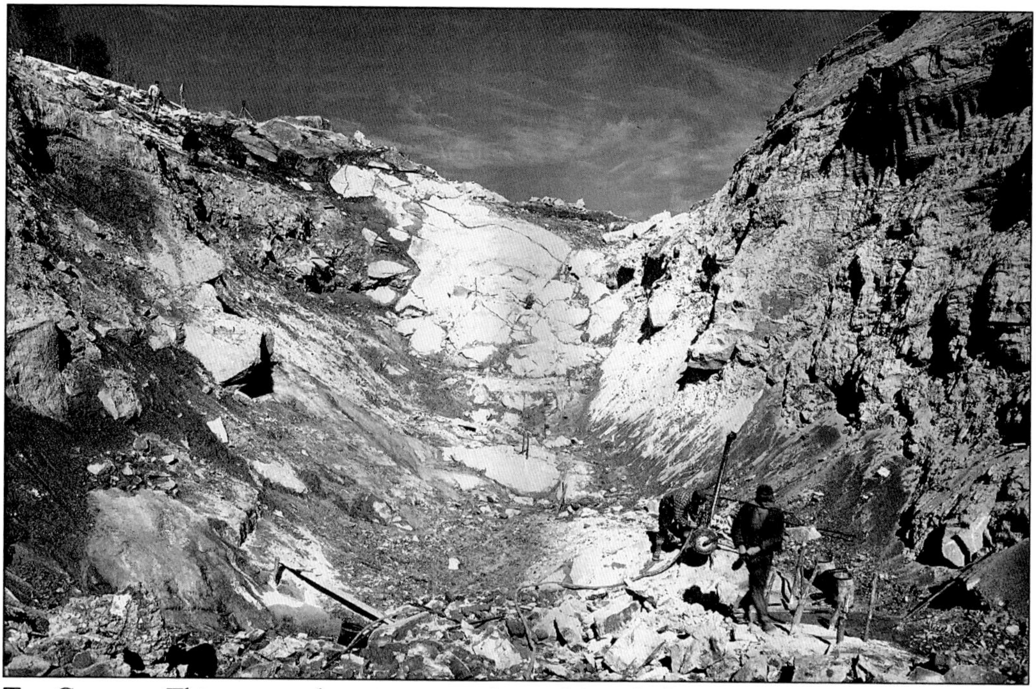

THE COULOIR. This man-made ravine, carved out of Appalachian bedrock, represents the high and the low of the Ashuelot River in the foreseeable future. The tunnel conveying the river 99 percent of the time will have its discharge portal at the lower right. At top center is the spillway crest. Separating the two is 50 vertical feet, representing some 10 billion gallons of water to be "stored" in upstream Surry.

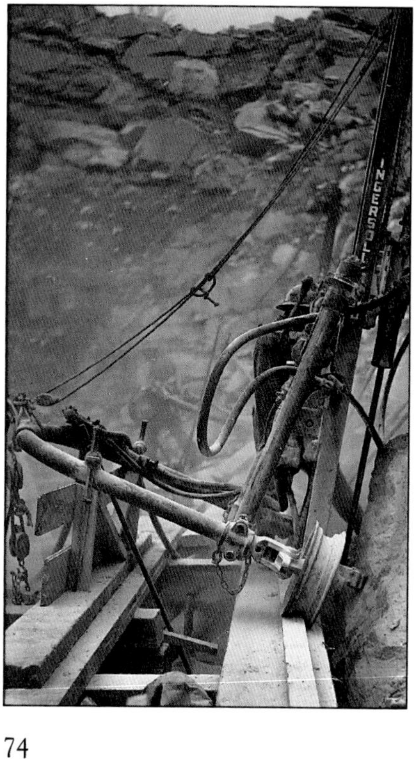

THE DRILL. Compressed air drove the rock drills, and jerry-built tracks provided the requisite purchase.

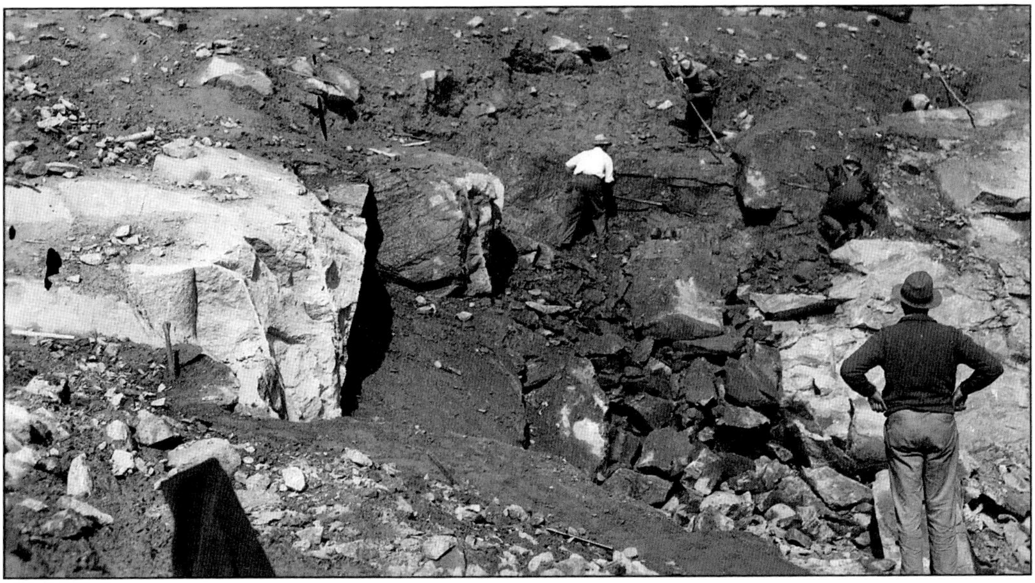

Rotted Ledge. We tend to regard stone as stone, but not all rock is solid. Workmen here remove "rotted" strata that have been compromised by weathering—that is, degraded by seepage. Compare the respective tints of the workface and the projecting ledge at the left.

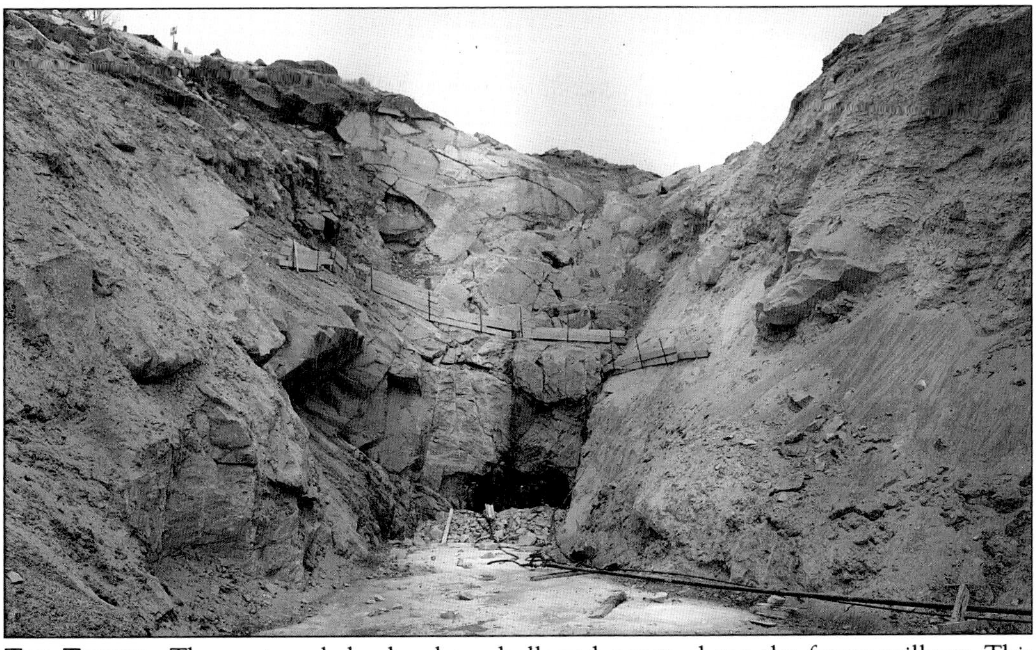

The Tunnel. The western ledge has been hollowed out to shape the future spillway. This photograph, from February 1940, shows drilling begun on the tunnel, the critical piece of a flood-control project. The channeled river will flow through the tunnel during normal weather conditions. During threatening situations, however, interior floodgates will cut off the flow, creating an expansive reservoir behind the dam. The storage pool, reaching a maximum of 970 acres (or 10.6 billion gallons) before it spills over the top of the weir, will relieve downstream sites of pressure from this watershed while other tributaries are accommodated past their respective crests.

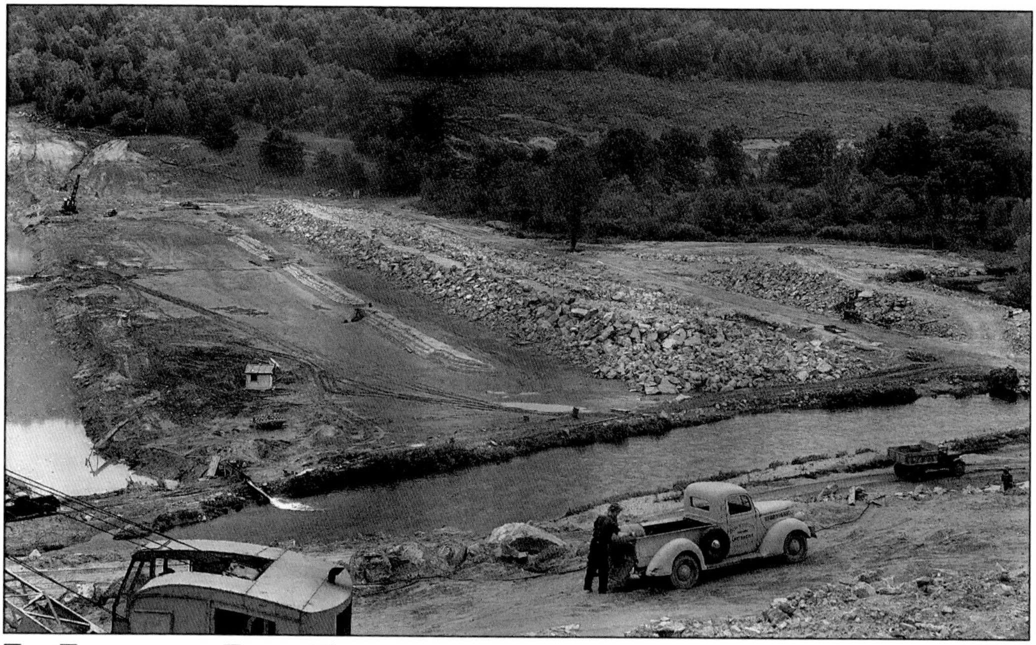

The Tools of the Trade. This view diagonally downstream from the approximate position of the future control house shows the modest equipment with which this refashioning of the landscape was achieved. Frank W. Whitcomb Inc., site-work subcontractor, remains in business in Cheshire County 60 years later. Subsoils for the dam foundation are being drained by pumping into the Ashuelot, channeled across the lower third of the picture. Barely visible along the tree line at the upper left is a stone wall, denoting an old pasture and, evidently, a property line.

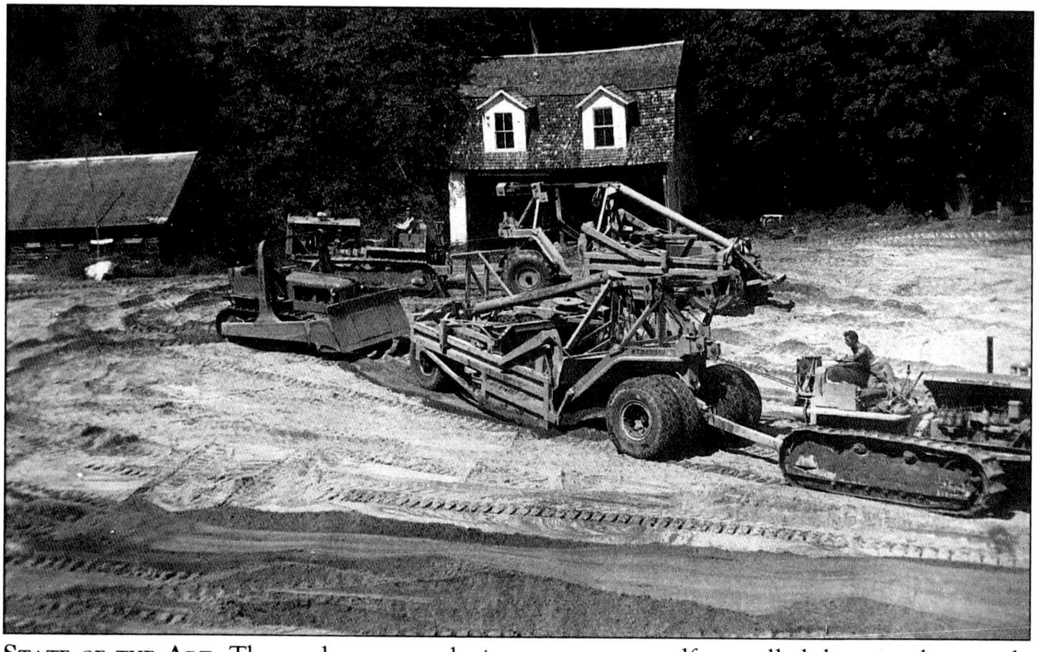

State of the Art. The grader-scraper device was not yet self-propelled, but simultaneously hauled and pushed by tracked bulldozers. Notice the condemned structures at the rear.

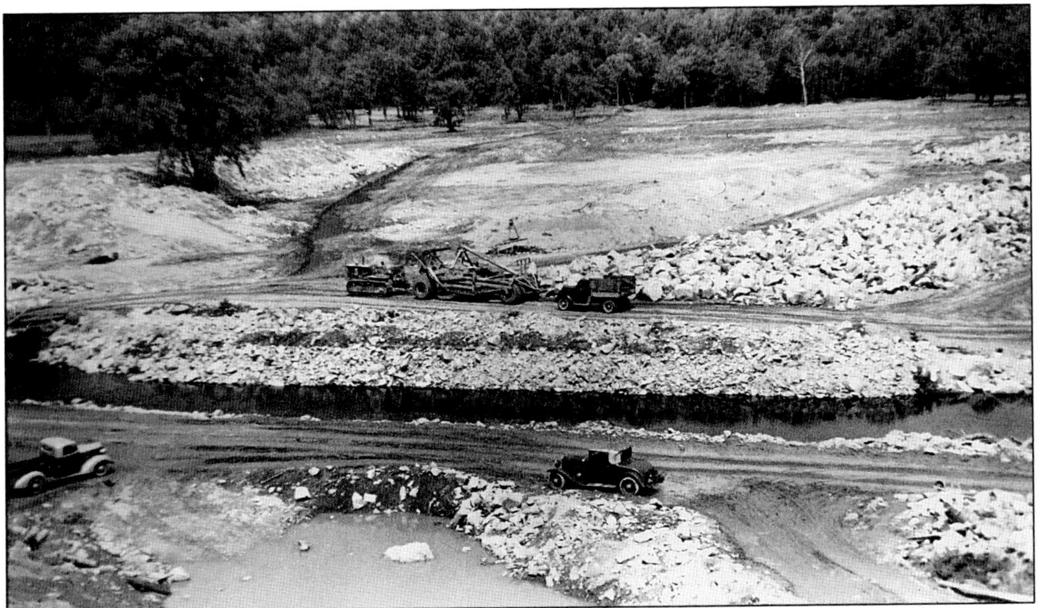

The Farmland Transformed. The tools may have been rudimentary by later standards, but with sufficient man-hours the farming resource base of Surry is being transformed.

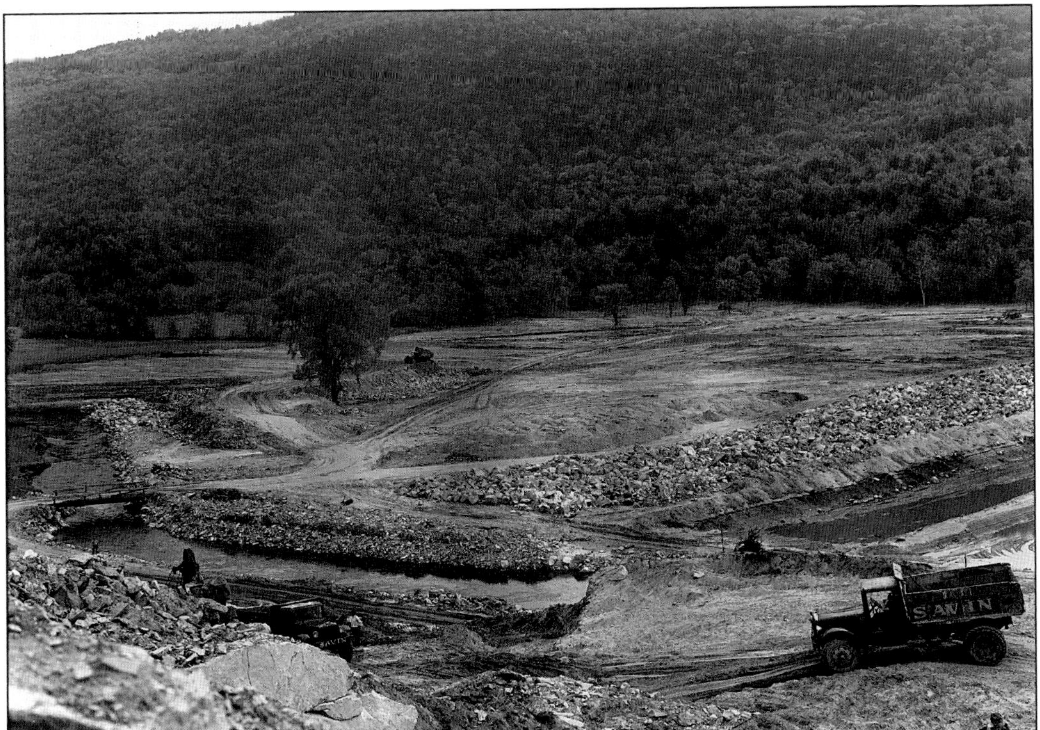

The Valley Floor. This view upstream, from June 1940, shows the intake channel (which will eventually flow through the tunnel) and the reworking of the valley floor. Savin Construction of Hartford, Connecticut, was general contractor. Visible at the far left is a healthy hay crop, ready for first cutting, at the Keller Farm.

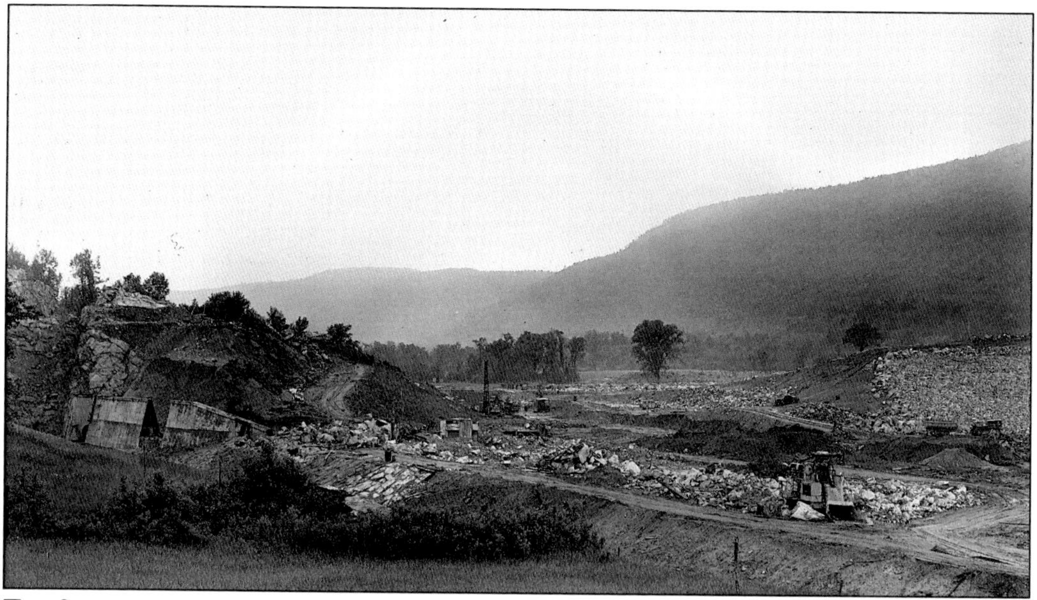

The Shape of Things to Come. This image from June 1941 shows the dam at approximately the halfway mark. At floodplain level remain various cofferdams and borrow areas, while the rammed earth dam takes shape on the right. It will eventually be raised to 86 feet above the valley floor and sheathed in riprap. At the left can be seen the discharge portal, concrete retaining walls, and laid derrick stone along the spillway channel. At the far left, the spillway remains an unfinished couloir in solid ledge.

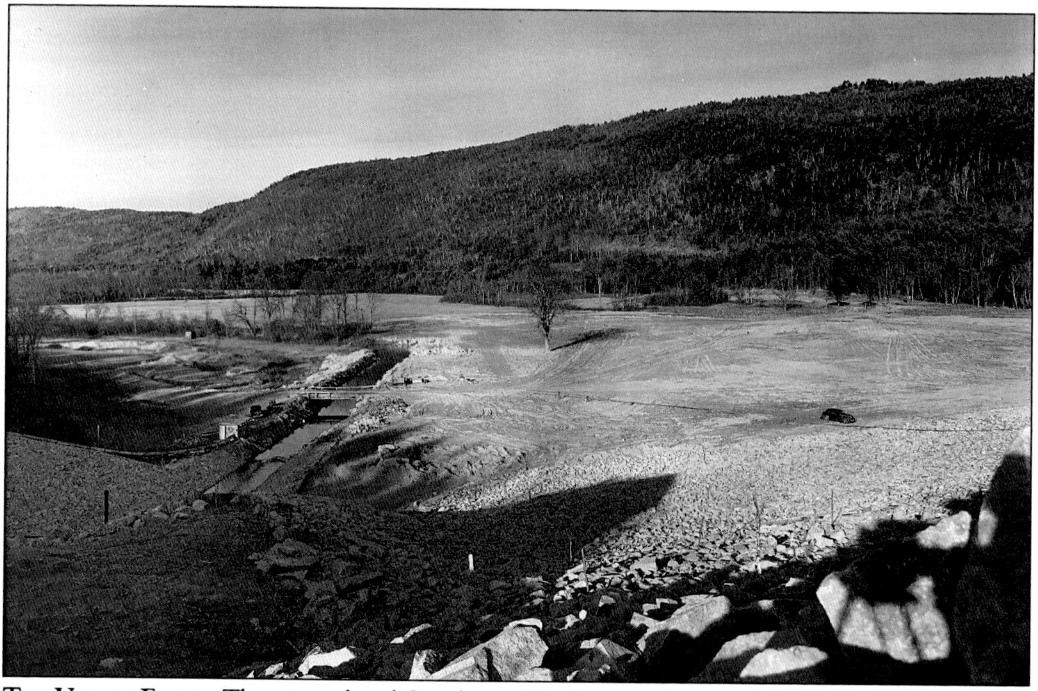

The Valley Floor. This view, dated October 1941, shows a change of seasons and of landscape. The photographer stands atop a carefully constructed wall of riprap, looking up a crafted intake channel, a hardened reservoir floor, and a sentinel tree now bereft of foliage.

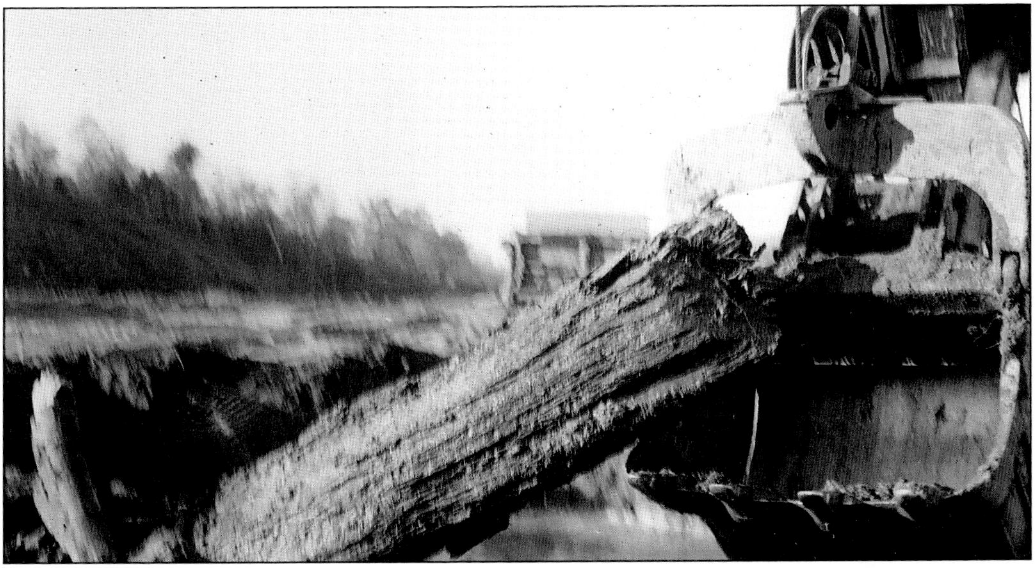

Sedimentary Archaeology. The excavation of the valley floor yielded some unexpected finds. Having scraped off the topsoil and then the sandy subsoils, workmen were startled to find another stratum of organic matter, within which were substantial timbers bearing ax marks. Here is one such find.

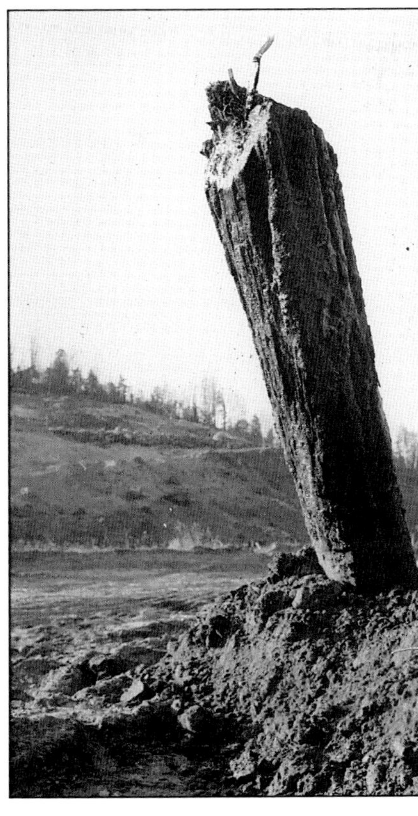

Archaeology. While professional archaeologists were not yet assigned to such major excavations, the workmen clearly regarded this find as deserving of documentation. The timbers presumably emanate from pioneer land clearing, felled and left to decay (or burn) but preserved by early flooding, which encased them in sediments immune to oxidation.

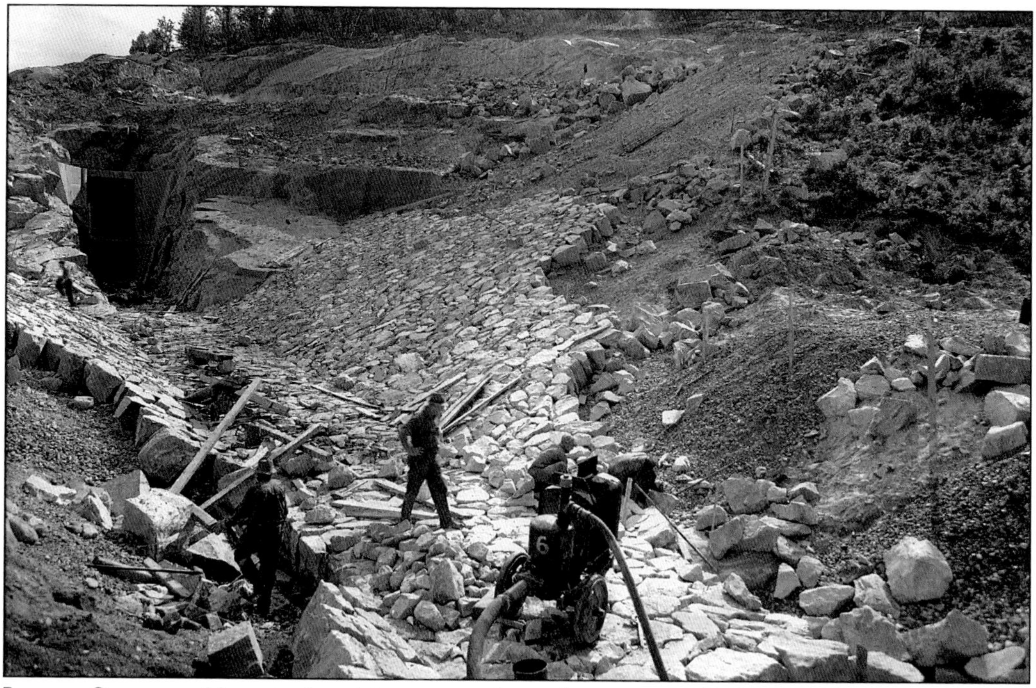

Intake Channel. Here, in the ultimate act of recycling, quarried ledge and blasted stone is laid to pave the intake channel. While a compressor is available for power assistance, the principal tools are those used in Egypt at the time of the pharaohs: levers, skids, inclined plane, and roller. The intake portal is shaped to receive the floodgate frames.

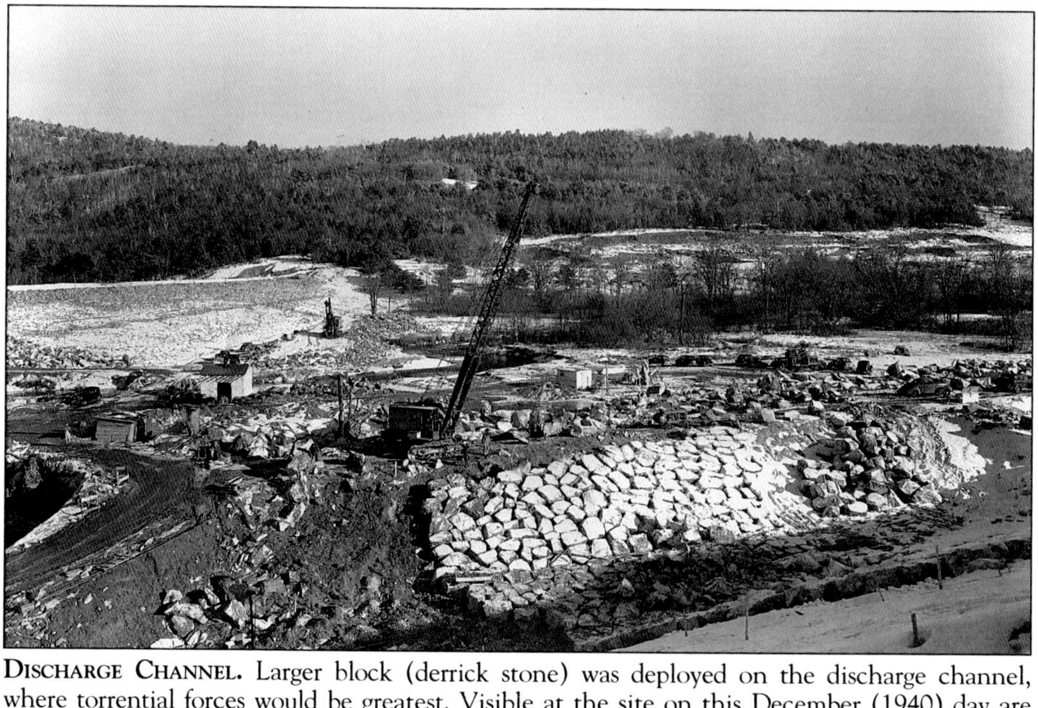

Discharge Channel. Larger block (derrick stone) was deployed on the discharge channel, where torrential forces would be greatest. Visible at the site on this December (1940) day are 14 workmen's automobiles, along with crane, compressors, power shovel, and one pickup truck.

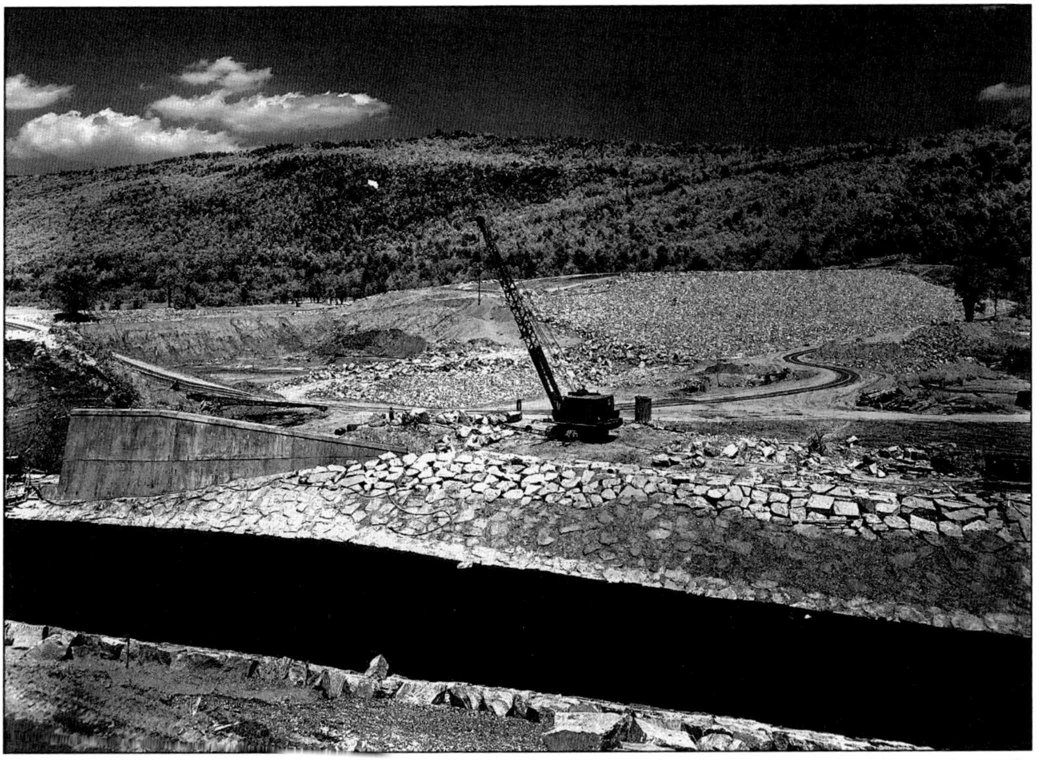

Paving. This striking photograph, taken six months later, shows the discharge channel nearly completed, reinforced with poured concrete abutments. The image is actually on infrared film, casting Surry Mountain in the likeness of an Ansel Adams photograph.

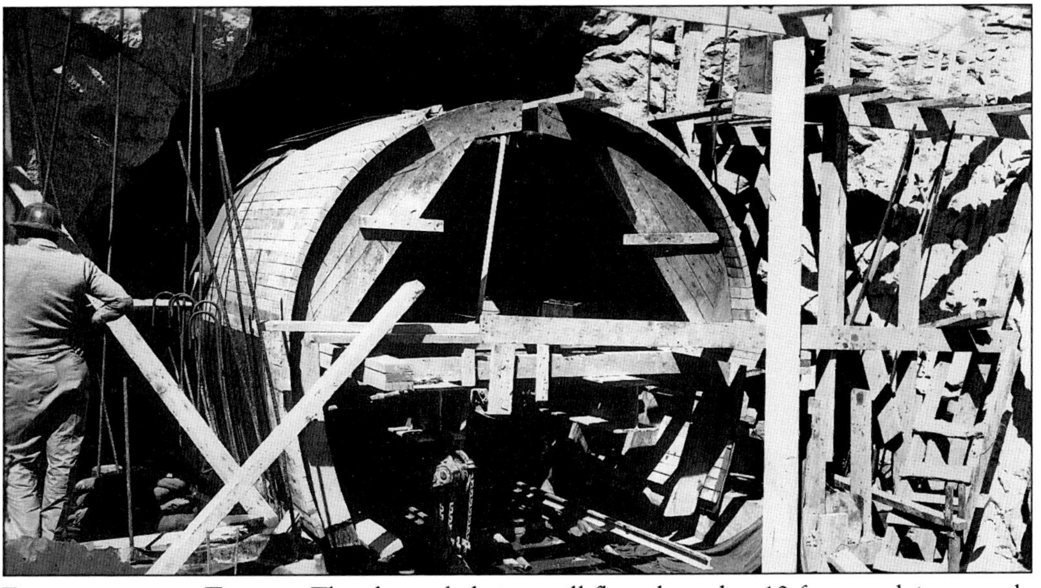

Fabricating the Tunnel. The channeled river will flow through a 10-foot conduit, recently drilled through the solid ledge of the west bank. The tunnel is finished by the application of a concrete skin. Workmen here build the form that defines the inner surface of the tunnel skin. The hard hat on this man is the only one noted in the photograph files of dam construction.

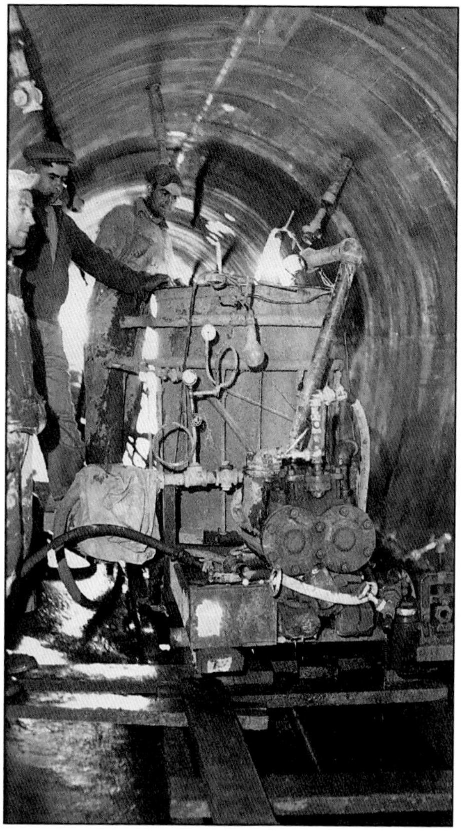

FILLING THE GAPS. Grouting is pressure-injected into the cavity between the concrete lining and the surrounding rock surface. Here is the pump equipment, mounted on skids.

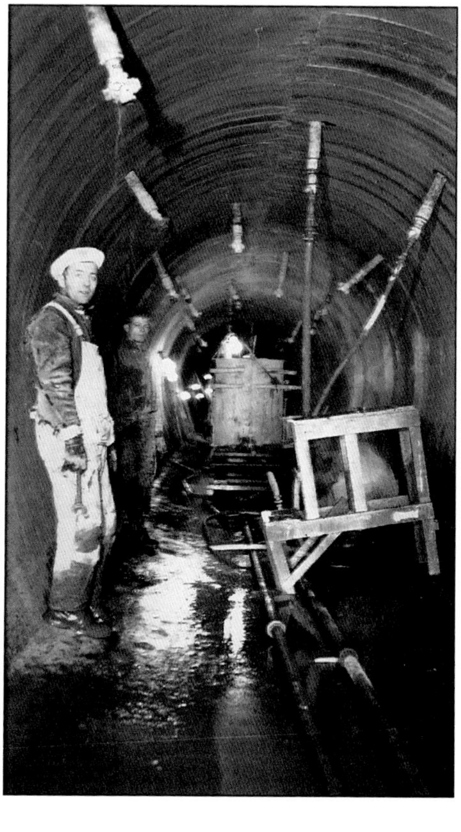

PUMPING. Hoses connect the pump to fittings drilled at 10, 12, and 2 o'clock. Gravity performs 50 percent of the job; the pump does the rest.

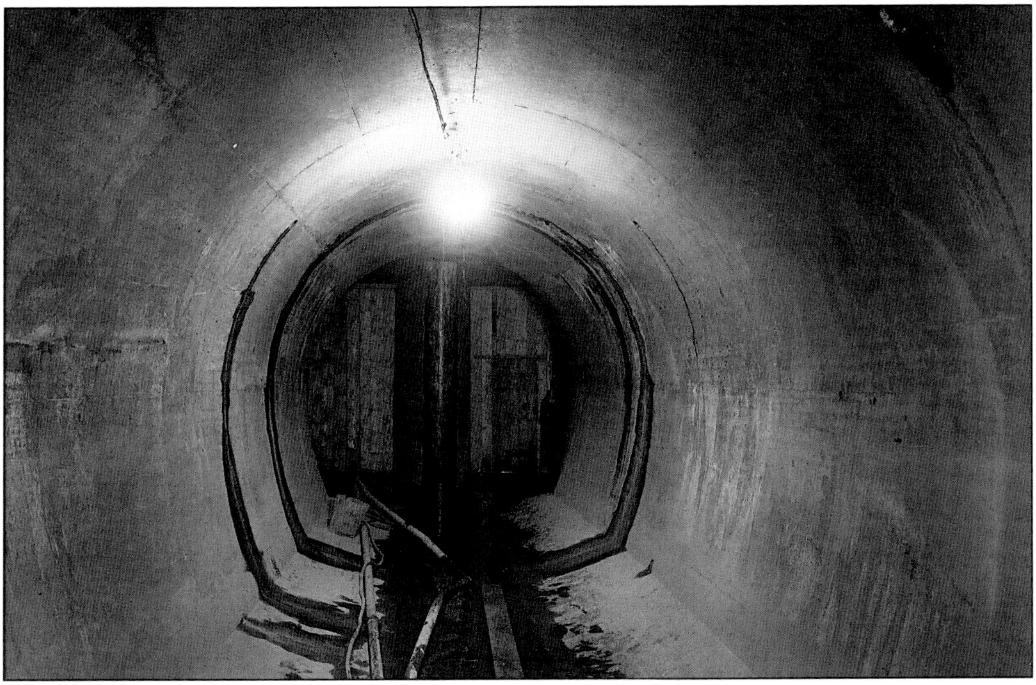

THE FINISHED TUNNEL. With the forms disassembled and removed, the new riverbed of the Ashuelot stands ready for inspection. The view is toward the floodgate frames. Notice the holes for grout fittings.

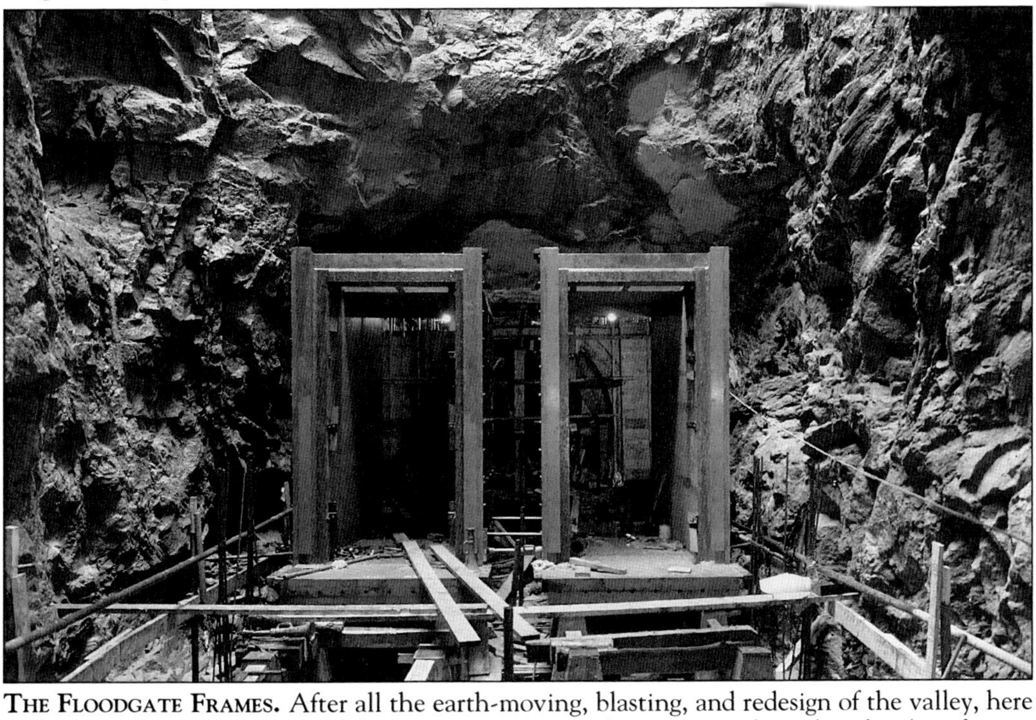

THE FLOODGATE FRAMES. After all the earth-moving, blasting, and redesign of the valley, here is the core element. Heavy steel frames are set in poured concrete pads, with re-bar (reinforcing steel that provides "backbone" for the concrete) visible everywhere.

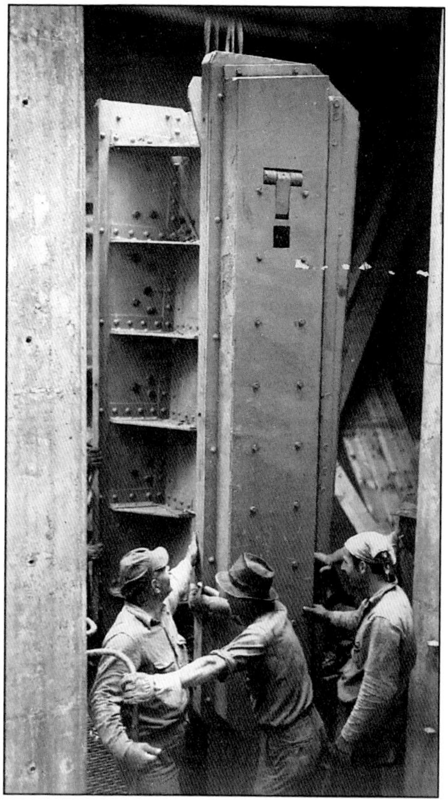

A Floodgate. Here, on August 14, 1941, workmen guide a prefabricated steel floodgate into the east-side service chamber. Two massive floodgates, each weighing five tons and raised and lowered by winched cables, make up the principal working parts of the dam. A third gate, mounted on tracks in a subfloor of the control house, is maintained on standby to address any failure of the primary gates. The three original gates, incidentally, were replaced in year 2000, after 58 years of service.

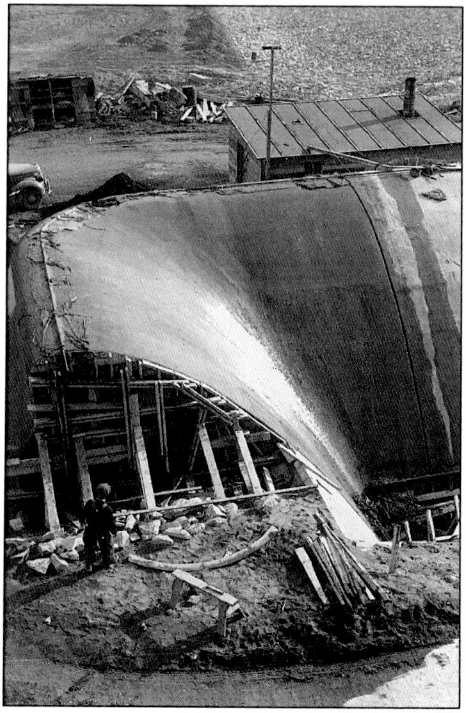

The Weir. In anticipation of the "One Hundred Year Event," when flood waters exceed the storage capacity of the reservoir, dam-builders must prepare a lip, analogous to that on a kitchen pot, to channel the overflow safely into the spillway. Called a weir, here is Surry's under construction, with an initial skim of concrete curing atop the formwork cribbing.

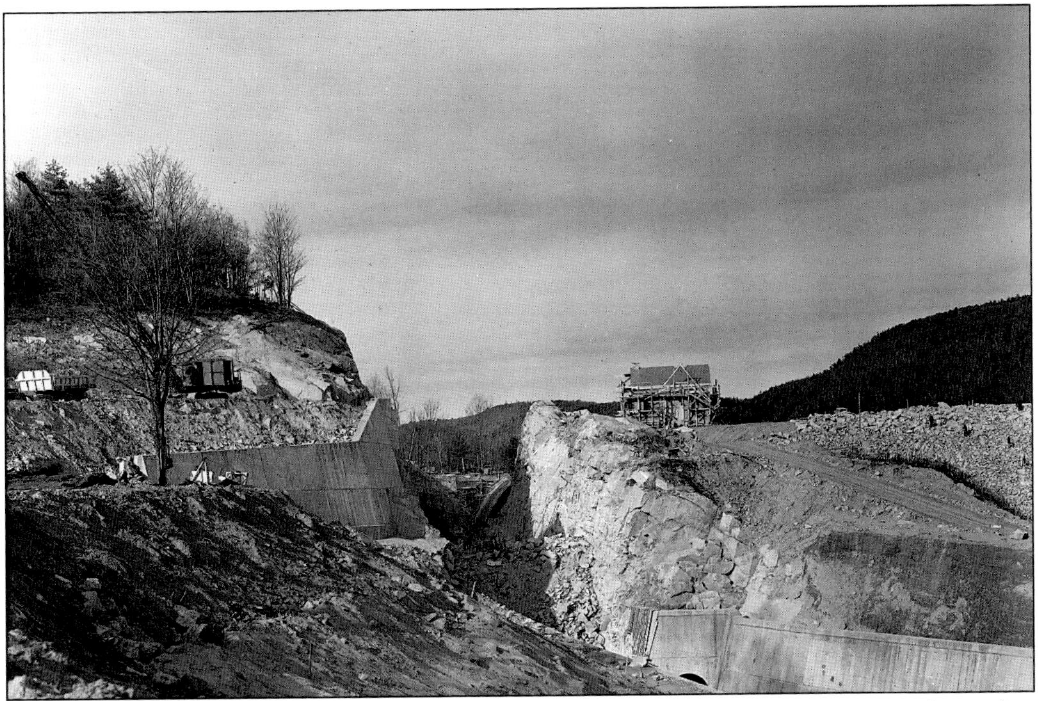

THE WEIR SECTIONS. This upstream view (October 1941) shows weir sections in relationship to the spillway channel and the control house under construction.

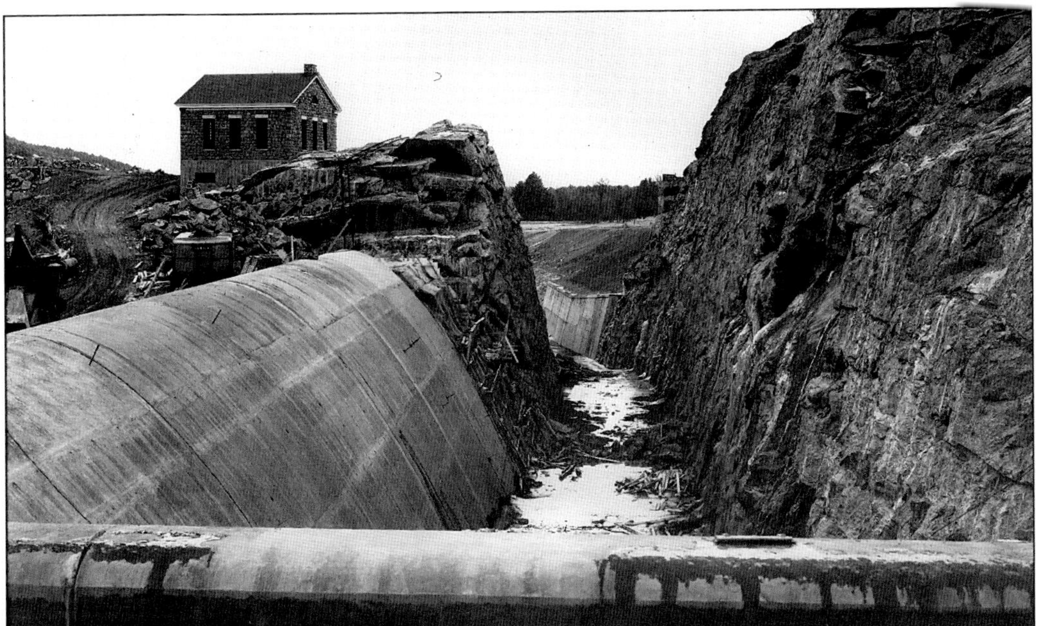

THE WEIR, LATER. This later view (January 1942) shows the progress of three months. Eighteen vertical feet separate the top of the dam (control house floor) and the top of the weir. Yet to be built is an access bridge across the spillway to the control house and roadbed of the dam.

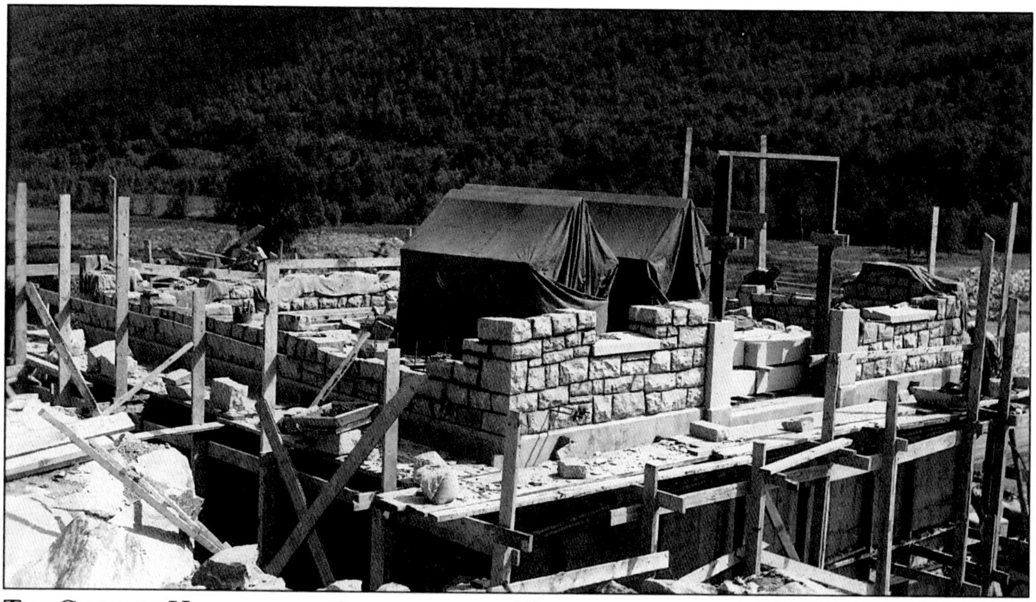

The Control House under Construction. The power equipment for raising and lowering the floodgates is installed in the control house. This handsome building is of masonry construction, in this case of coursed ashlar block.

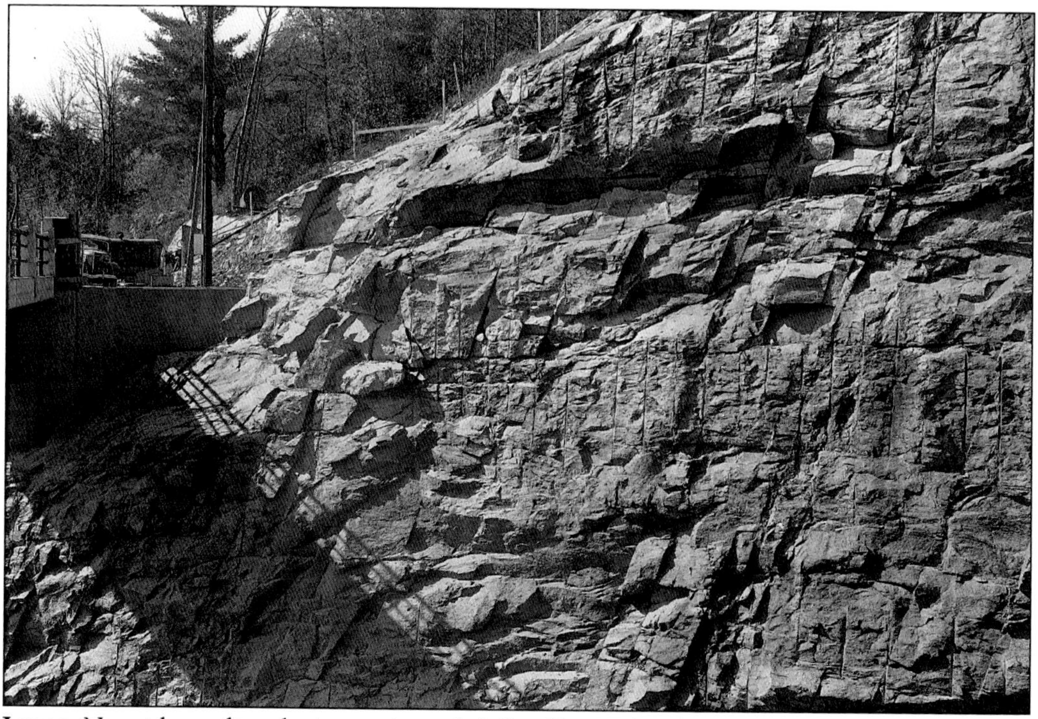

Ledge. Notwithstanding the ingenuity and skills of latter-day Americans, as exemplified by the Army Corps of Engineers, the surest counter to a natural force as potent as a flood is another natural force. Here is the bedrock by which New Hampshire identifies itself—the Granite State. Forming the west side of the spillway and anchoring the entire structure in *terra firma*, the wall of ledge before us shows more than 75 dynamite borings.

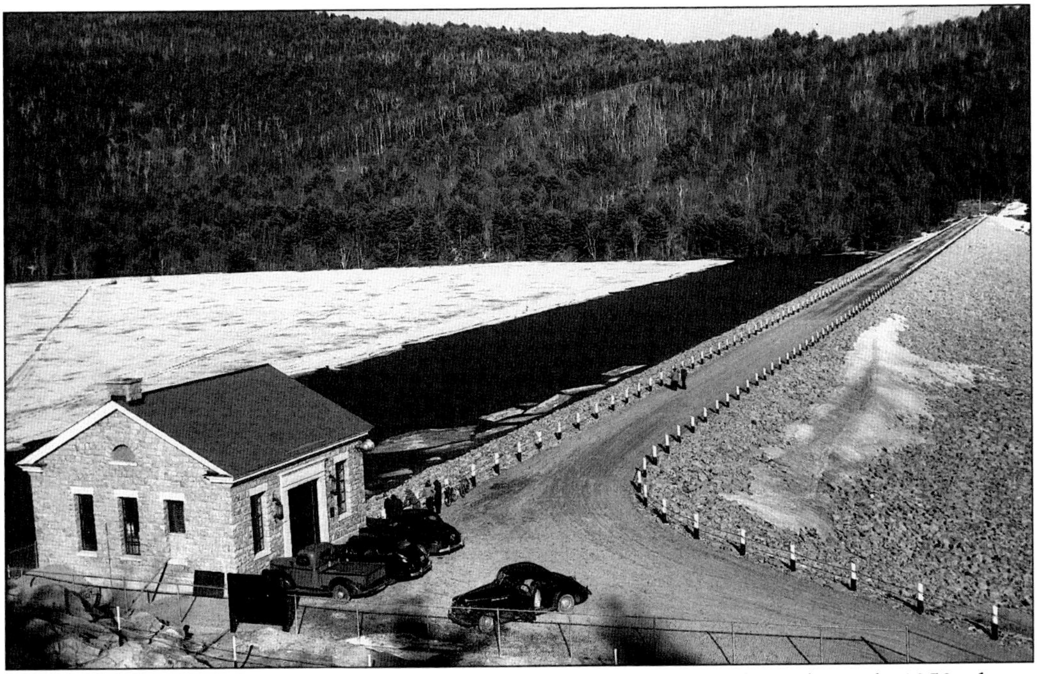

Completion—the Dam at Work. A wintry (but undated) scene from the early 1950s shows visitors inspecting high water in the late winter. Notice the handsome control house, finished now with classical trim.

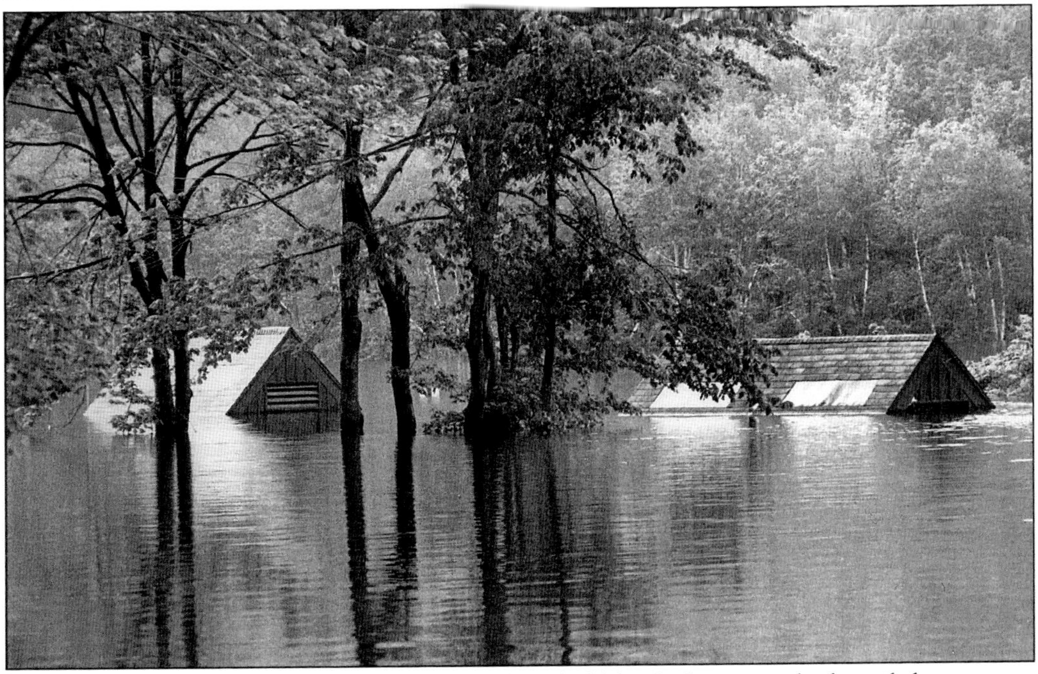

Flooding, 1979. When floodgates are closed to hold back this watershed until downstream pressures subside, one consequence is a predictable but unavoidable flooding of the public recreation area above the dam. Here is one such event in May 1979, following heavy rains on melting snowpack. The bathhouses are being bathed. (KS.)

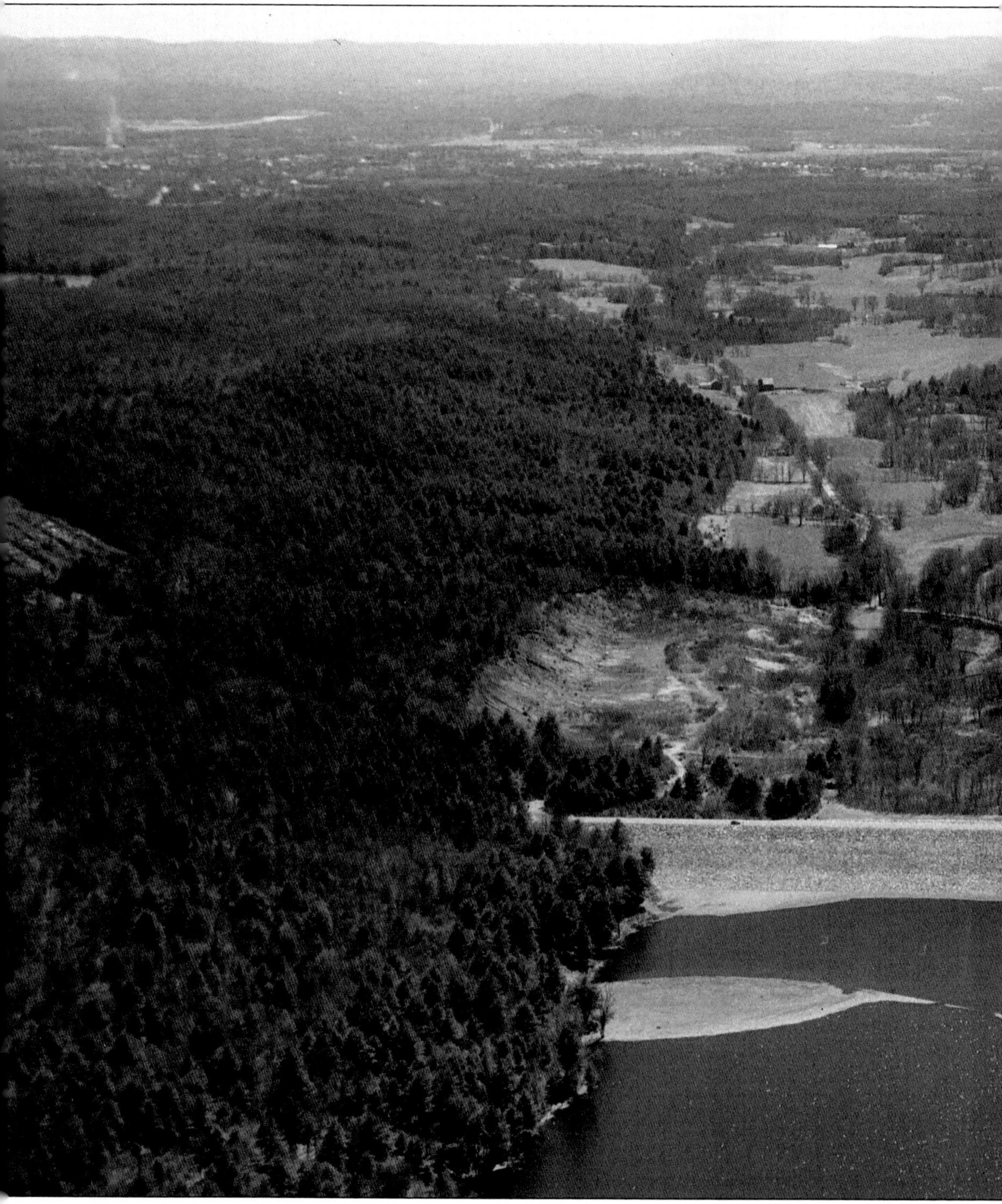

RISING WATER, 1958. This aerial view shows the big picture: a drowned valley above the dam, a dry valley below the dam, and the city of Keene (upper left), oblivious to the head wall of water poised four miles north of it. By extrapolation, one could substitute Springfield, Massachusetts, and Hartford, Connecticut, for Keene and imagine the many billions of gallons

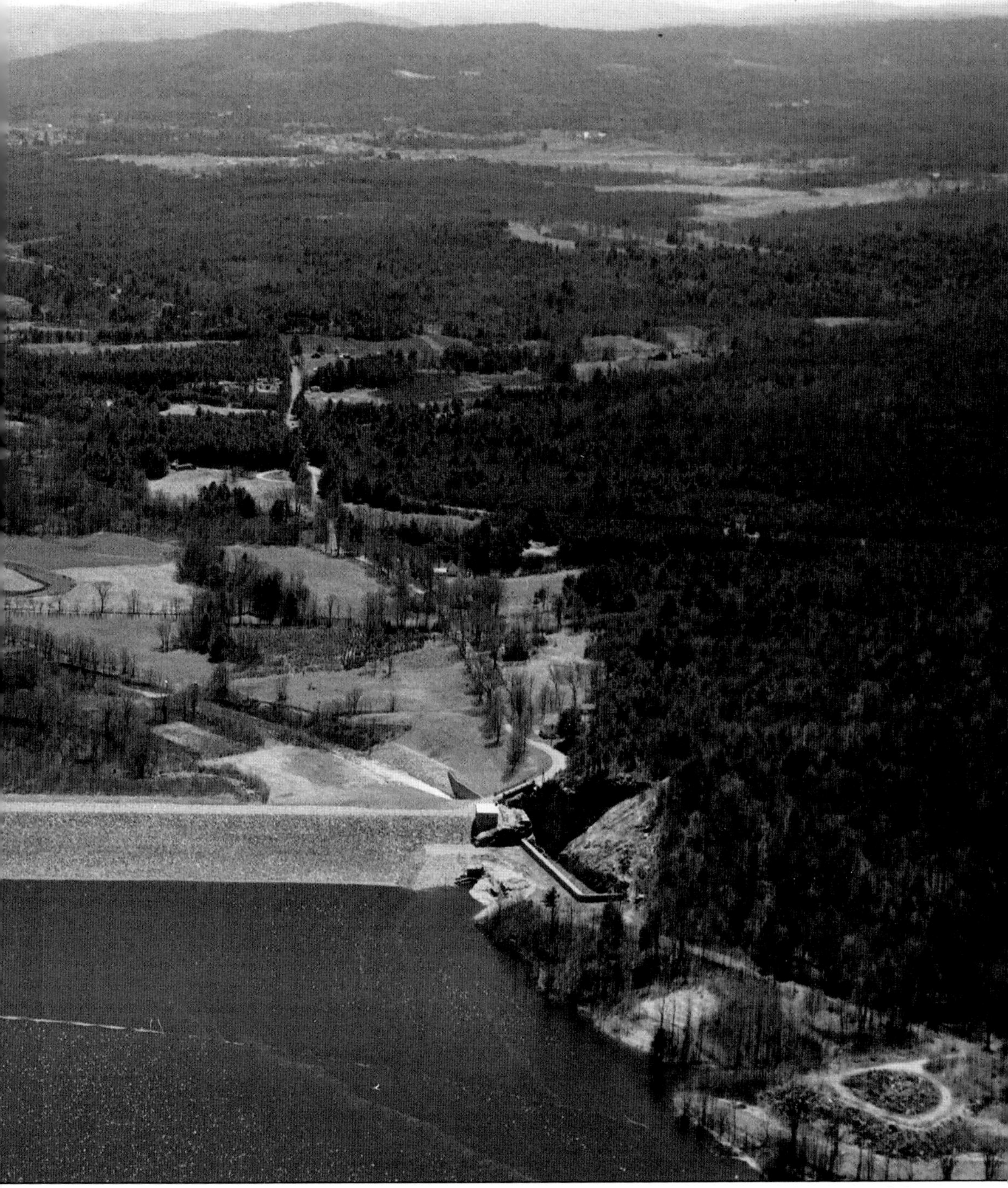

of water withheld by the 10-or-so flood-control dams then in operation on tributaries of the Connecticut River. The photograph was taken 15 years after completion. Construction scars have healed. Spring runoff and April rains, however, have contributed to a rapidly rising reservoir. A log boom has corralled timber cut off Surry Mountain during the winter.

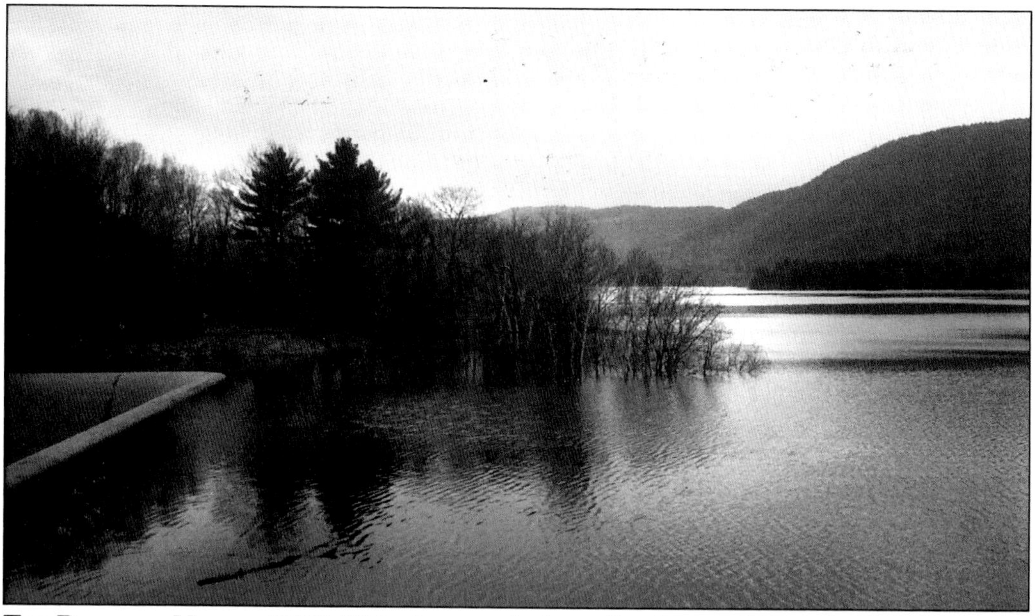

The Drowned Valley, 1987. This photograph shows flood-control at work: a flooded valley, water rising by the hour to the lip of the spillway weir. Army Corps of Engineers headquarters in Waltham, Massachusetts, receives a steady stream of data by satellite and land lines from its 16 dams in the Connecticut River Basin. Surry and its companion dam, Otter Brook, kept gates sealed, triggering the first ever spillway discharge.

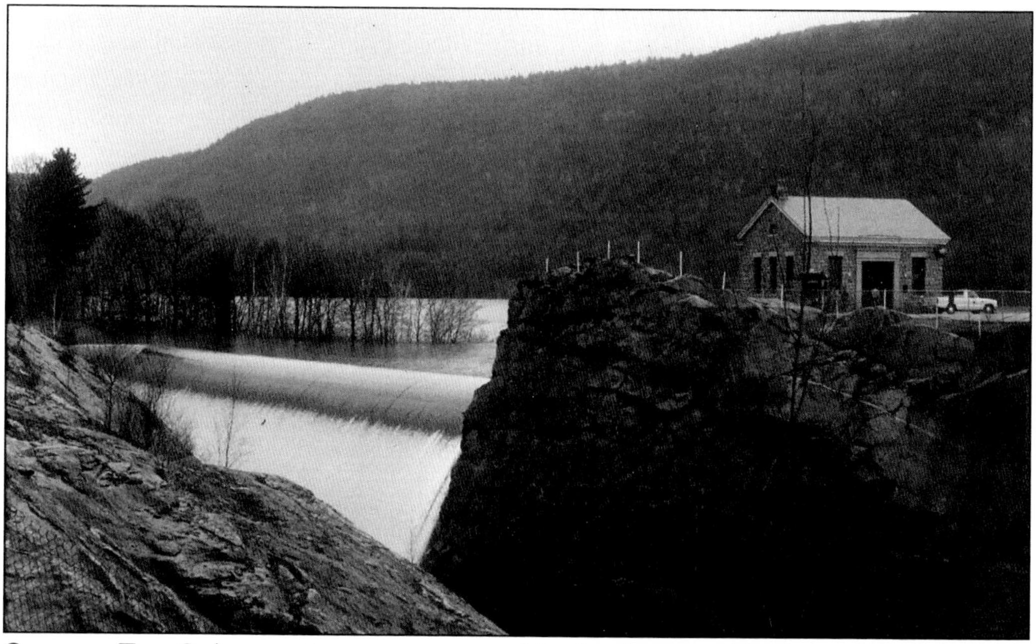

Over the Top. Only once since construction of the dam have pool levels reached the spillway crest. Here, for the photographic record, is the event, dated March 30, 1987, when rapid snowmelt combined with persistent April rains to reach capacity. By design, the stored pool of water at crest totals 10.6 billion gallons and covers nearly 1,000 acres of Surry countryside.

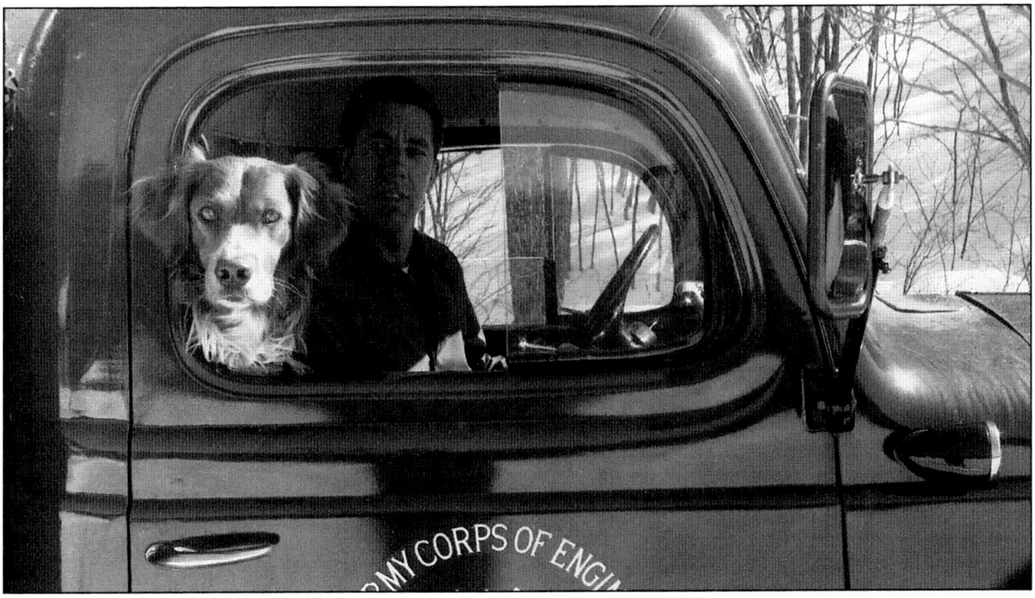

THE DAM AND THE TOWN. Once the trauma of dislocation and construction had passed, the town of Surry adjusted to its new landscape and new rhythms of life. For its part, the Army Corps of Engineers also reached out to the town, establishing face-to-face relationships, supporting the work of local committees, maintaining the flood-control area as an improved habitat for both natural use and human appreciation. For many, the face of the federal government in Surry was Vern Guyette, dam director of the 1960s and 1970s, photographed exactly as many encountered him.

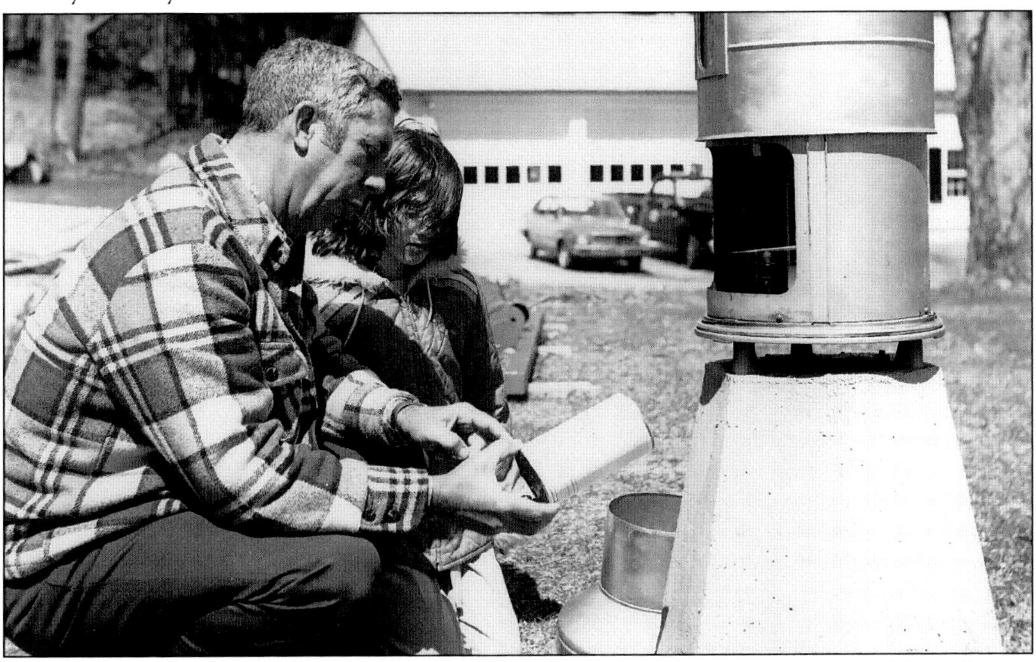

TAKING THE MEASURE. The Army Corps of Engineers maintains an active public relations program, with guided hikes, tours, slide presentations, and so on. One program of long standing is support of education. Here, Vern Guyette shows a Surry student the workings of a rain gauge.

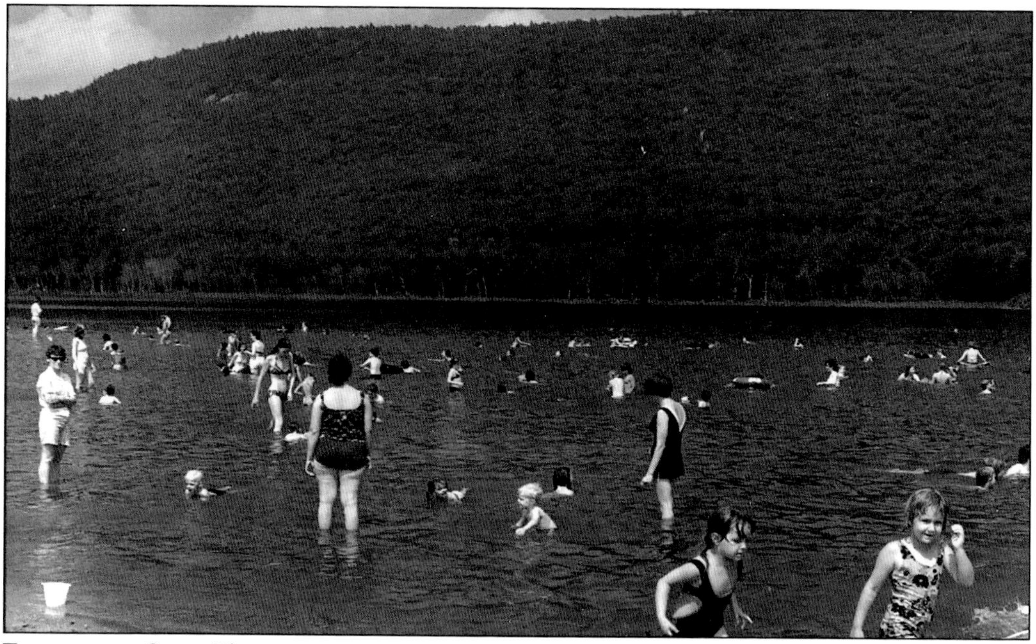

Fun in the Sun. The swimming area attracts the largest numbers of users (during season), reaching as many as 100,000 persons in the era before the Army Corps of Engineers instituted admissions fees at its sites. At Surry, a 600-foot beach was created near Green Pond, where ice was once harvested (see chapter 2). The depth of the pool is currently maintained at 15 feet. (KS.)

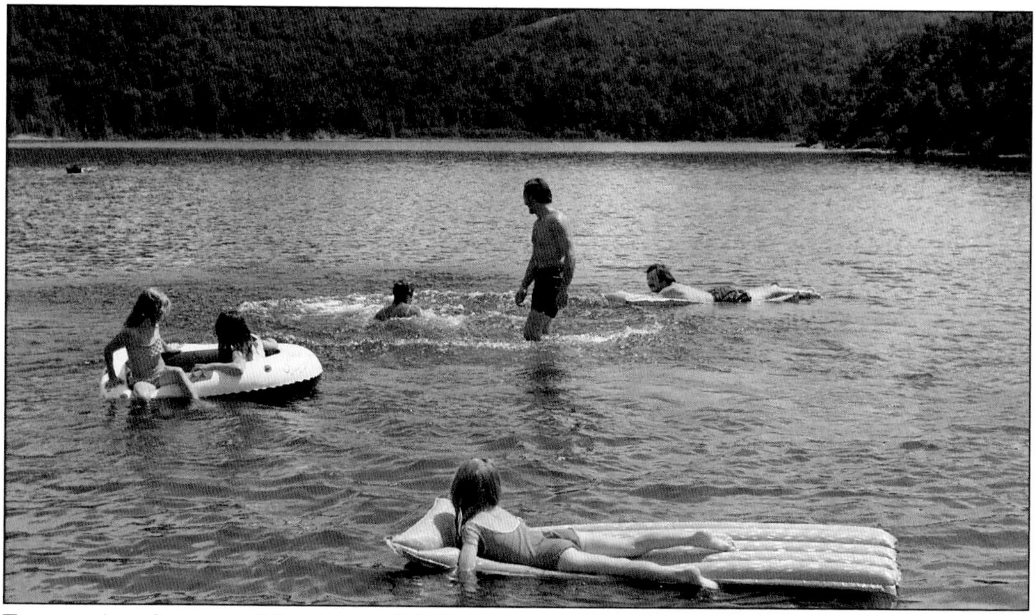

Fun in All Seasons. Hunting and fishing are permitted, as well as canoeing, sailing, and motorboating. Hundreds of birdhouses have been erected to support cavity nesters whose habitat has suffered (bluebirds and wrens, for example). The undisturbed environment of the flood-control zone has brought black bear, mink, otter, muskrat and other less frequent species to Surry Mountain.

Five

From Agricultural Village to Recreational Suburb

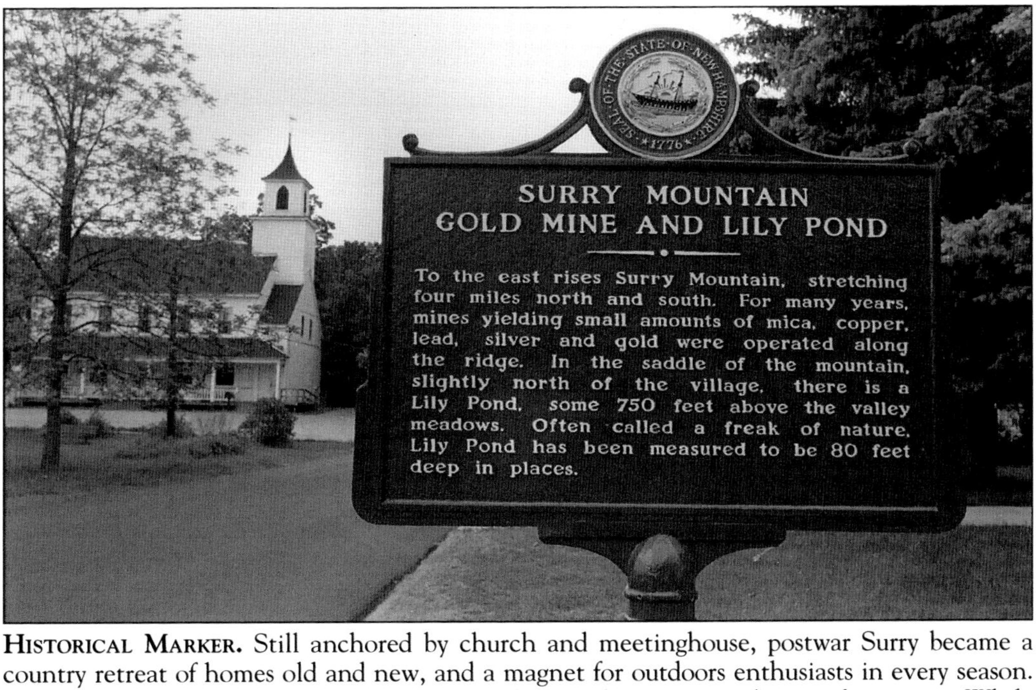

Historical Marker. Still anchored by church and meetinghouse, postwar Surry became a country retreat of homes old and new, and a magnet for outdoors enthusiasts in every season. The state historical marker bespeaks the advent of tourists, seeking information. While agriculture surely has declined in economic and social significance, it is Surry's virtue that the spirit of community continues unabated. This chapter tracks the development of contemporary social institutions (consolidated schools, fire company, library) and distinctive culture (community theatre, self-government, Scouts, cultivation of historical awareness). Finally, it celebrates some remarkable individuals who have made magnanimity the hallmark of their citizenship of Surry.

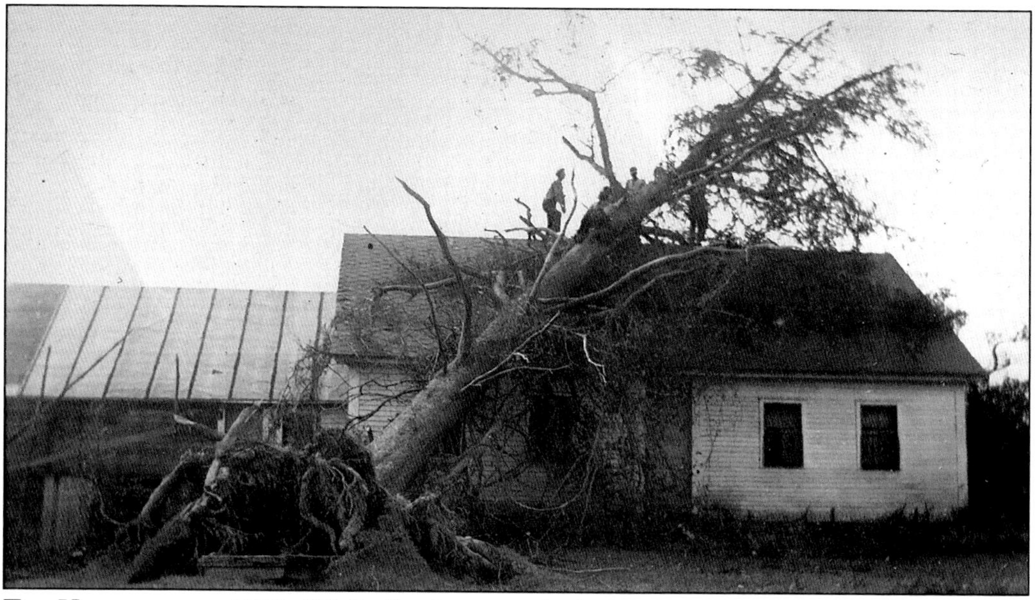

The Hurricane of 1938. While flooding was the longer-lasting consequence inland of the storms of 1936 and 1938, the hurricanes caused copious wind damage across New England as well. Here at the Anderson-White-Britton Farm on Mine Ledge Road, a dooryard maple nearly as old as the house has been stripped of foliage, shorn of limb, and torqued out of the rain-soaked ground.

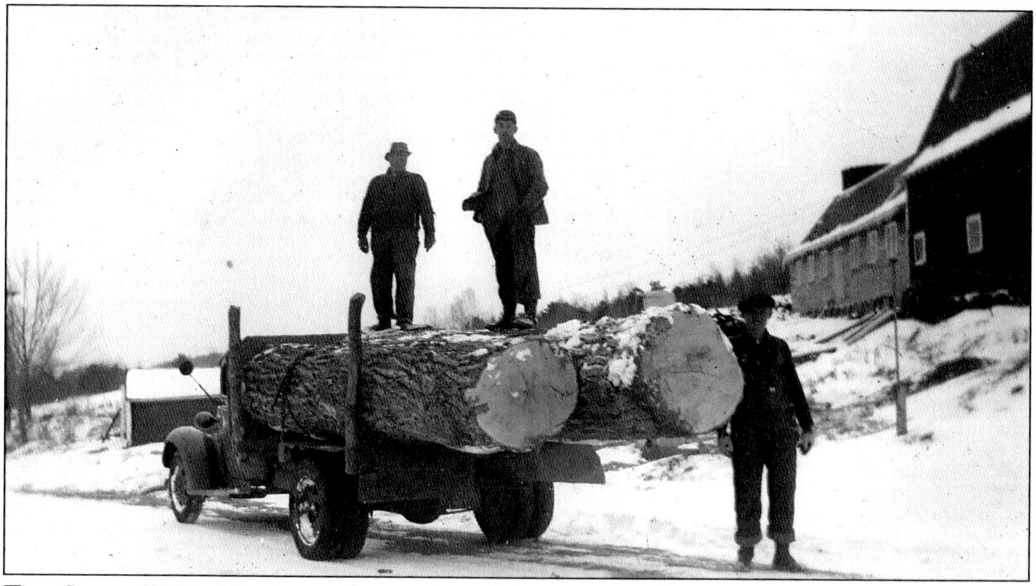

Two Logs, 1940. Hurricane cleanup lasted for years. In fact, seven decades-plus after the storms, swaths of timber can still be found in inaccessible regions, slowly decaying in parallel southwest-northeast formations. Here, in 1940, the Wilbur Farm, no doubt using oxen, skidded these beautiful hardwood sawlogs to a landing where they could be muscled onto a truck bound for the mill.

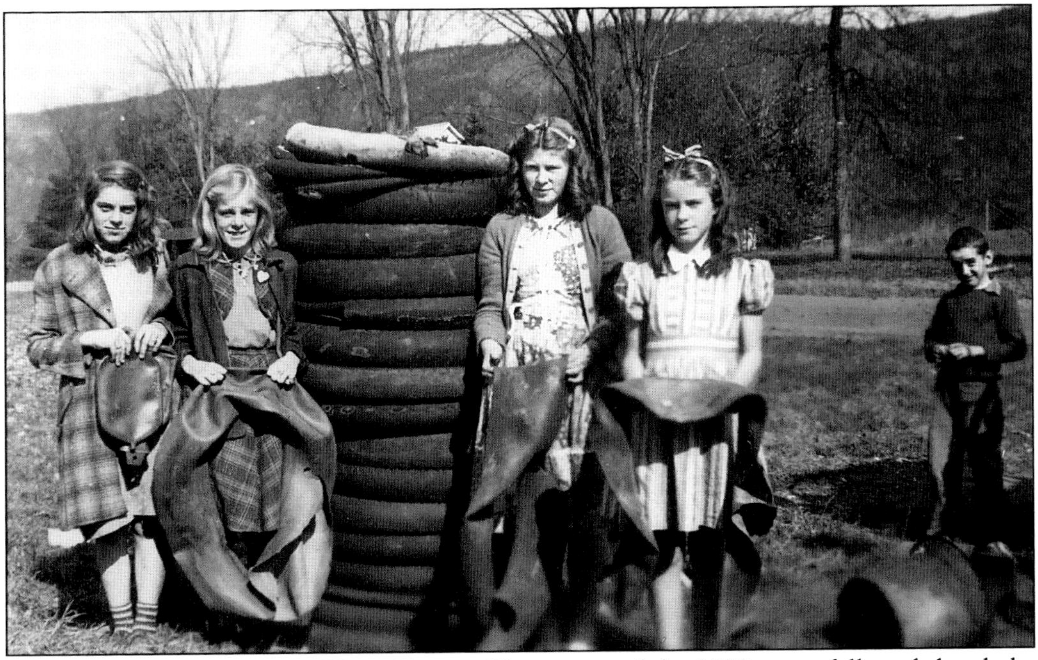

The World War and the Home Front. The storms of the 1930s were followed shortly by the winds of war across the oceans. Once the United States joined combat following Pearl Harbor, civilian life changed even in pastoral Surry. Patriotic schoolgirls led the way in this local effort at recycling, then called a "scrap drive." Shown, from left to right, are Florence and Lillian Davis, Lillian Martin, and Constance Young displaying the rubbery fruits of their 1942 door-to-door campaign, while Peter Malcolm watches shyly from the shadows. In addition to the inner tubes and tires, is that not a hot-water bladder in Florence's hands? Below is the metals pile. Plowshares may not be evident, but stovepipe and hayforms are recognizable Surry contributions to the American arsenal. The crude verse of the sign captures the raw nationalism of the people angered by an act of war.

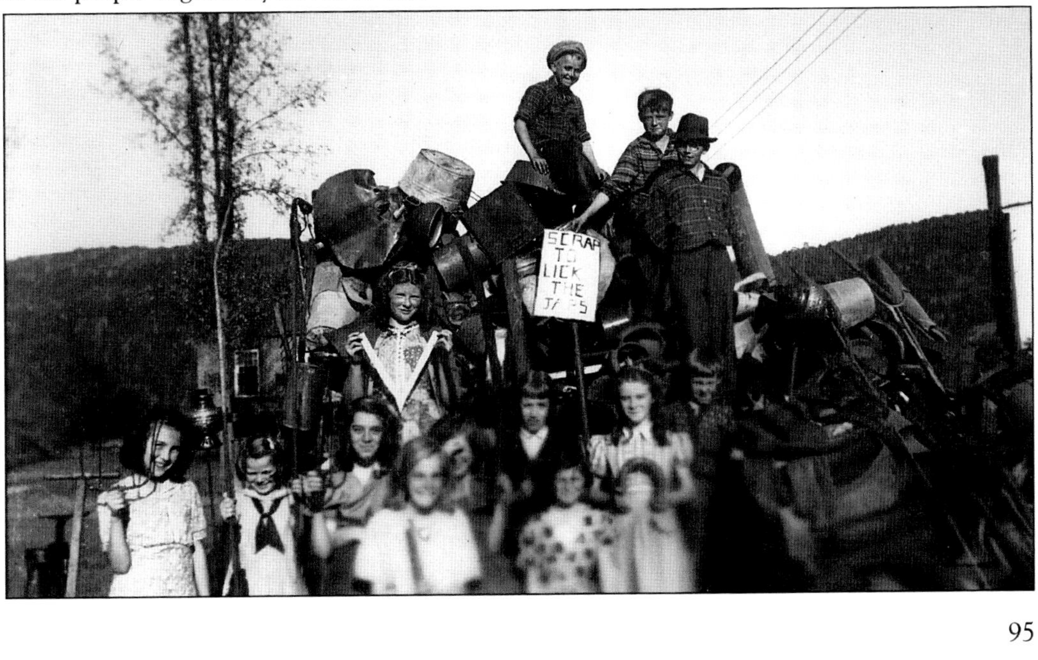

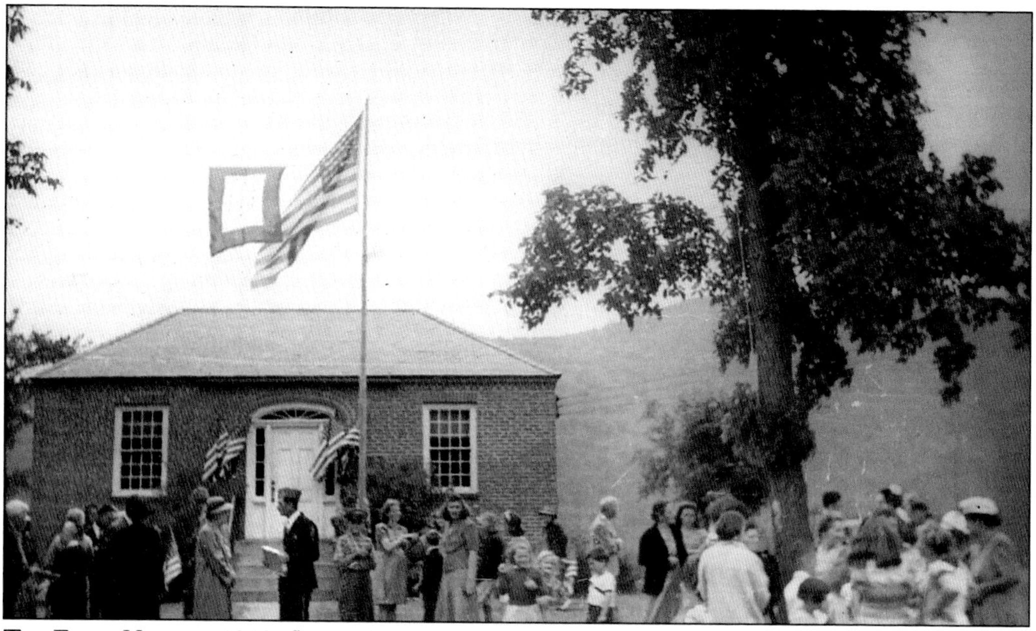

THE FLAG. Here is a 1940s flag raising at Reed Free Library in support of U.S. servicemen, whose tranquil domestic lives have been swept up into the global chaos called World War II. While elders, children, and young mothers have gathered on the lawn, notice there are no young men.

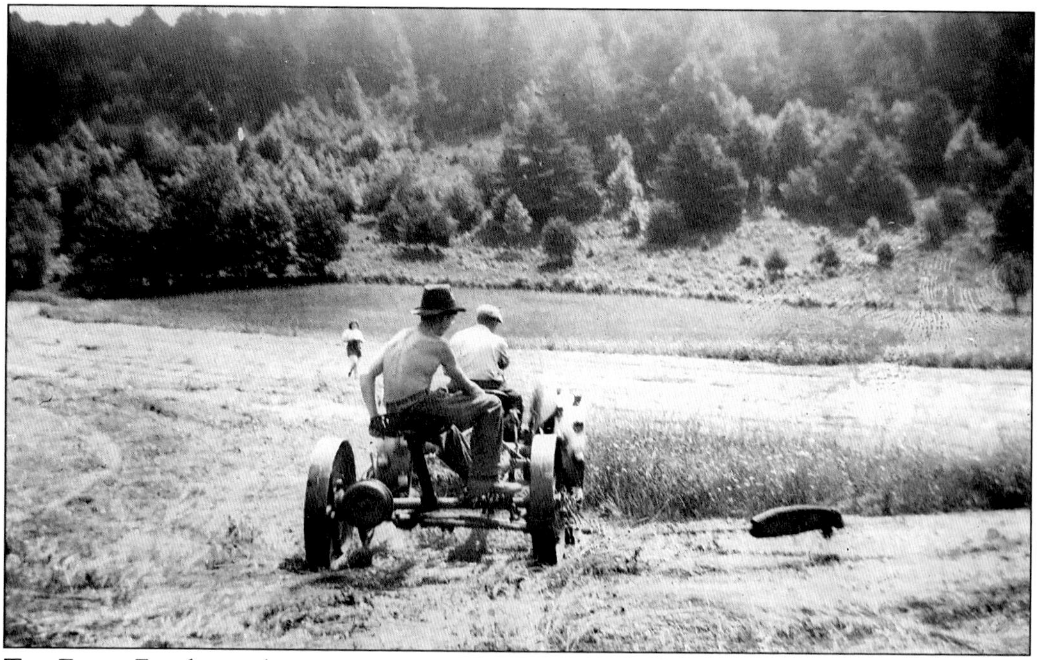

THE FARM. For those whose age or circumstances prevented enlistment or conscription, farm work became more onerous, with fewer able hands and a backdrop of worry and uncertainty. One laborsaving device, the tractor, had gradually gained acceptance in the conservative countryside. Ernest and Samuel Ball here ply a towed cutter bar from a 1941 Ford tractor on a sloping mowing. Samuel Ball shortly thereafter entered the navy, one of five Ball sons to do so.

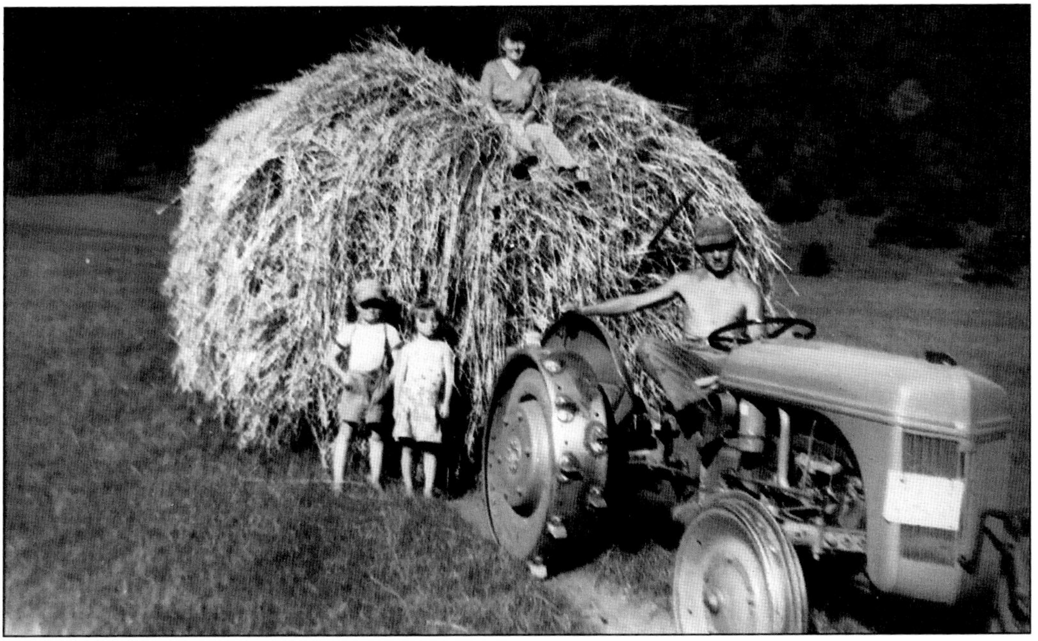

A LOAD OF HAY. Other members of the Ball family escort a load of hay to the barn. The hay has been turned and dried, raked, and pitched onto the wagon, all to be reversed at the hayloft. The sun is low, as another long day on a labor-pinched wartime farm draws to a close. Judging by the lush growth, this is a prime second cut of late July or early August.

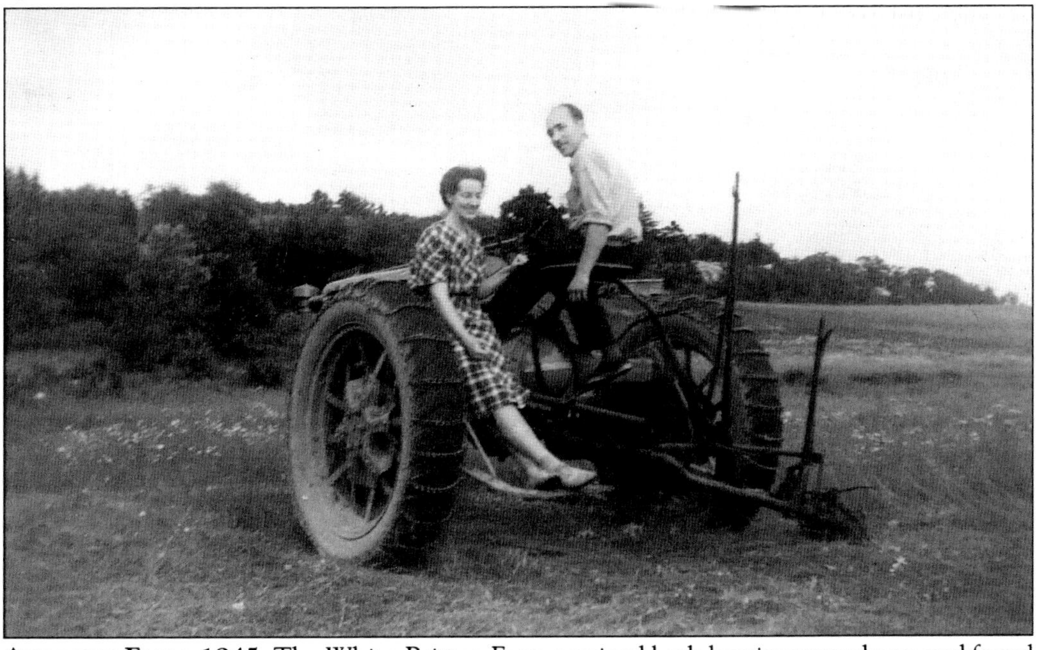

ANDACRES FARM, 1945. The White-Britton Farm survived both hurricanes and war, and found new ownership in Arnold and Jean Anderson in 1943. Here, the Andersons pause for a break on their 1919 Farmall, grateful that the 25-year-old tractor can still plow the upland soils of Mine Ledge Road. As of this writing, in fact, both the tractor and a 1938 Dodge farm truck remain operational at Andacres Farm.

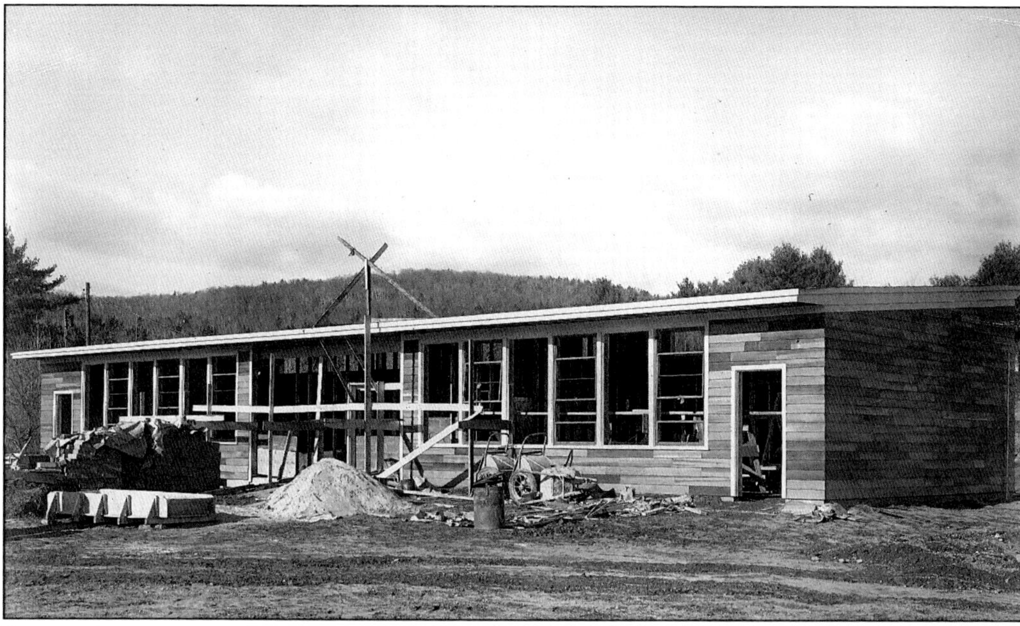

SURRY ELEMENTARY SCHOOL, 1950. World War II has ended; Surry Mountain Dam is operational; and a new village bypass has just opened (Route 12A). We know with hindsight that an American economic and demographic boom started in the late 1940s. Improvement was in the air. Right on cue, Surry built a new school on the bypass, with two classrooms, kitchen and dining room, and auctioned off its one-room schoolhouses. By 1955, a third classroom had to be made of the five-year-old dining room.

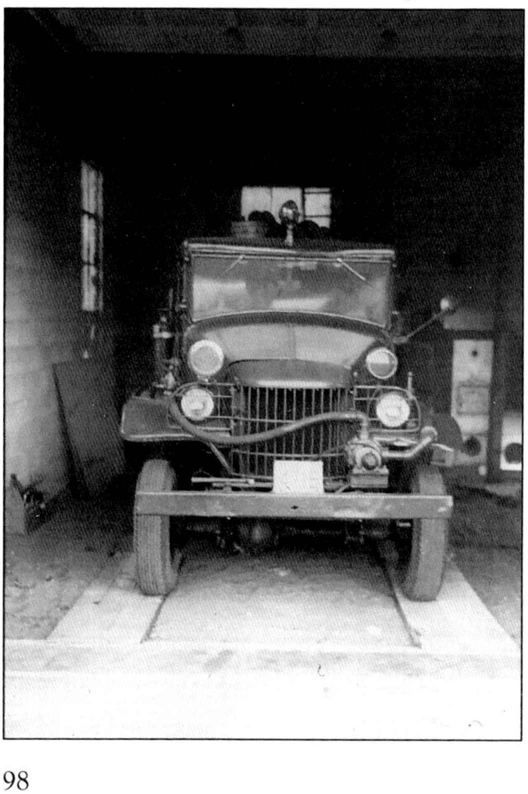

SURRY'S FIRST FIRE ENGINE, 1955. Improvements continued. Individuals belonging to the Surry Development & Improvement Association organized the Surry Volunteer Fire Company in 1954 and proceeded to home-build this first fire engine from a military-surplus truck. A station was built opposite the school on land donated in memory of Mabel H. Kingsbury. Founding fire wards were Ernest Ball, Calvin Frink, and Horace Pickering.

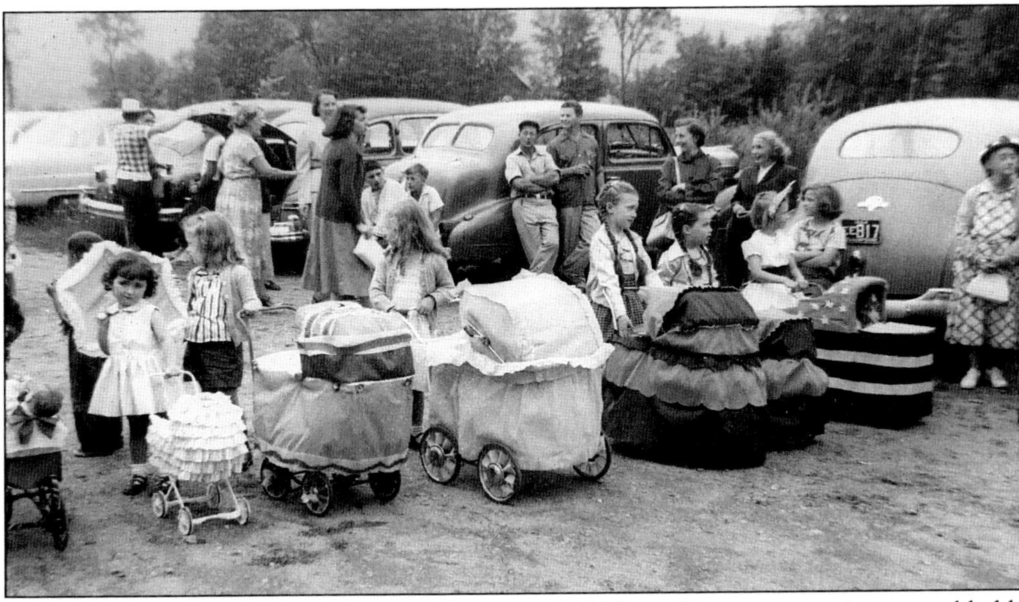

OLD HOME DAY, 1950S. Surry began celebrating Old Home Day as soon as it was enabled by statute in 1899. On a designated day in August, the community remembers its history with sundry parades, picnics, and performances. Here is a 1950s edition at the dam, featuring a doll parade. Pram mistresses include Laura Frink, Marilyn Ball, and Sherry Ball. Notice the patriotic motif of the doll carriage on the right.

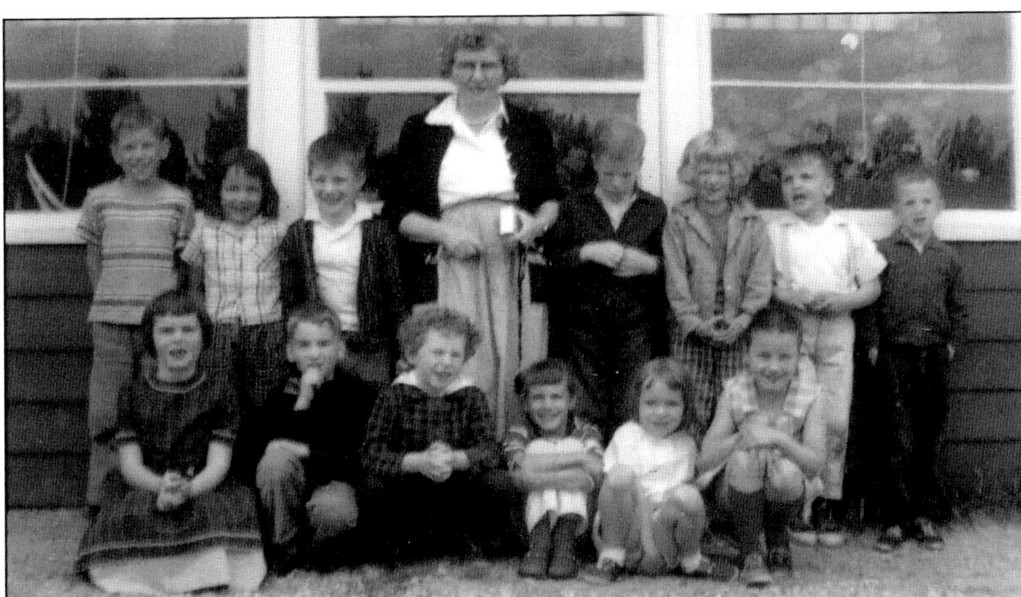

SURRY ELEMENTARY SCHOOL, 1961. Here at the close of the 1960–1961 school year is the combined first- and second-grade class at Surry Elementary School. Shown, from left to right, are the following: (front row) Margaret Aldrich, Timothy Haynes, Marilyn Ball, Patty Gilbert, Bonnie Smith, and Dora Tenney; (back row) Denis Abrams, Robin Wood, Mark Rhoades, teacher Ruth Connors, Philip Crotto, Sandy Cummings, Peter Wilbur, and Danny Smith. Ruth Connors taught an entire generation of Surry children in her 40-plus-year career.

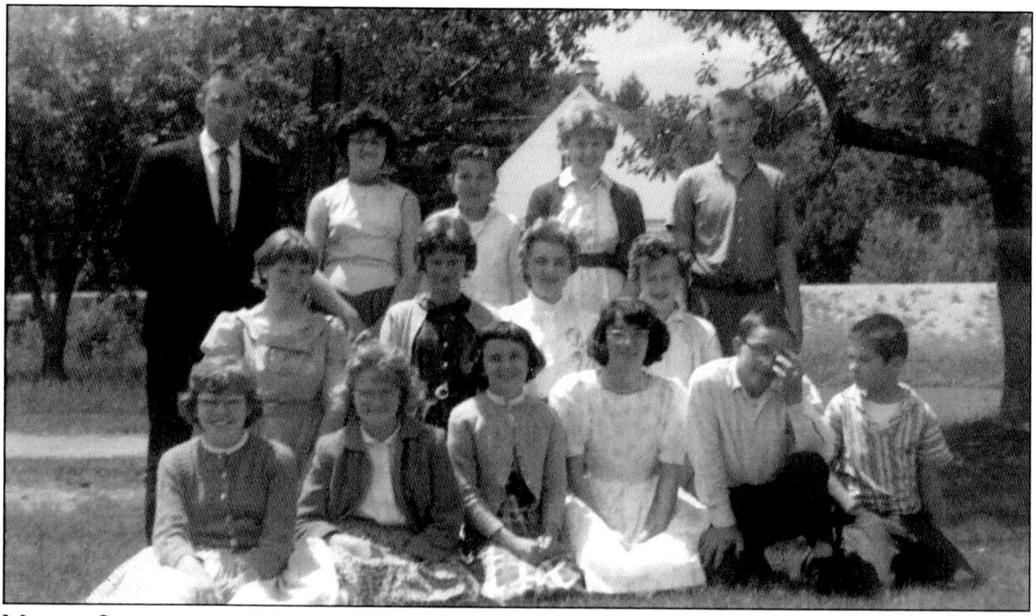

MIDDLE SCHOOLERS, 1961. Members of the combined seventh- and eighth-grade class pose for end-of-year pictures. They are, from left to right, as follows: (front row) Patty Kent, Susie Cummings, Linda Smith, Pat Brown, John Hallowhill, and Ernie Guyer; (middle row) Cheryl Lorette, Nancy Reid, Linda Rhoades, and Onley Clough; (back row) teacher Edward Fairbanks, Gwen Woods, Mike Lorandeau, Jane Darling, and Timothy Dean.

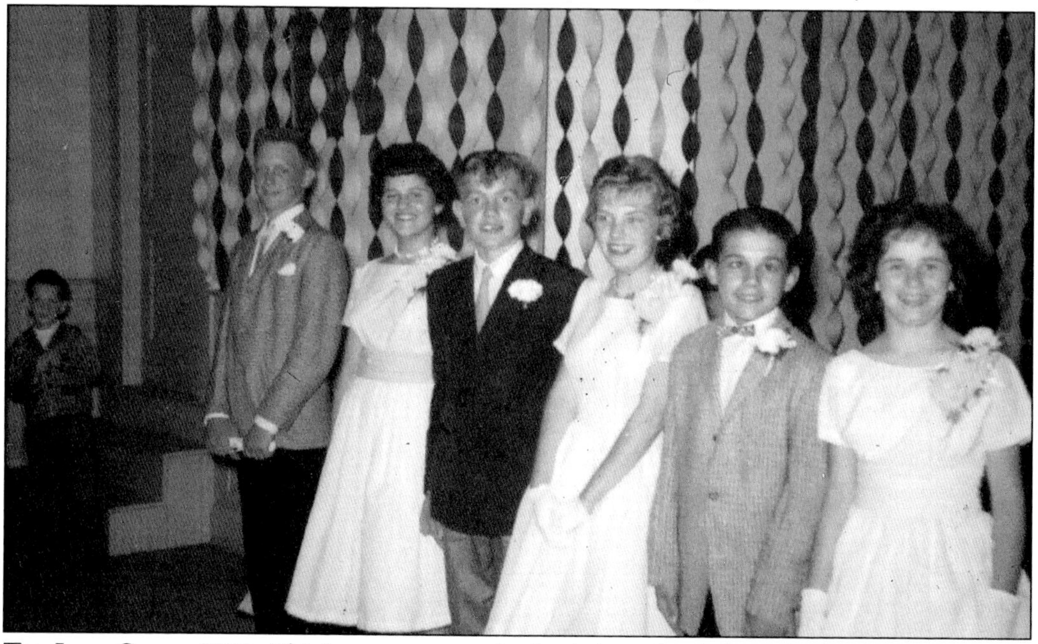

THE LAST CLASS, 1962. This happy group is the final class of eighth-grade children to graduate from Surry Elementary School. Having joined a regional district with seven other towns in 1961, Surry hereafter bused its seventh- and eighth-graders to the new Monadnock Regional High School in Swanzey. Enjoying their historic moment are, from left to right, James Martell, Gwen Woods, Michael Lorandeau, Linda Rhoades, Ernest Guyer, and Linda Smith.

THE LIBRARIAN. The Reeds may have funded it, and others may have served on its board of trustees, but here is the Surry native who created the Reed Free Library, as defined by its collections. Lois Ball Anderson concluded her 40 years of service as librarian (1927–1966) with the "glad-ful" thanks of a community of readers, students, and users.

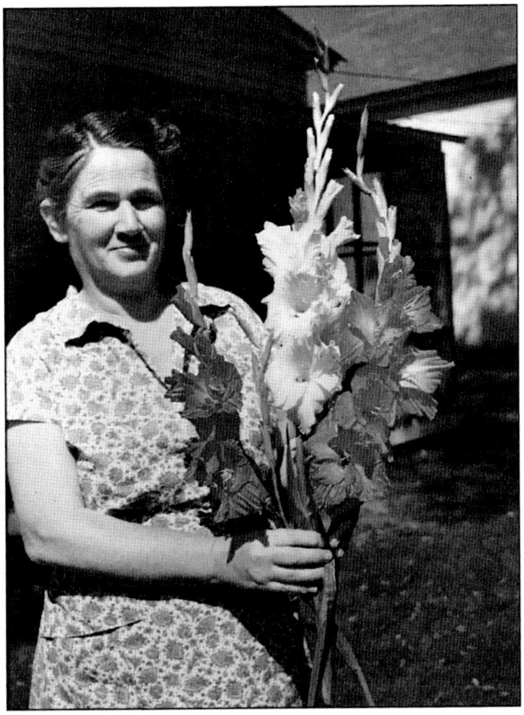

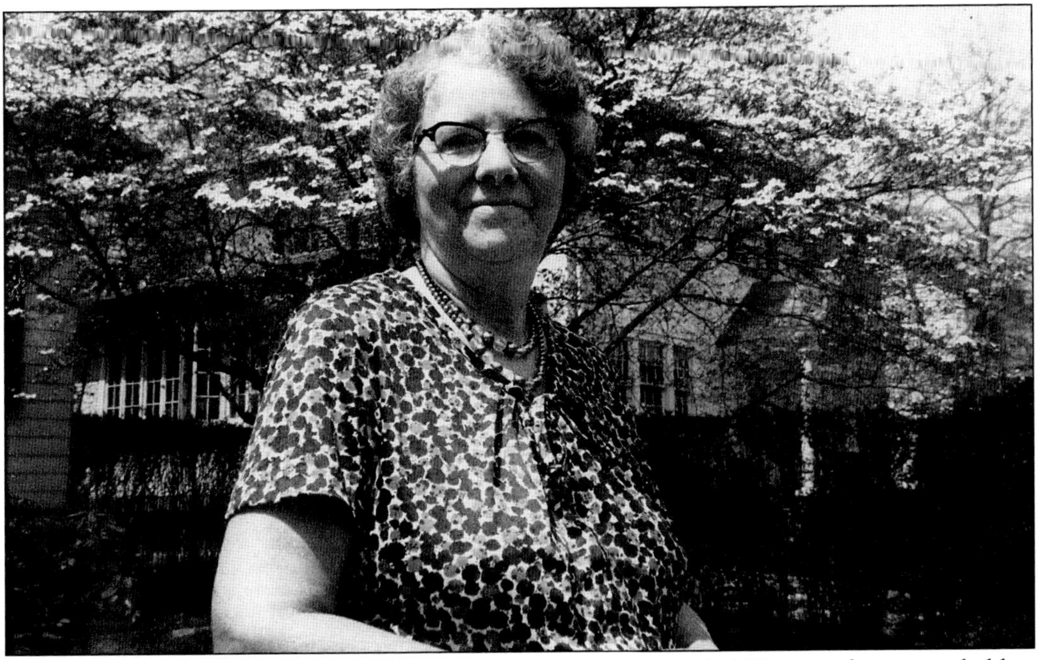

THE POSTMISTRESS. Another valued community servant was Isabel Young, who succeeded her father and served as postmistress for more than 30 years. Both father and daughter processed and distributed the mail from their house (see page 52), and old-timers retain fond memories of apiary-shipped bees escaping their containers during a hot weekend hold for pickup, of gift wheels of cheese ripening with offensive consequences awaiting an addressee's return, and of other interesting arrivals. Isabel Young also served on the school board for five years.

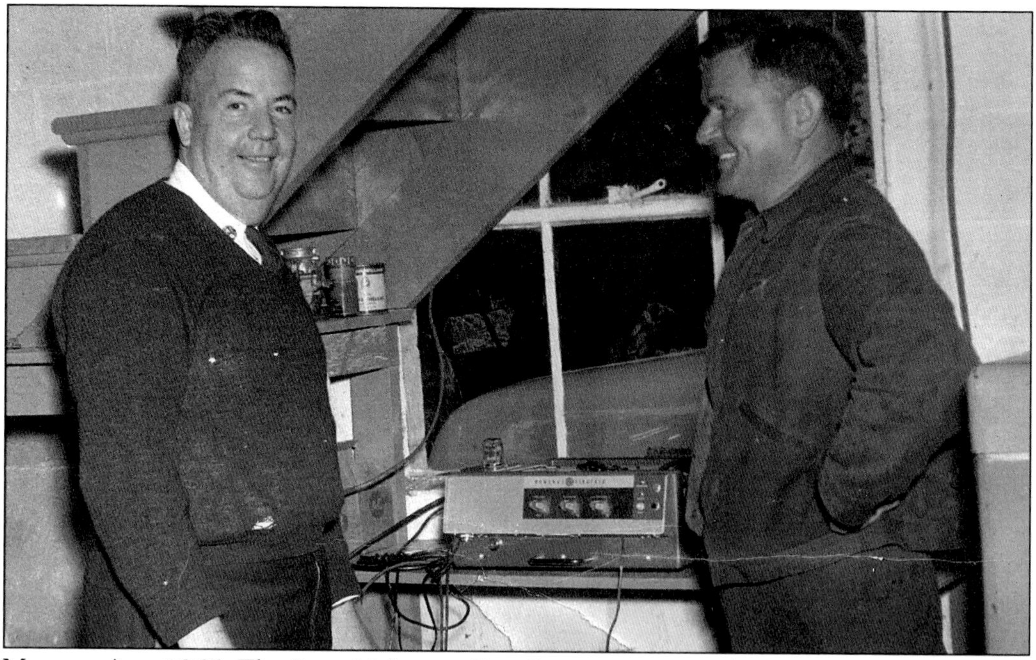

Mutual Aid, 1965. The Surry Volunteer Fire Company possessed a fire engine and a station and several trained firefighters. Next came "networking." The company was accepted in 1965 into the regional mutual aid network. Centralized communications and training brought common standards and equipment to tens of member towns, as well as immediate contact and emergency backup for multi-alarm events. Bob Callahan and Cal Frink appreciate the new radio base station.

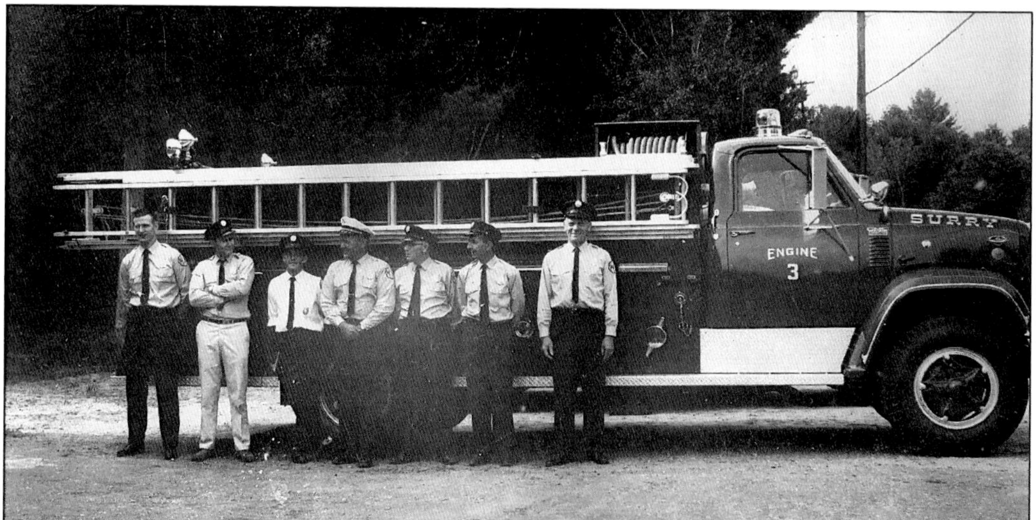

Surry No. 3, 1968. Continuing improvements to social overhead capital led voters at the 1967 town meeting to endorse the purchase of a brand-new fire truck. No. 1 had been war surplus. No. 2 had been a used truck rigged with a pump for backcountry brushfires. No. 3 was a 1967 Maxim bought for $18,000 from the manufacturer. Taking proud possession of the new insurance-abating vehicle are, from left to right, John Berglund, Henry Blewett, Bob Traquair, Cal Frink, Herb Ball, Gil Pride, and Dwight Wrigley.

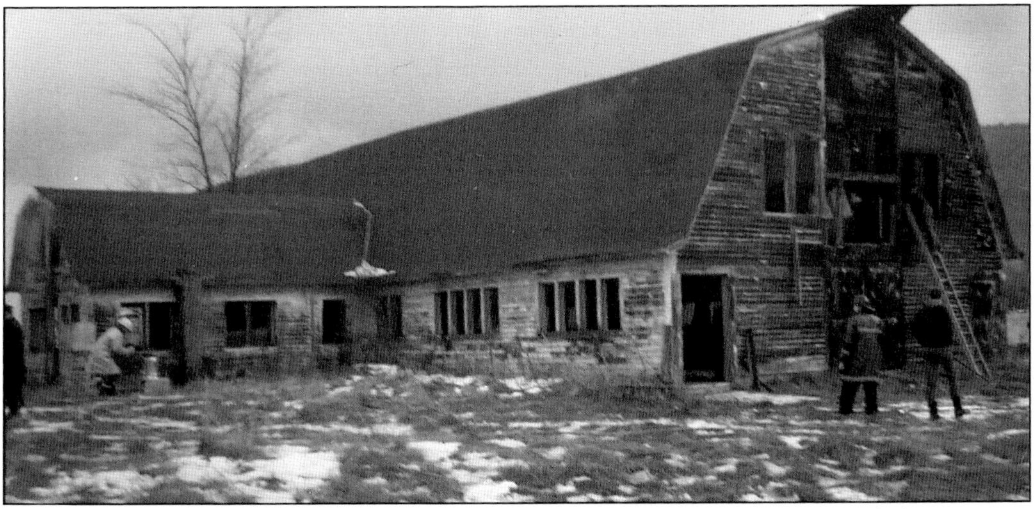

A Doomed Dairy. New England dairy farmers have struggled to compete with larger, more efficient farms in New York State and farther west. Smaller landholdings mean smaller herds, bringing less efficiency. When the younger generation declines to assume the unrelenting responsibilities of tending the herd, the painful moment of truth arrives. This farm, having auctioned off its cattle in the summer of 1968, waits as the Surry Fire Department prepares to torch the barn (a well-built gambrel with wainscoting throughout) as a training exercise.

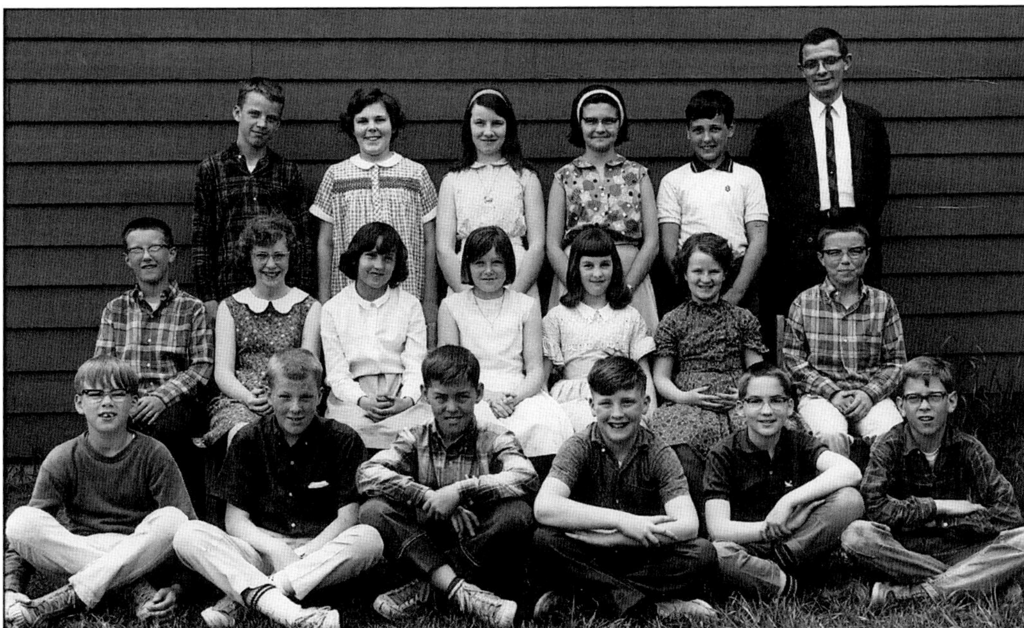

Plaid, Sneakers, and Hair Bands. It must the 1960s, and the teacher's necktie clinches it. Teaching principal of Surry School Donald Black poses with his fifth- and sixth-graders in 1966. Students, from left to right, are as follows: (front row) Roy Blake, Philip Crotto, Tom Aldrich, Mark Rhoades, Timothy Haynes, and Dennis Abrams; (middle row) Douglas Kennison, Marilyn Ball, Robin Wood, Verna Lorette, Peninnah Haynes, Nancy Everett, and Wayne Kennison; (back row) David Everett, Margaret Aldrich, Dora Tenney, Susan Smith, and Charles Munson.

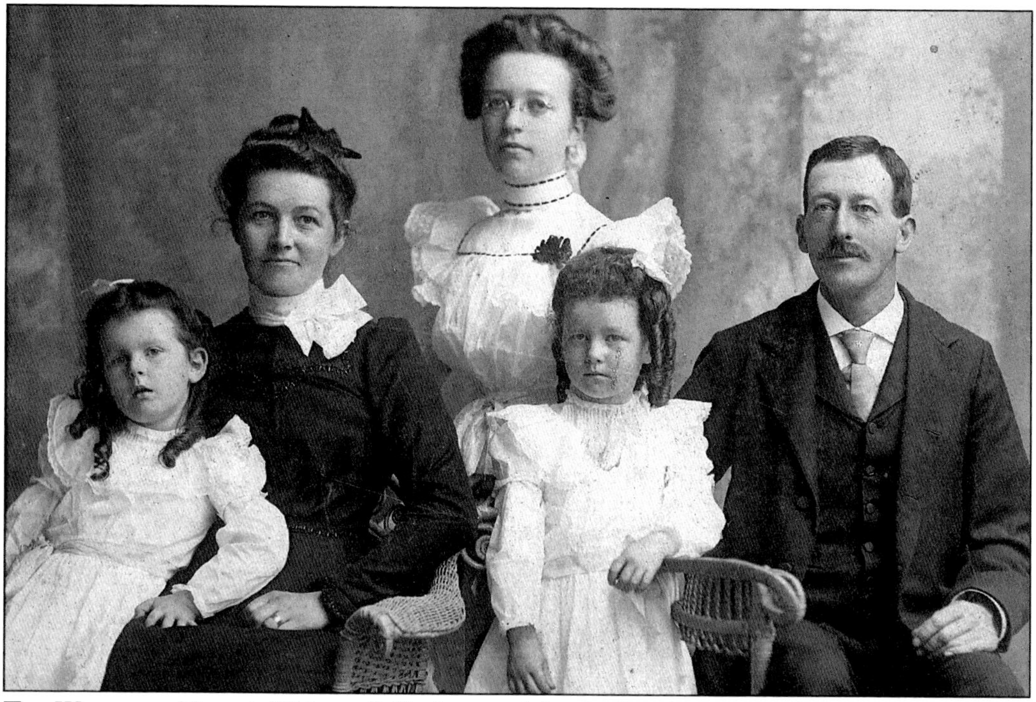

The Websters. Victoria Webster Ball, along with her husband, Ernest Ball, figured prominently in 20th-century Surry life. In this family portrait taken at the dawn of the century are, from the left to right, Victoria's twin, Elizabeth (both born in Alstead); mother Sarah Jane (born in California); sister Mabelle; Victoria Ball; and father Herbert M. Webster.

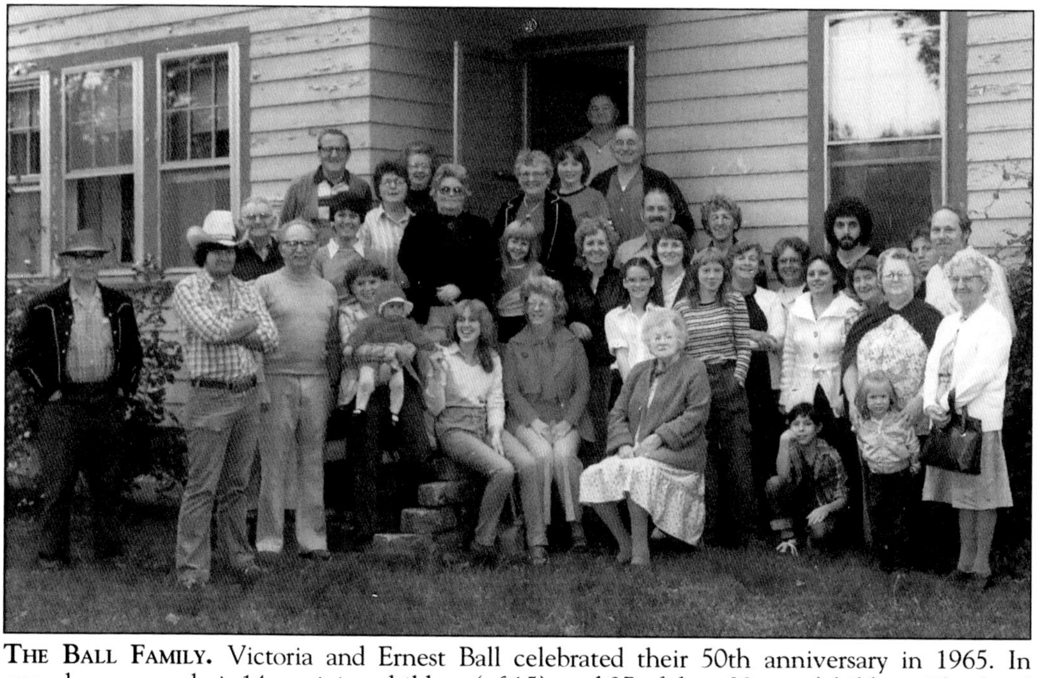

The Ball Family. Victoria and Ernest Ball celebrated their 50th anniversary in 1965. In attendance were their 14 surviving children (of 15), and 27 of then 30 grandchildren. This loyal Surry clan holds a family reunion annually in conjunction with the town's Old Home Day.

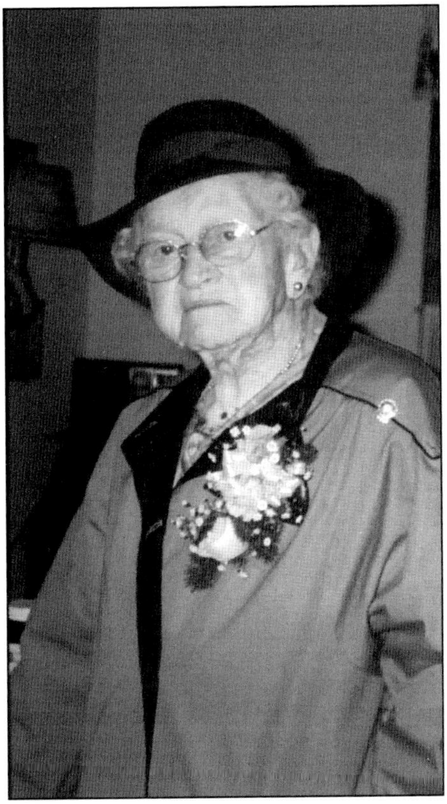

A Birthday Party for Victoria Ball, 1987. Unofficial matriarch of a community in which her presence loomed large (forbidding daughters to milk cows, for example, lest it become women's duty), Victoria Ball enters her 90th birthday party wearing a characteristic chapeau. She served as supervisor of the voting checklist for 27 years, and helped inspire and fund the updated Surry history.

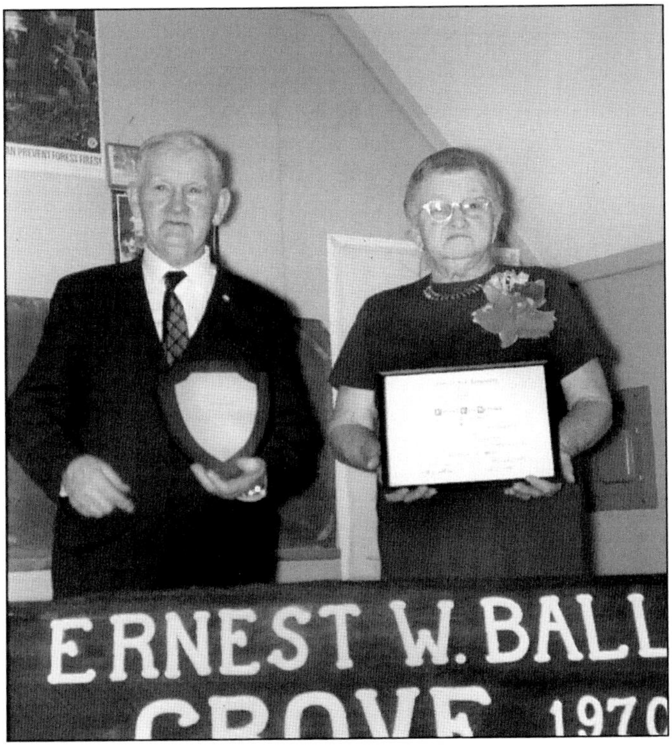

The Ball Grove. At this fire station ceremony in 1970, Ernest and Victoria Ball are honored by the dedication of a donated tract of adjoining land as the Ball Grove. Too moved to "muster" a smile for the camera, longtime fire warden Ernest Ball was remembered for his faithful town service as road agent, dump tender, police chief, school board member, and selectman.

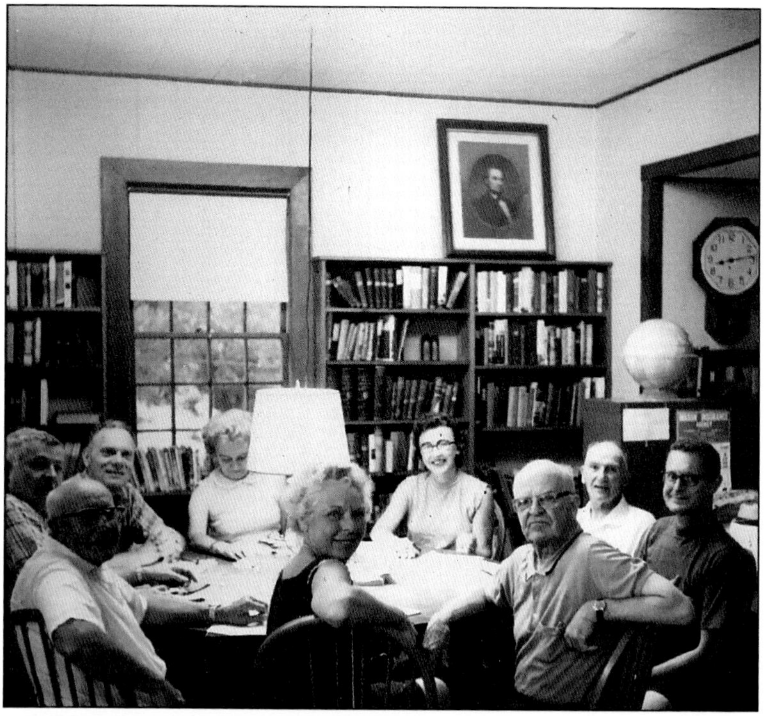

THE BICENTENNIAL, 1969. Surry was one of those Colonial towns whose local bicentennial antedated the national one, in this case celebrating incorporation in 1769. Here is the planning committee at an 8:00 a.m. meeting at the Reed Free Library: from left to right, Leo Vogel, Floyd Britton, Dwight Wrigley, Mary Tracy, Jackie Swan, Dorothea Kitlan, Harold Kendall, Chick Nims, and Dick Kitlan.

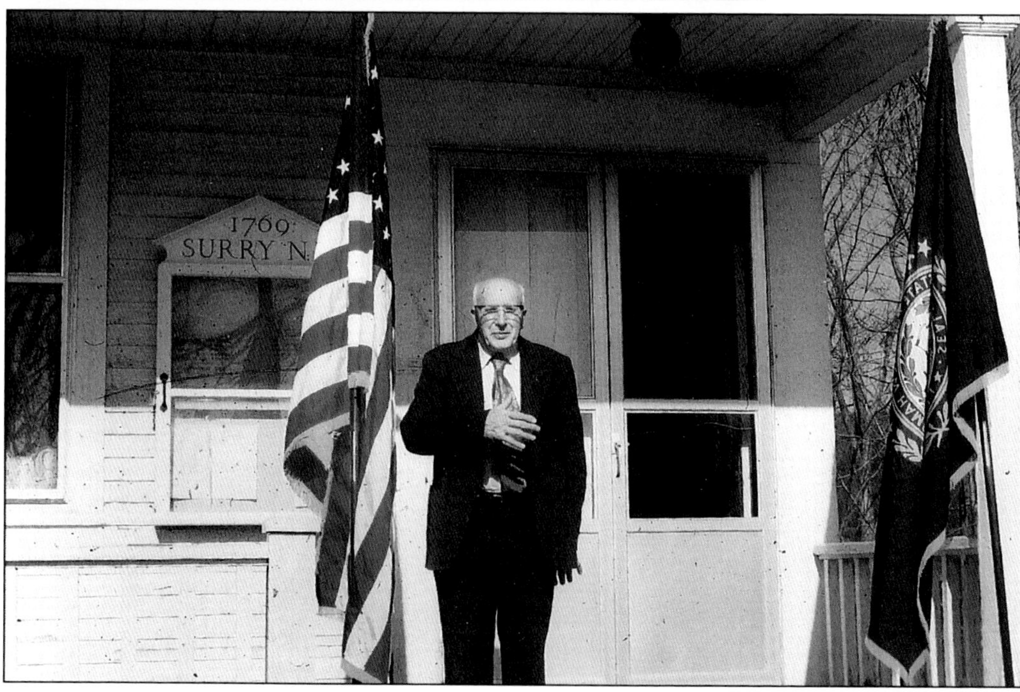

A TOWN FATHER. Floyd Britton waxes patriotic on the steps of Surry Town Hall on Election Day of 1972. Flanked by national and state flags and a civic building in use for 200 years, this loyal son of Surry drove the school bus with unbending punctuality, worked as town clerk (33 years), tax collector (19 years), and served on the planning board (11 years) and the zoning board (25 years).

The Gaol. Among the meetinghouse's many uses had been as a jail, or gaol (British variation). Here, Floyd Britton good-naturedly models (1973) the iron lockup removed from town hall after a century's service. Towns installed such facilities in the hard decades after the Civil War to deal with "tramps"—often demobilized, traumatized veterans who wandered the countryside, unable to settle down.

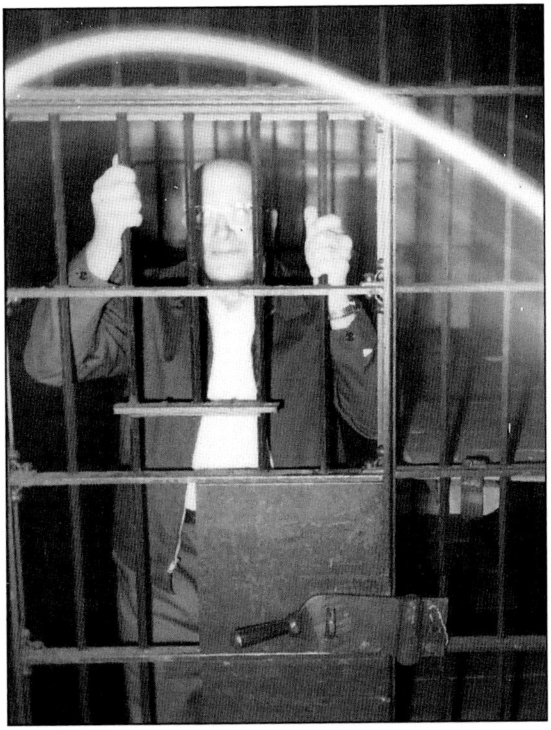

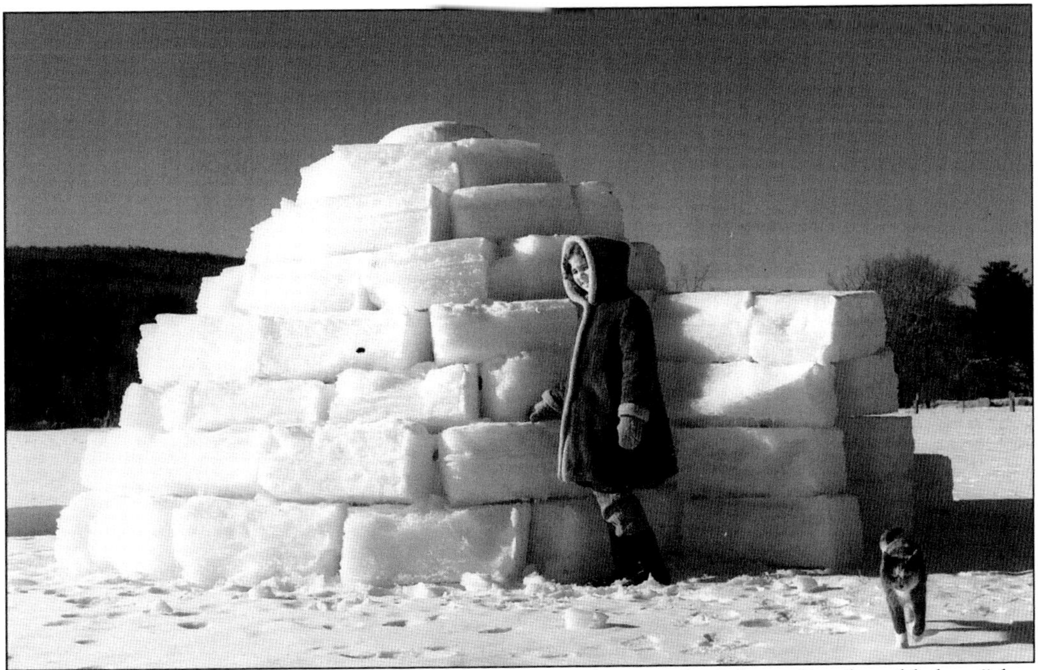

An Igloo, 1973. Elders often say winters are not the equal of those "in the old days," but whenever a hard winter strikes, a resourceful youngster will take advantage. Whereas ice harvesting once meant stock for the straw-lined icehouse and home icebox (if not cash income), for Rachel Haynes and cat, it meant experiential learning, or "how the Eskimos live." (KS.)

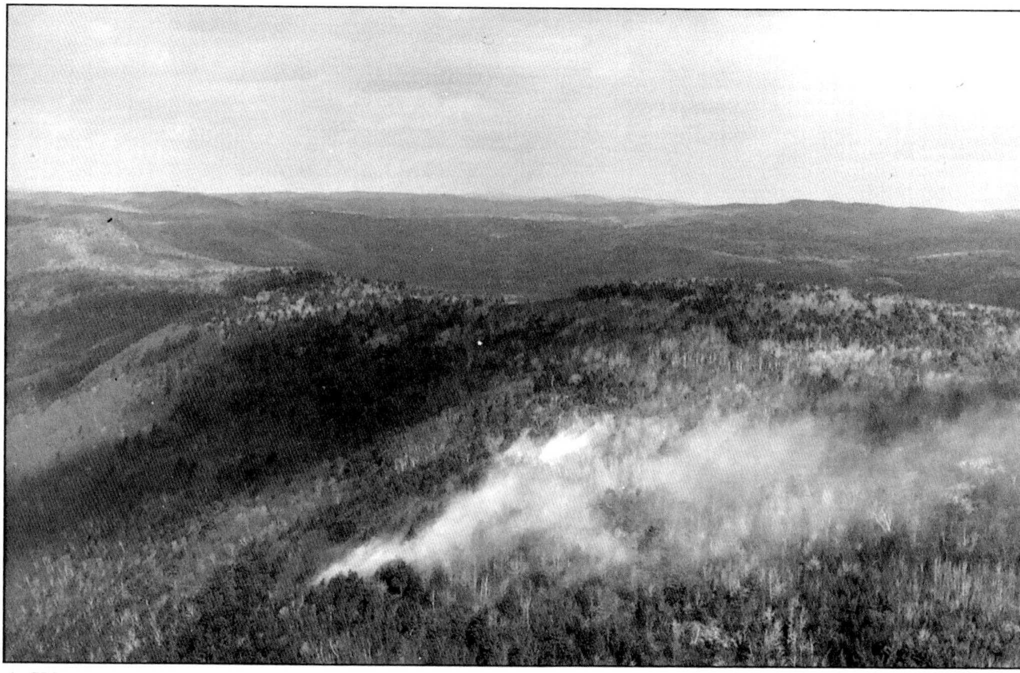

A Wildfire, 1973. Timber and brush in inaccessible areas, such as mountain ridges, is always vulnerable to combustion in drier years, even in a river-reservoir town such as Surry. Here, in the autumn of 1973, is a wildfire on the mountain threatening to migrate to neighboring towns. Surry appealed for help, with reassuring results (below). (KS.)

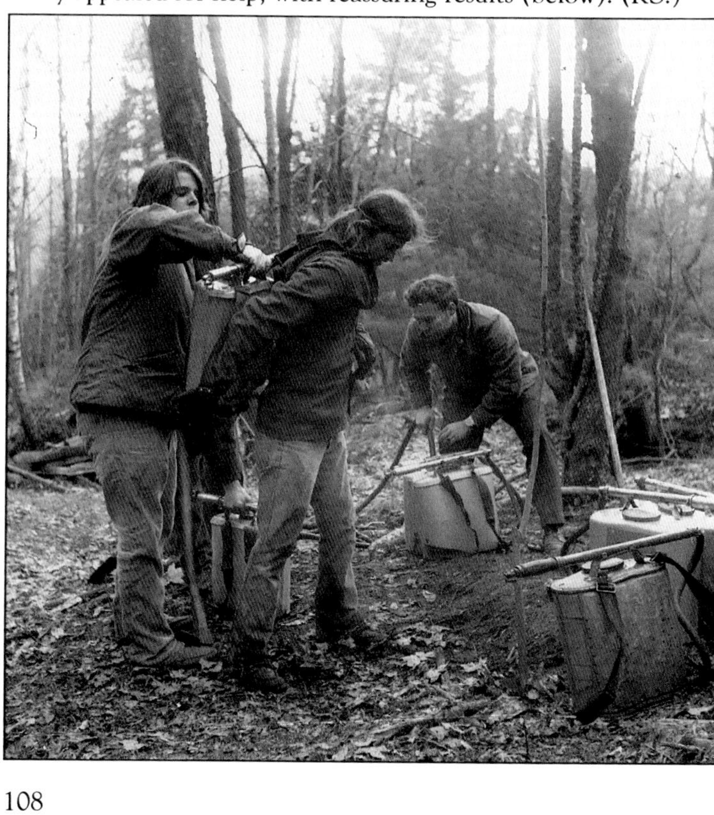

Gender-Neutral Firefighting, 1973. Wildfire is crisis. American fire departments learned from the 1960s onward that there were many environmentally conscious young women who would gladly go to the fire lines to help save habitat or an ecosystem. Here, volunteers from Keene State College don their water packs to help Surry quell its weeklong wildfire. (KS.)

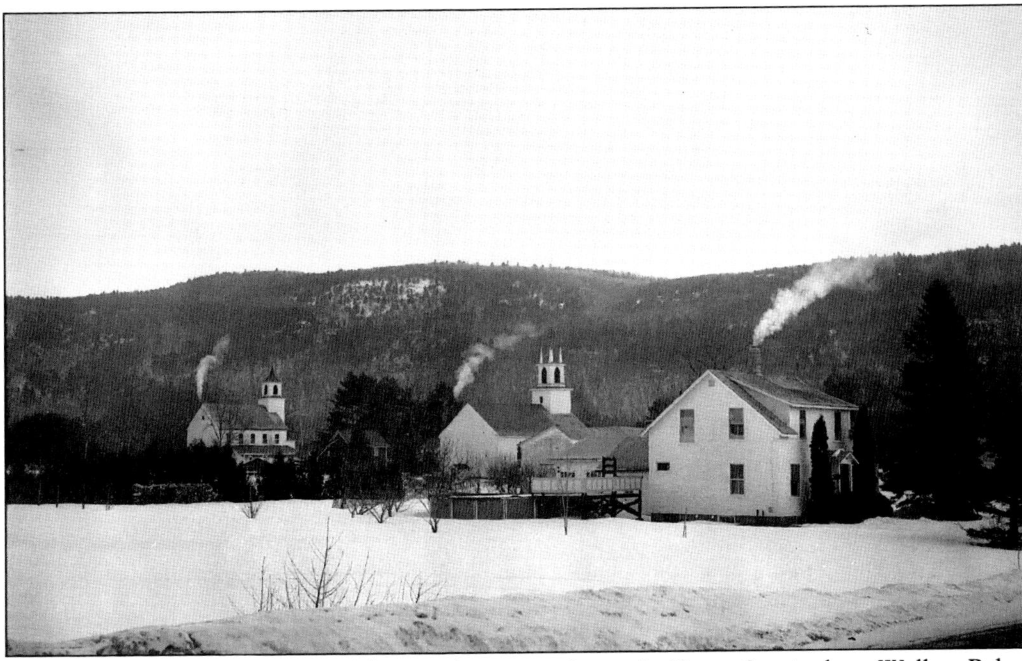

VILLAGE SMOKE, 1978. The first full-time photojournalist at the Keene Sentinel was Wallace Baker, whose daily commute to work led him, if he so chose, past Surry village. It was a choice often made, resulting in a frequency of documentation of this handsome village out of all proportion to its newsworthiness. Here, facing its namesake mountain on a bone-chilling February morning, the town struggles to warm up living and working spaces for the day ahead. (KS.)

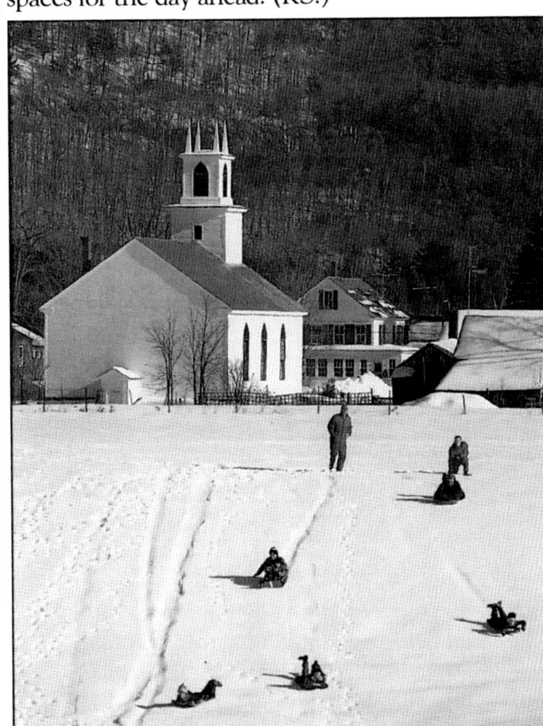

WINTER FUN, 1970S. Children sledding behind the village church became the poster image of Surry for a decade or so, appearing as a New Hampshire postcard and as the cover image on an issue of *New Hampshire Profiles* magazine. Here, Lloyd Soderberg (coincidentally principal of Surry School) has just dispatched another child out onto the untracked slopes of life.

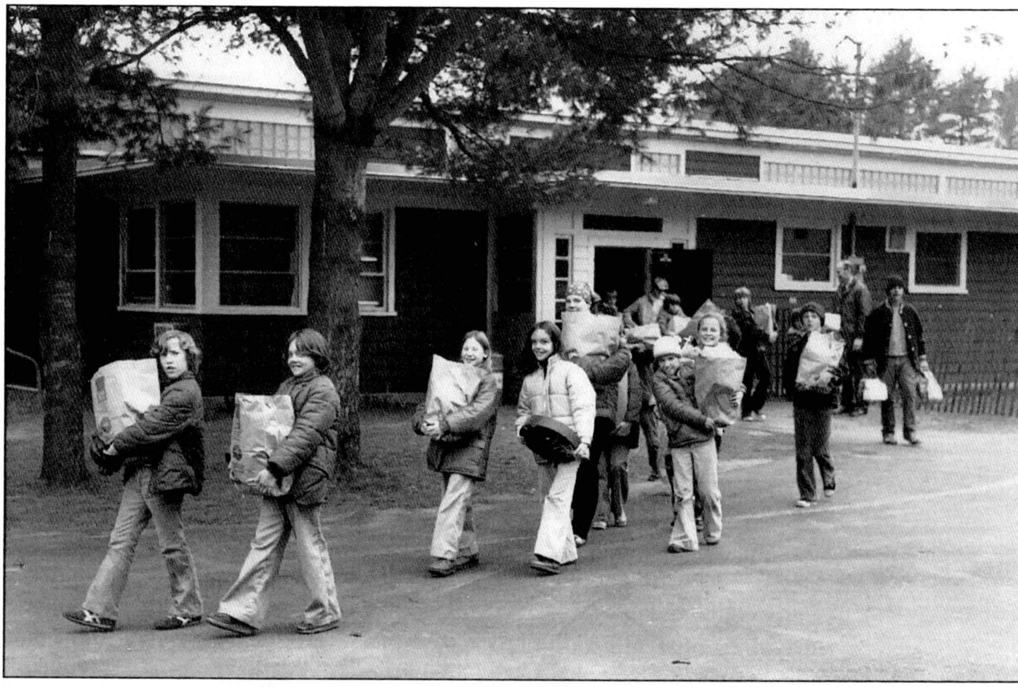

MOVING DAY, 1977. The new Surry school needed additional expansion by the 1970s. To facilitate construction of an addition, school classes were conducted in both the village church and town hall for eight months. Epitomizing the do-it-yourself move, Surry pupils lug sackfuls of educational supplies one mile from their school on the state highway (Route 12A) to the old town hall. There is warm irony in an 18th-century building "rescuing" a 30-year-old one. (KS.)

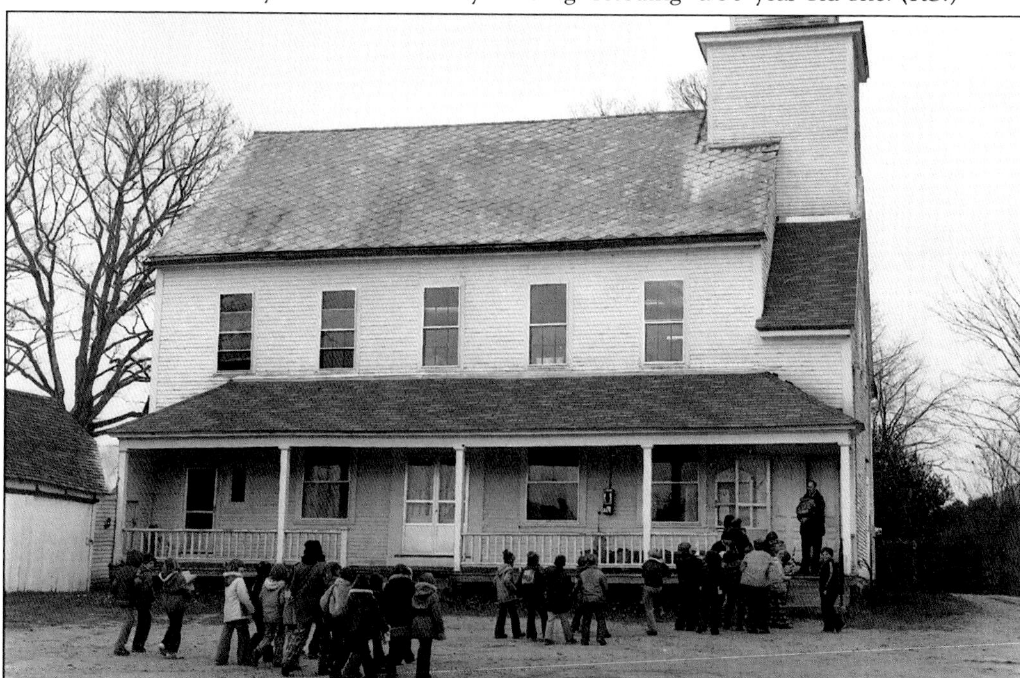

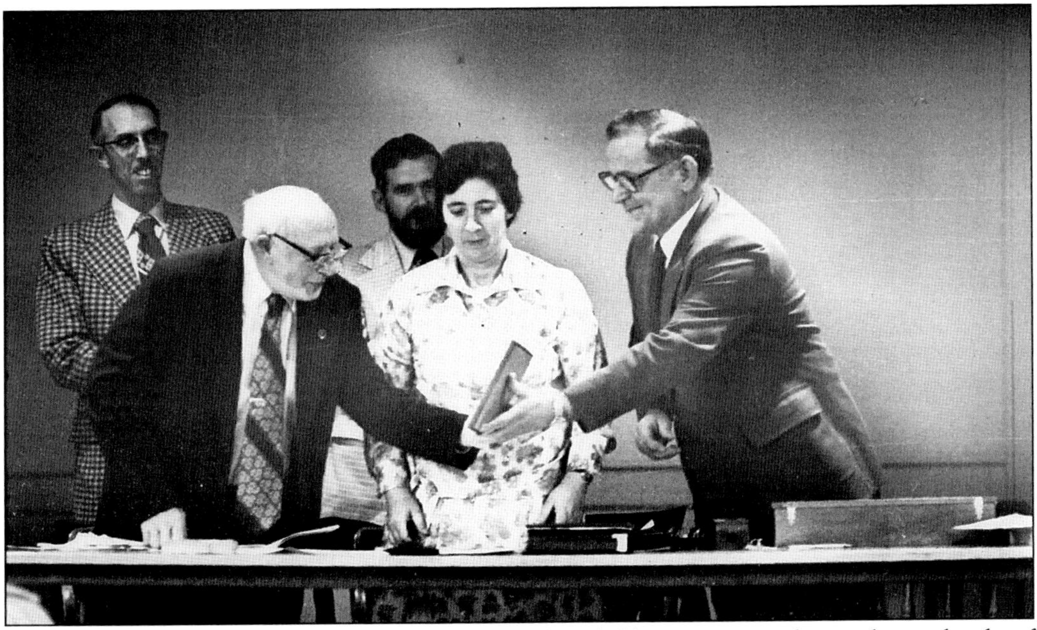

A Job Well Done, 1978. Floyd Britton (second from left) reciprocates the southpaw thanks of Calvin Frink, moderator (right), on March 1, 1978, for his 33 years as town clerk. Paula Lorette (center) prepares to step into the well-worn clerk's shoes, while Selectmen Hugh Clark (left) and Carl Lorette (third from left) applaud the dedicated service.

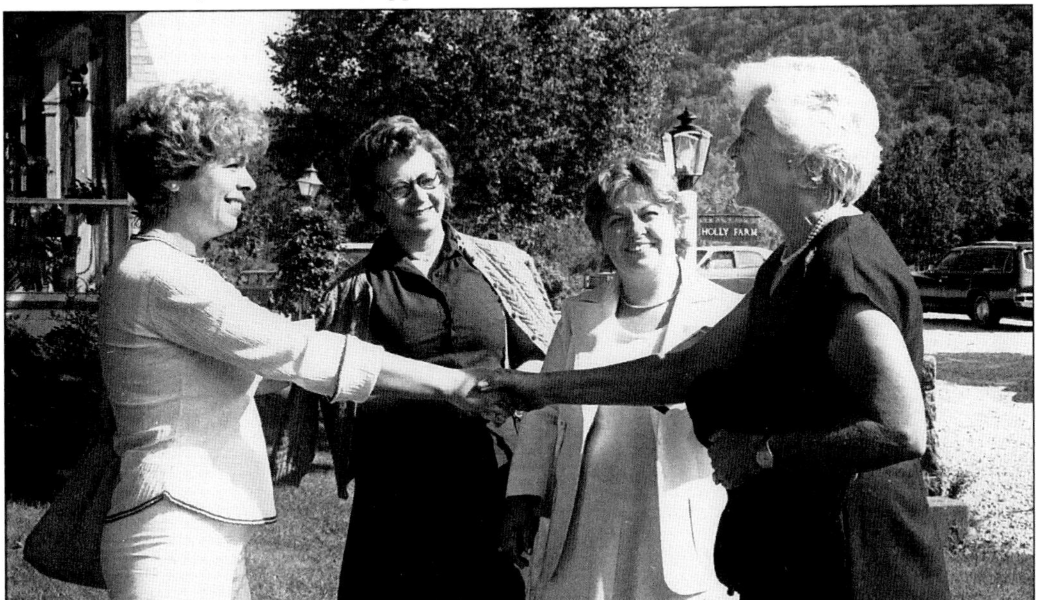

First Lady, First Mother. First-in-the-nation presidential primaries ensure visits to New Hampshire by most aspirants to the highest office. In August 1979, Barbara Bush, soon to become a vice-presidential spouse, arrives at a Cheshire Women's Republican Club picnic at Holly Farm. She is welcomed by president Kiki Chakalos, an unidentified woman, and Arietta Rigopoulos. Barbara Bush was First Lady from 1988 to 1992 and became "First Mother" to Pres. George W. Bush in 2001.

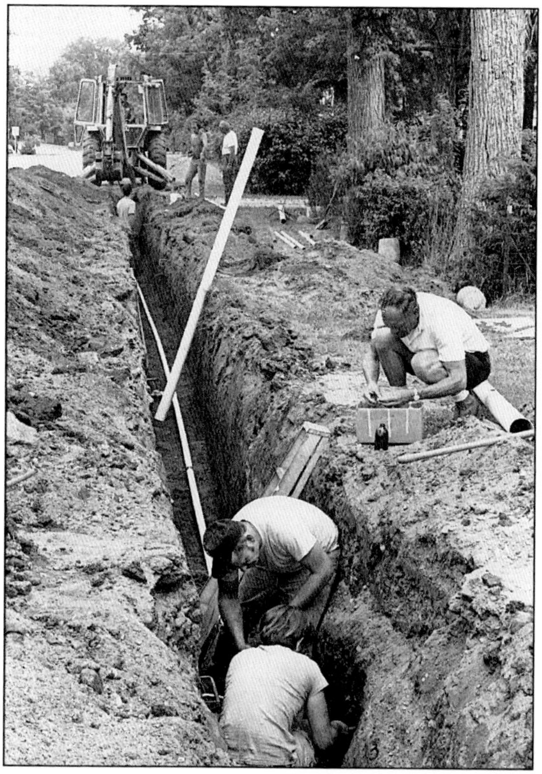

A Big Dig, 1978. That such a diminutive community should have its own utility is most improbable, but in fact the Surry Village Water Company has piped water to some 17 homes in the village from an uphill spring since 1823. In 1978, users replaced all the piping—mains and service connections—in a do-it-yourself project. Backhoe and all labor was volunteered, to the bemusement of the media. Resultant national publicity made Surry's project the "shunt seen 'round the world." Pictured, from front to back, are Bill Bigelow, Lloyd Soderberg, Dwight Wrigley, Paul Haynes, and others, trenching through town. (KS.)

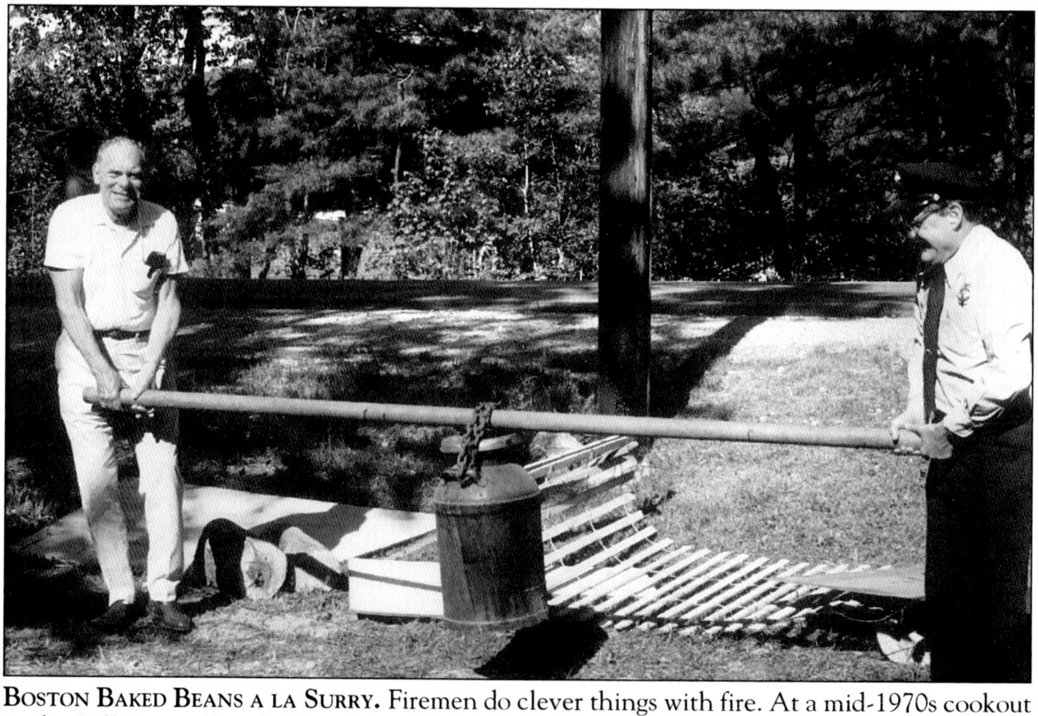

Boston Baked Beans a la Surry. Firemen do clever things with fire. At a mid-1970s cookout in the Ball Grove, Dwight Wrigley and Ainslee Phillips hoist a sizzling 40-quart milk can filled with beans from the fire pit where they have been baking for 10 hours.

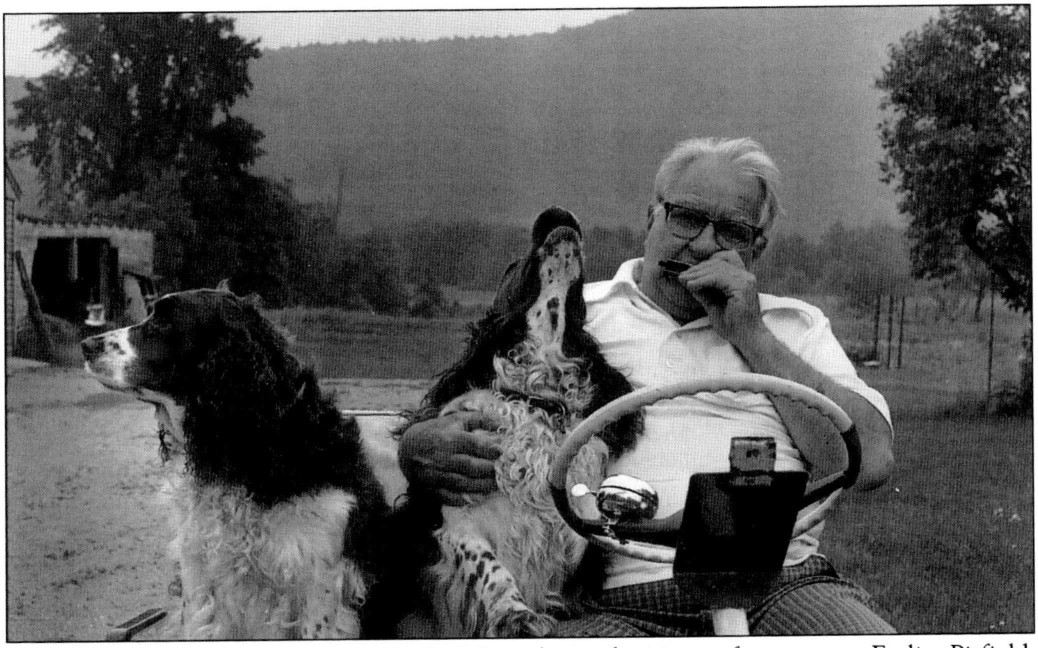

ONE PIED PIPER OF SURRY, 1978. Another devoted citizen of town was Emlin Pitfield. Medical circumstances limited his mobility to a golf cart, but that did not prevent his playing a constructive and ubiquitous role in the village. He embellished community life with harmonica serenades. Anxious to please, his spaniels were ever ready to harmonize. (KS.)

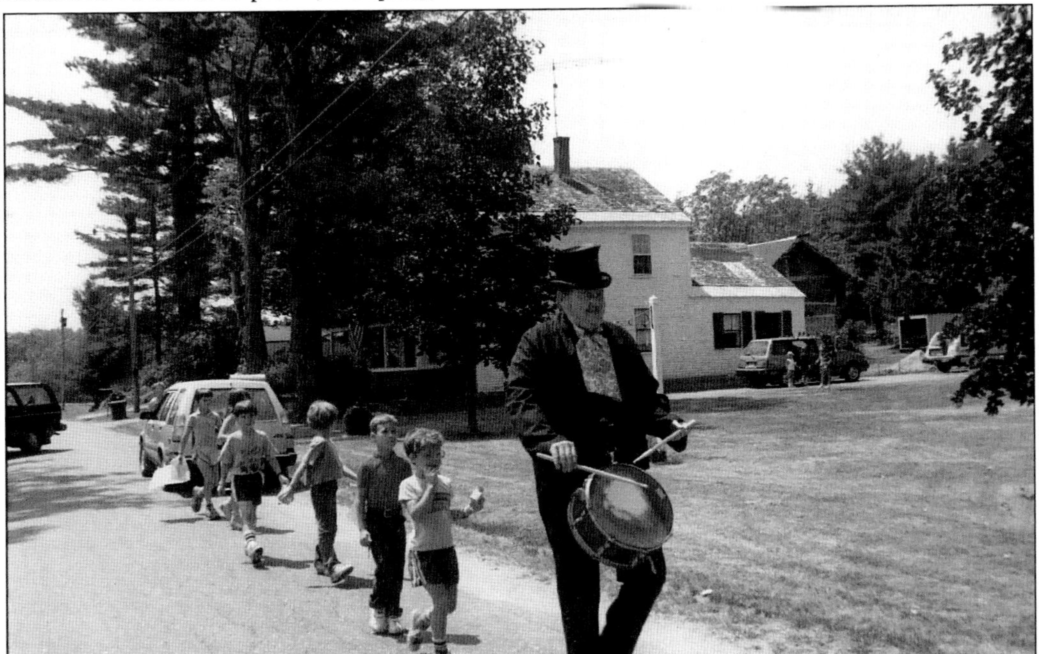

ANOTHER PIED PIPER OF SURRY, 1988. Harold Pike retired from teaching only to begin volunteering for the Surry Recreation Department as teaching "chairperson of summer school under the old sycamore tree." Here, he leads his "merrie band" down the Great Road to the crafts project of the day.

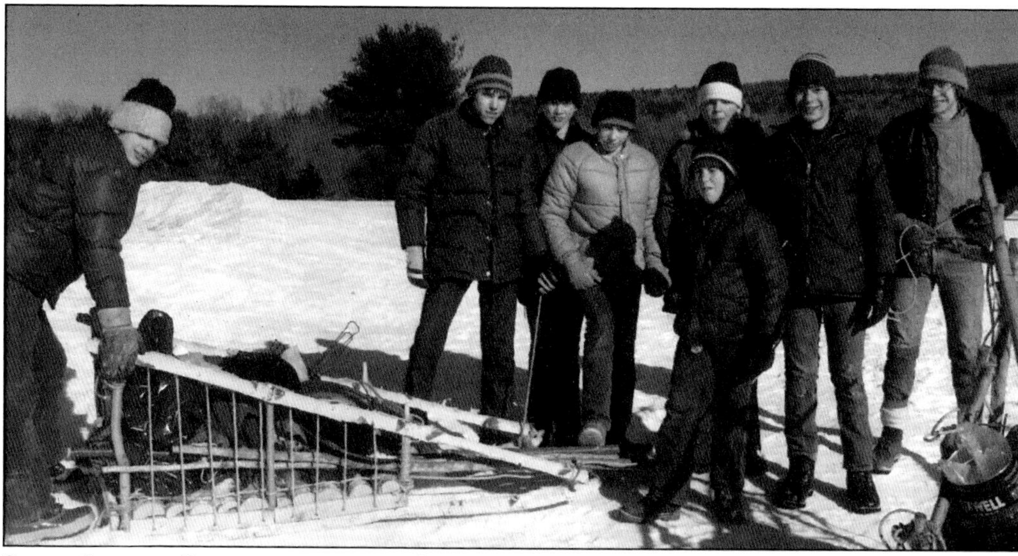

SURRY SCOUTS. Scouting remains vital in Surry, thanks to the unwavering sponsorship of the Volunteer Fire Department. Here is Troop 289's Klondike team of 1978. The sled is handmade, carrying supplies for designated activities at stations along the all-day course. Exulting in their team performance at the conclusion of the day, are, from left to right, Tim Small, David Vitale, Bruce Soderberg, Bobby Stillings, Joe Gilliland (front), Chris Dyer, Dave Medvidovsky, and Bill Fosher

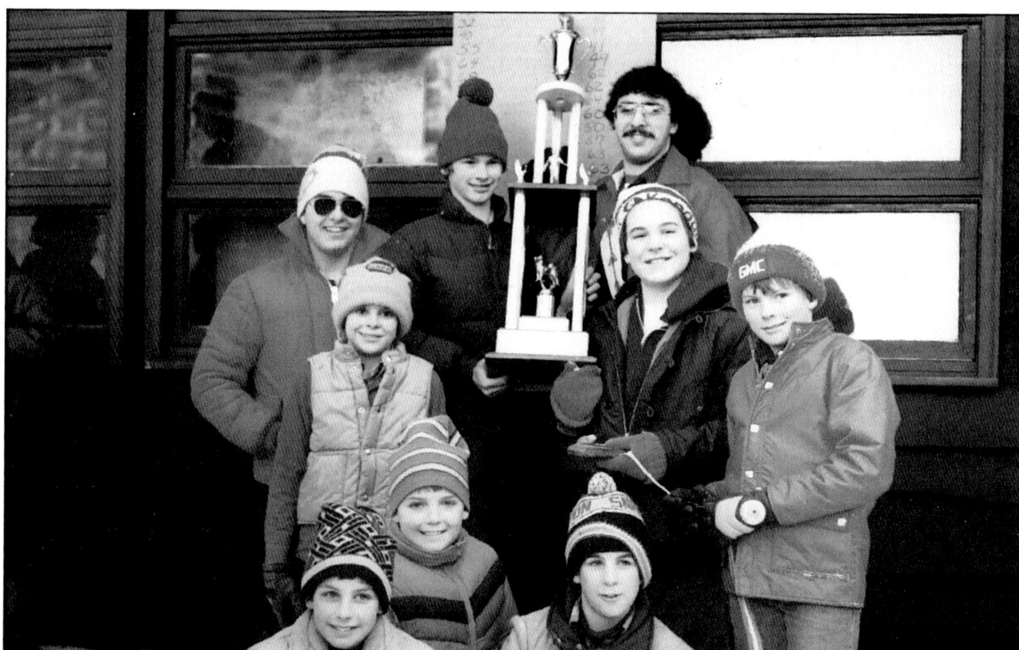

NEW HAMPSHIRE KLONDIKERS, 1983. Five years later, Troop 289 won the statewide Klondike competition. Savoring the achievement are the following: (kneeling, from left to right) Scott Dejnak, Kevin Wilbur, and Dan Small; (clockwise from the vested Scout) Todd Bissell, Roger Wilbur, Tim Bienvenu (accepting trophy), Kevin Acorice (New Hampshire Scout representative), Tom Dyer, and Randy Wyman.

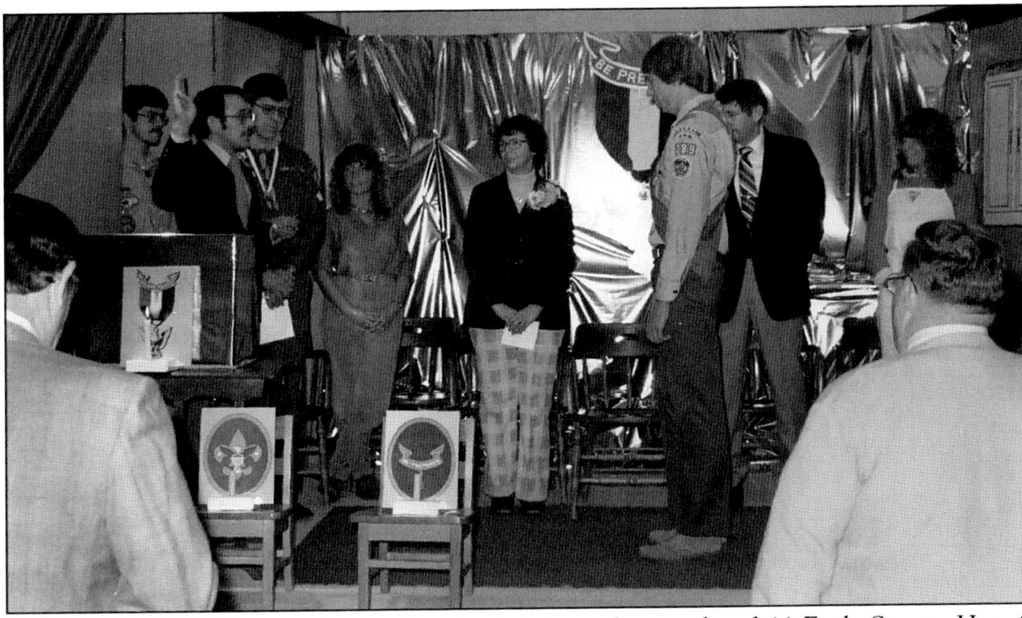

EAGLE SCOUT. With a population of under 900, Surry has produced 11 Eagle Scouts. Here is one solemn induction from 1982. Robert V. Stillings II is raised to the rank of Eagle, while state Sen. Clesson Blaisdell Jr., watches from the left. On stage, from left to right, are Scoutmaster Peter Bissell, William Bigelow, David Bohannan, sister Robin Stillings, mother Beulah Stillings, father Robert Stillings, sister LeeAnn Stillings, and James Dyer.

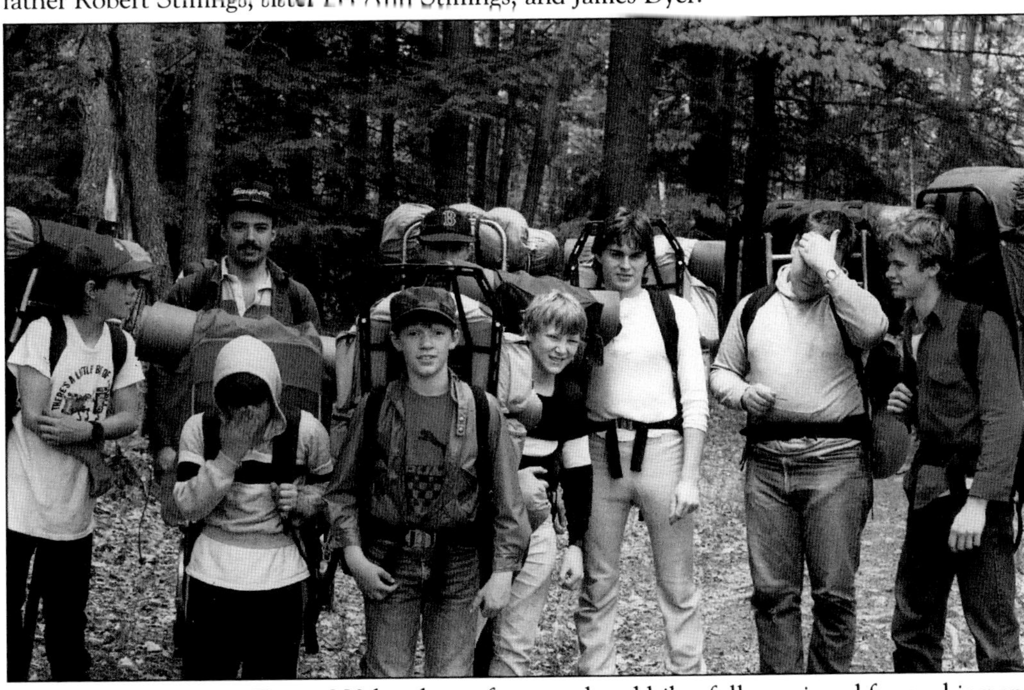

OVERNIGHTER, 1988. Troop 289 heads out for a weekend hike, fully equipped for cooking and sleeping in the open. Shown, from left to right, are the following: (front row) Erik Russell, Scott Beaudine, Jim Kent, Jamie Ball, Jeff Bissell, Tom Dyer, and Tim Bienvenu; (back row) John Lorette and Robert Denslow.

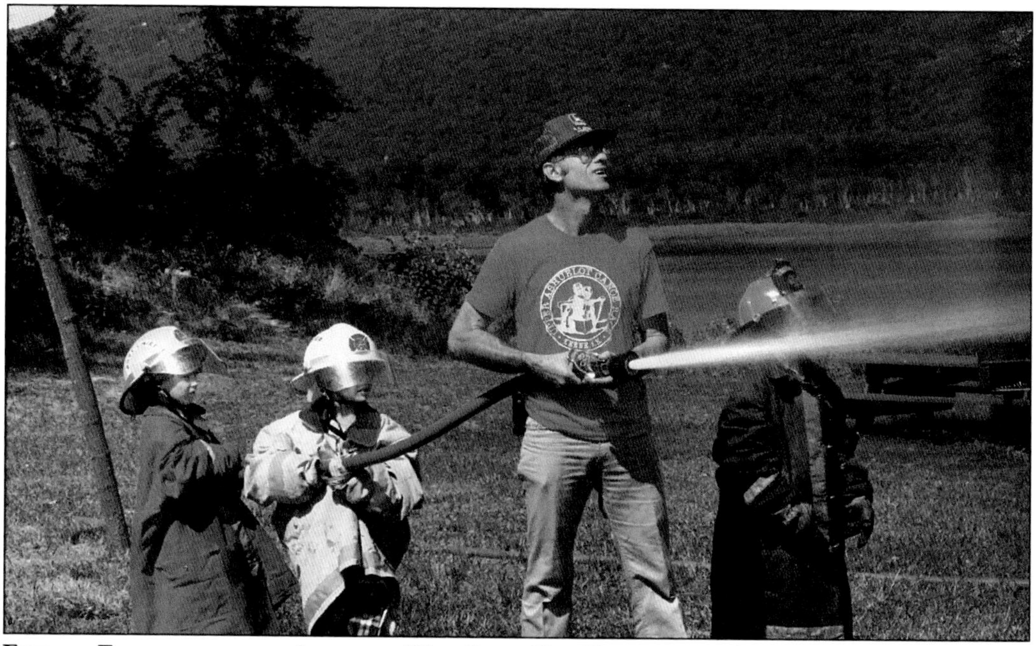

Future Firefighters of America. The Surry Fire Department does its part at Old Home Days to prepare the next generation to share the burden of keeping a small community secure. Tom Dutton is assisted at this muster by suitably garbed hose-persons in keeping a target ball aloft.

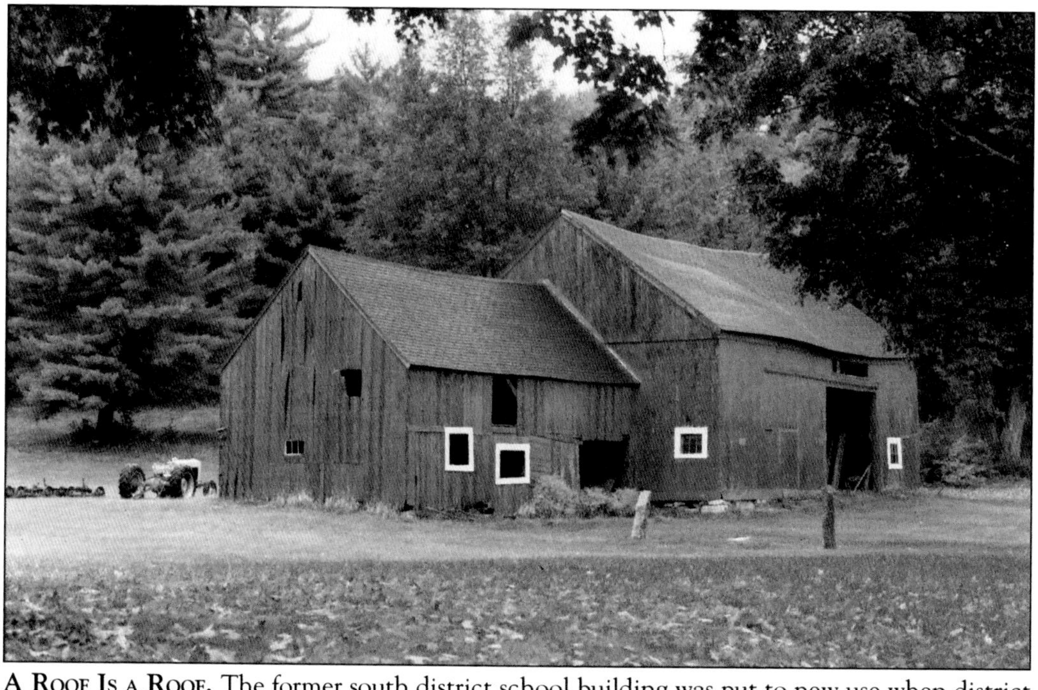

A Roof Is a Roof. The former south district school building was put to new use when district education was abolished in favor of centralized instruction. All the one-roomers were auctioned off. Most were removed to alternate sites to become homes. This little building (left) was snugged up to the Wilbur-Arnold barn as an extra shed for the farm.

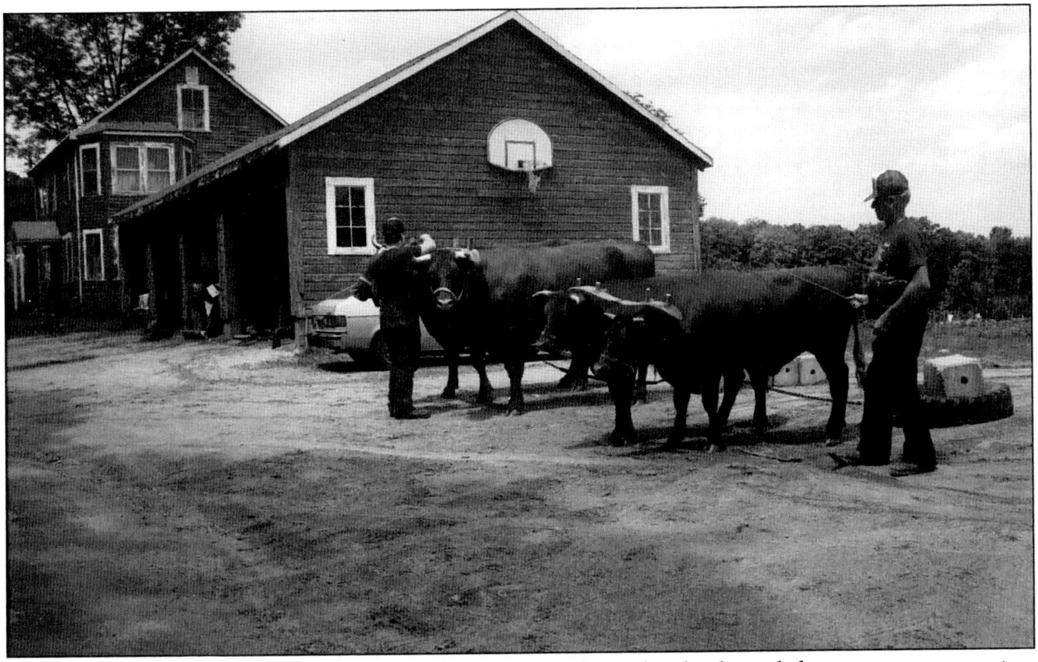

Yoked Oxen. Surry may have evolved into a residential suburb and four-season recreation center, but vestiges of its agricultural identity endure. Here on the Wilbur Farm in 1989, yoked oxen are put through their paces by Jonathan Miller and Howard Wilbur in preparation for competition at county fairs throughout the summer.

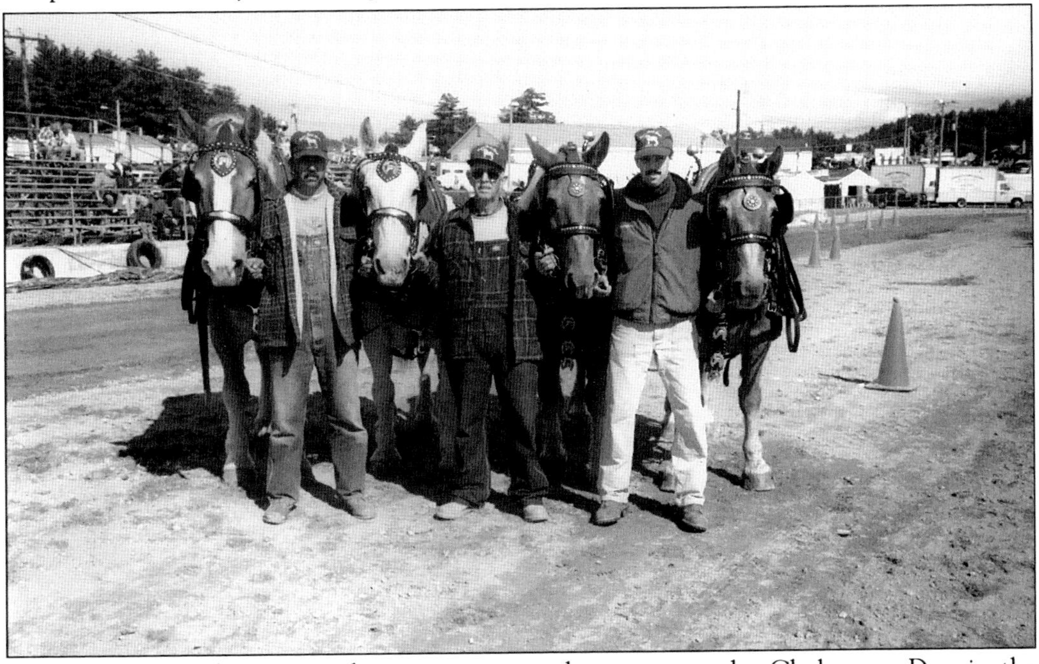

Draft Horses. Three men, three generations, three names—the Clark men: Durwin the son, Hugh the paterfamilias and selectman, and Matthew the grandson—proudly surround themselves with prizewinning horses Dan, Dan, Dan, and Dolly. This photograph was taken at the Deerfield Fair in the year 2000.

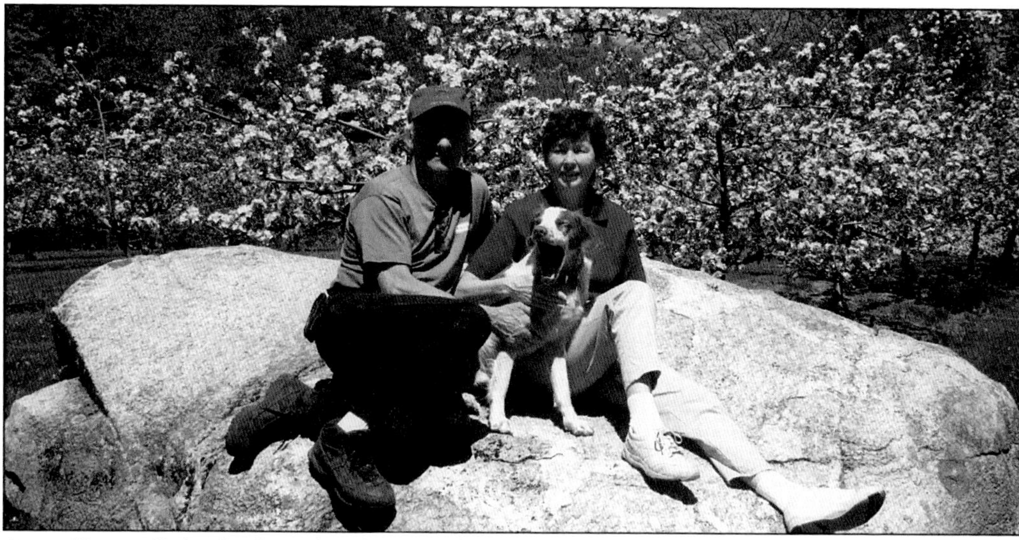

APPLE PLACE. Rebirth of another Surry tradition is an apple orchard created (1982) and operated by the Bienvenu family. For a town that once had 20-plus cider mills (beverage of choice for homesteaders), it is apt that orchards be an enduring mode of farming. The Bienvenus maintain 700 trees in 10 varieties, and make their own apple boxes of local pine. Here, Roger and Elaine Bienvenu take a break on their very own glacial erratic during blossom season.

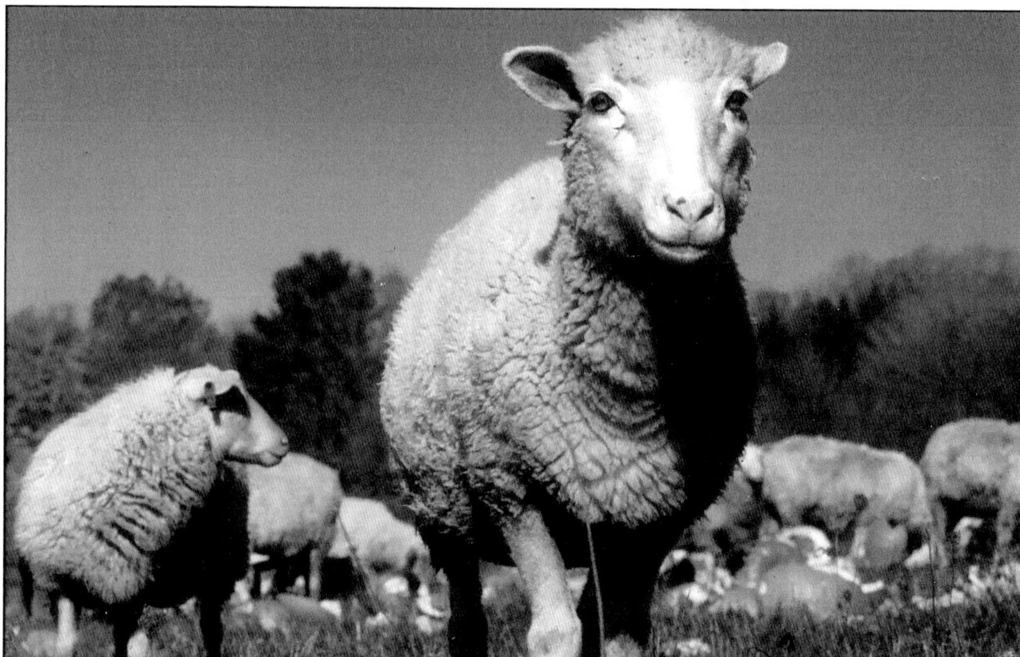

"THAT SHEEP MAY SAFELY GRAZE." Another agricultural revival for Surry has been the return of sheep raising. Bill Fosher began building his herd of two dozen in 1990, wintering them within bleat-shot of Surry Town Hall. April lambing raises the count to 60 or 70. His Border collies Molly, Bess, and Tweed help herd the sheep on upland summer pastures and transmission line corridors for Bellwether Solutions, LLC. The sheep here feast on scores of pumpkins, an annual windfall from Keene's Pumpkin Festival.

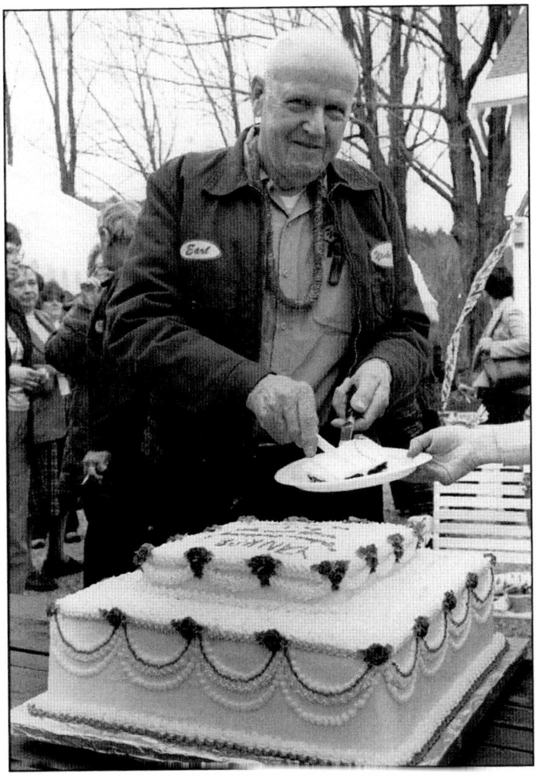

"PLAIN TALK." Earl Proulx is well known to readers of *Yankee* magazine as the veteran author of the "Fix-It" column, now called "Plain Talk." Born in Marlborough, he acquired his diverse construction skills with local firms (Arthur Whitcomb, Ralph Payne, Sears Roebuck), working on local projects from fire ponds to the Hinsdale Race Track. He supervised maintenance at Yankee in Dublin from 1973 to retirement in 1979, whereupon he was named the fix-it columnist. His second career is now in its third decade. Meanwhile, he built his own home in Surry, served as selectman for 12 years, and headed the restoration of Surry Town Hall. He is shown having his cake at retirement from *Yankee* in 1979 and then figuratively eating it, too, 20-plus years later.

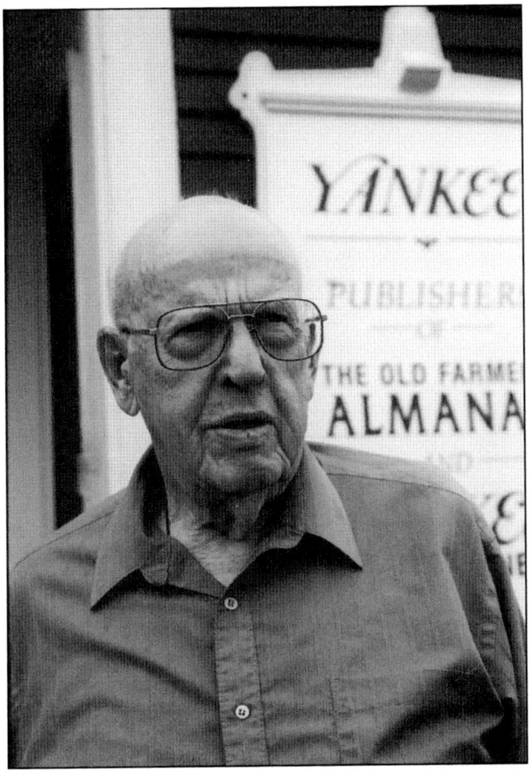

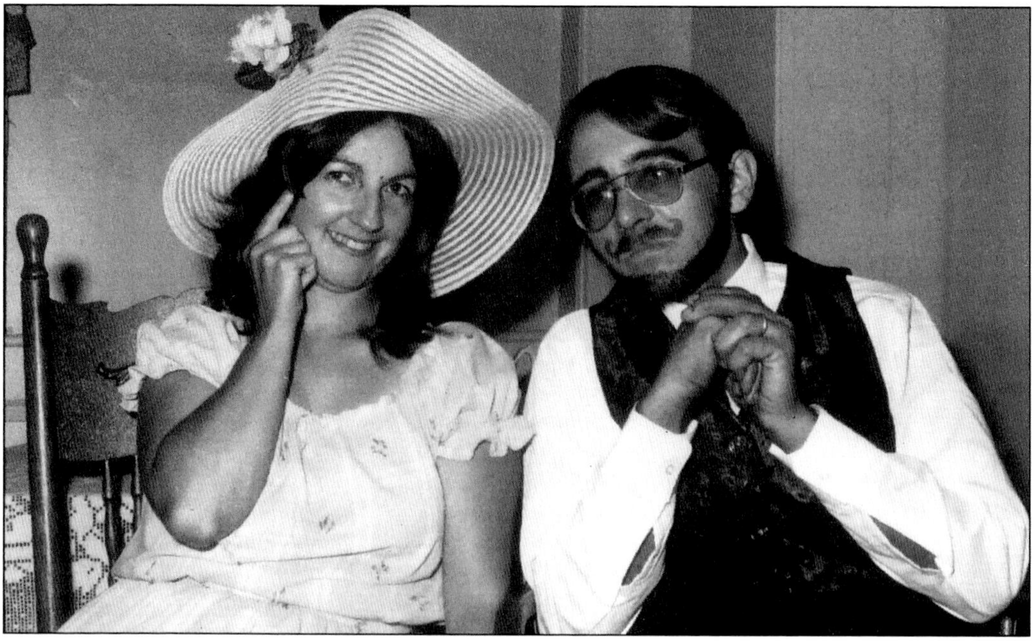

THE SURRY PLAYERS. Community theater is a binding force in many small towns across the country, but who would expect a community of 600 to 800 in late-20th-century America to generate the energy and talent and dedication to produce a new play annually for a quarter century? Surry succeeded. The 1979 premiere *Aaron Slick from Punkin Crick* had Sheila Breton and Bill Bigelow in prominent roles.

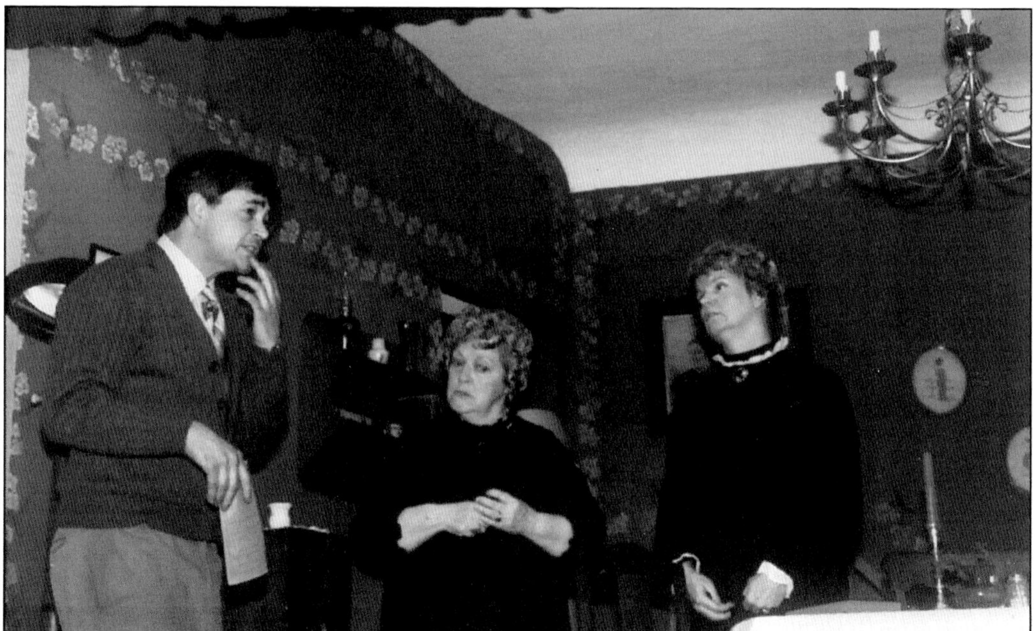

ARSENIC AND OLD LACE, 1988. "But they died so peacefully," a startled Mortimer (John Denis) is reassured by his aunts (Marilyn Jarvis and Maureen Bigelow) in the 1988 production of *Arsenic and Old Lace*.

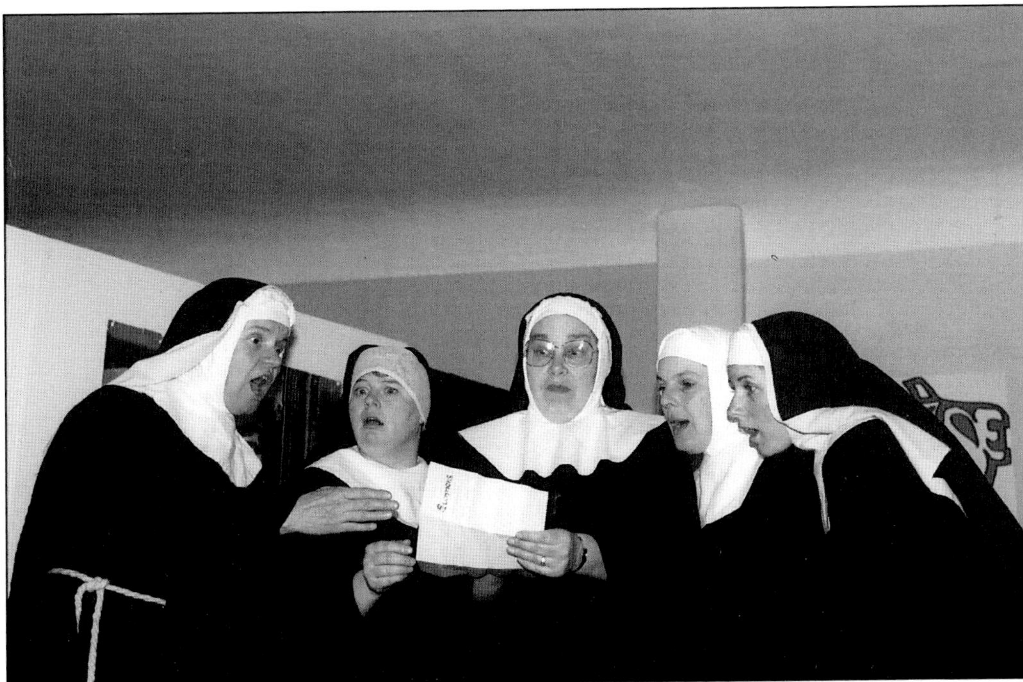

NUNSENSE, 1992. Mother Superior (Trish Metivier) reads the notice from the board of health to the alarmed Little Sisters of Hoboken (Maureen Bigelow, Susan Wolterbeek, Leslie Carlson, and Mona Anderson).

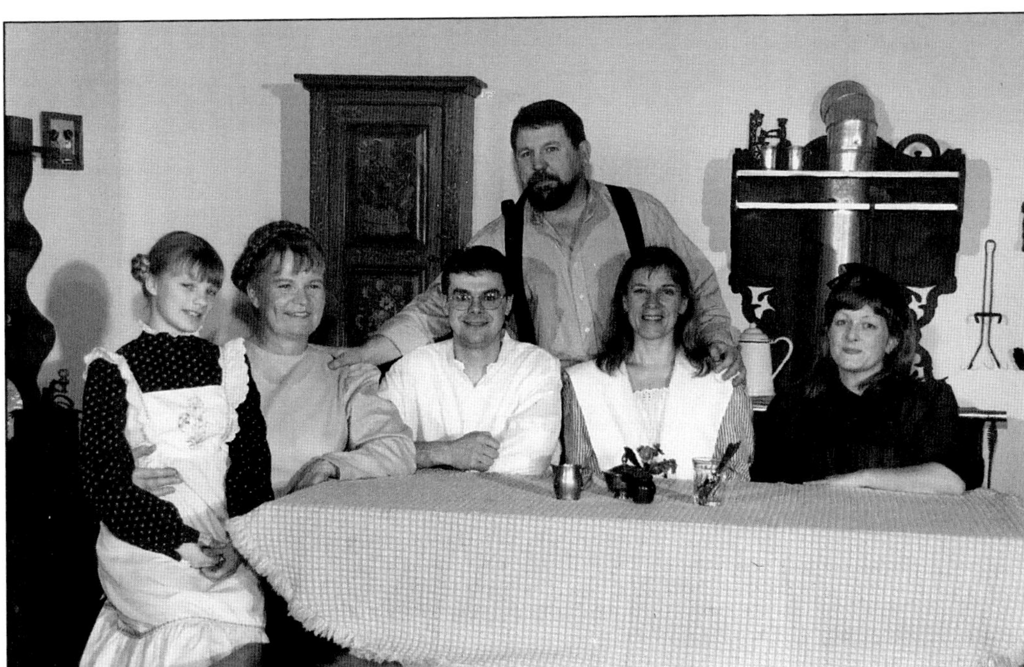

***I REMEMBER MAMA,* 2000.** Samantha Bissell, Maureen Bigelow, Todd Bissell, Ken Little, Mona Anderson, and Tracy Cushing make up a happy Mama's family in this millennial production.

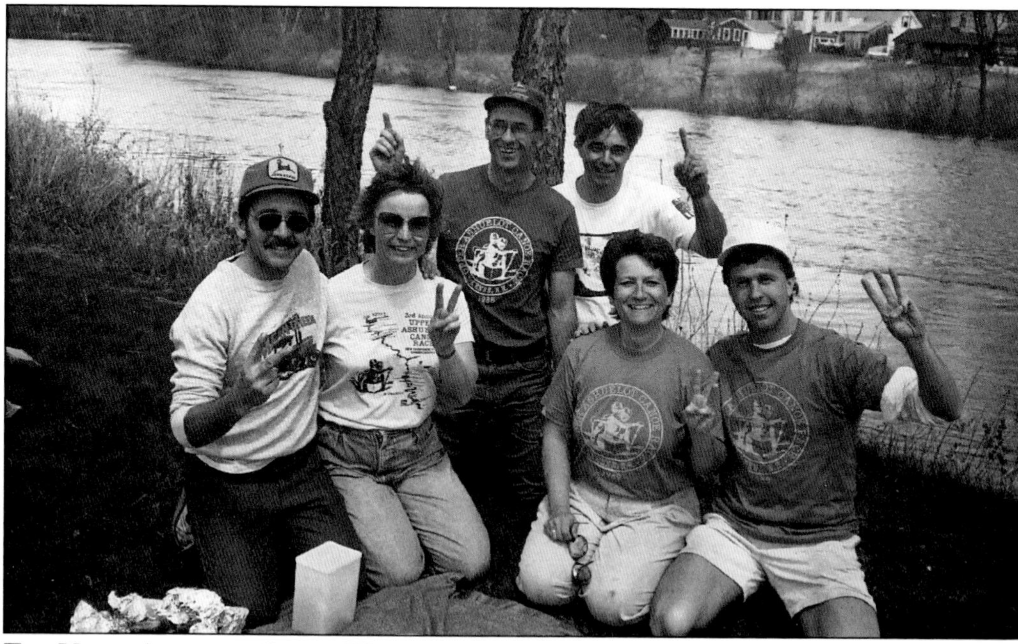

THE UPPER ASHUELOT CANOE WINNERS. Canoe and kayak races take place on the Ashuelot and its major tributaries annually during spring runoff. This high-water canoe race on the main stem was swept by Surry boats. Winners are Bill and Maureen Bigelow (second place), Tom Dutton and John Denis (first place), and Linda Denis and Tim Lawlor (third place).

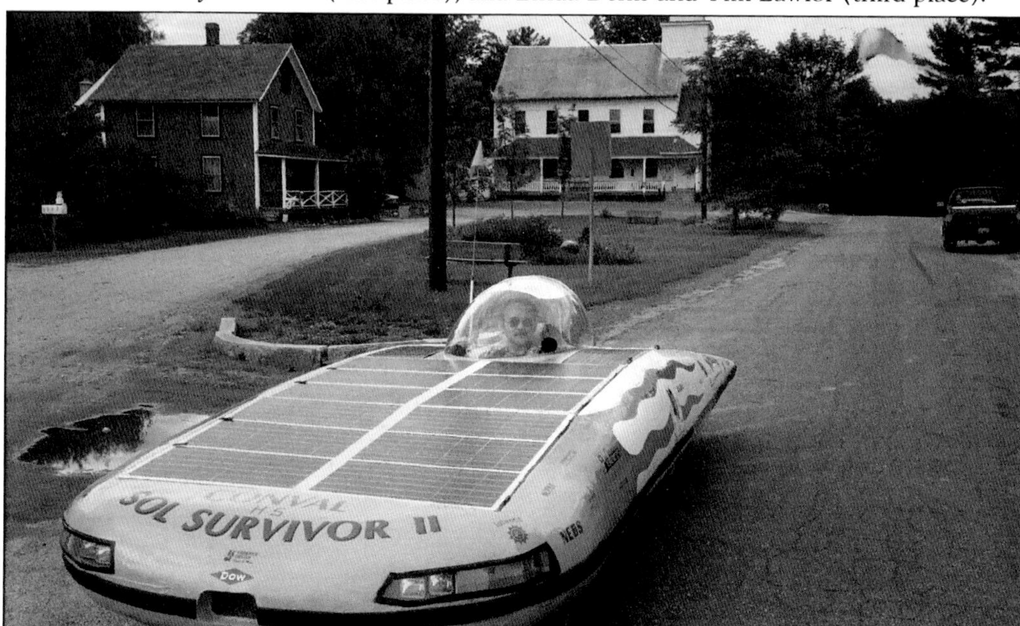

SOL SURVIVOR. Surry teacher Bill Bigelow encouraged his industrial arts classes at Conval High School to apply eco-friendly technologies to real-world situations. His students designed a solar-powered car that beat competing models from MIT, Harvard, Dartmouth, and others in the American Tour de Sol competition. Here, the teacher gets to drive Sol Survivor II (1992) through 200 years' worth of Surry history, figuratively nudging his town into its third century.

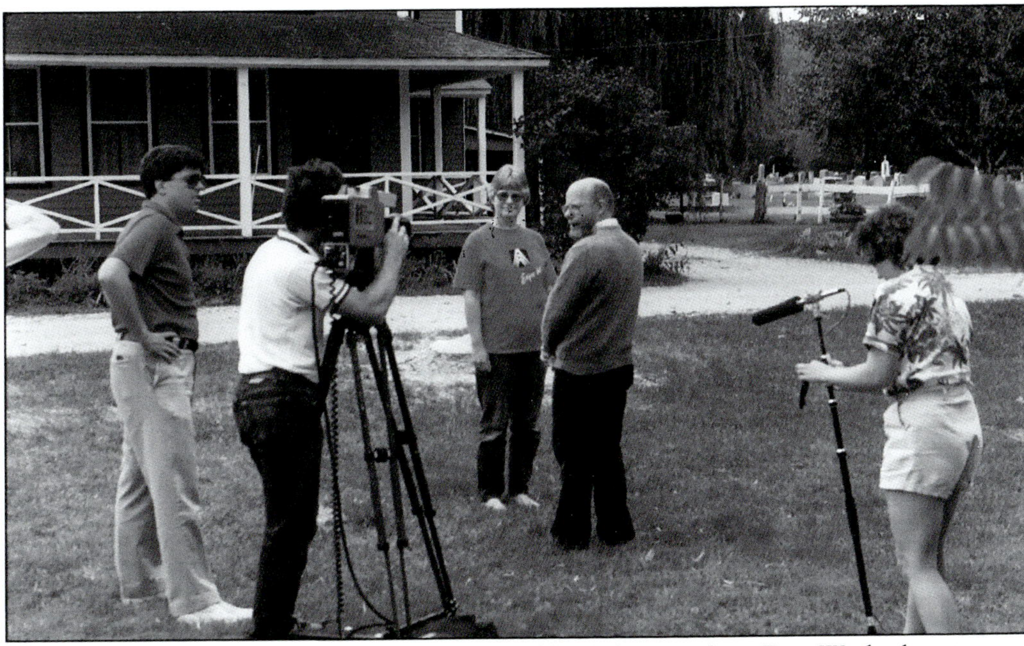

The Surry Documentary. New Hampshire Public Television host Fritz Wetherbee prepares to interview Mary Fosher on Surry history in the mid-1980s for the popular program *New Hampshire Crossroads*. Surrounded by television production staff, this veteran teacher gracefully adjusts to her carefully scripted "lesson plan" skating off in unanticipated directions.

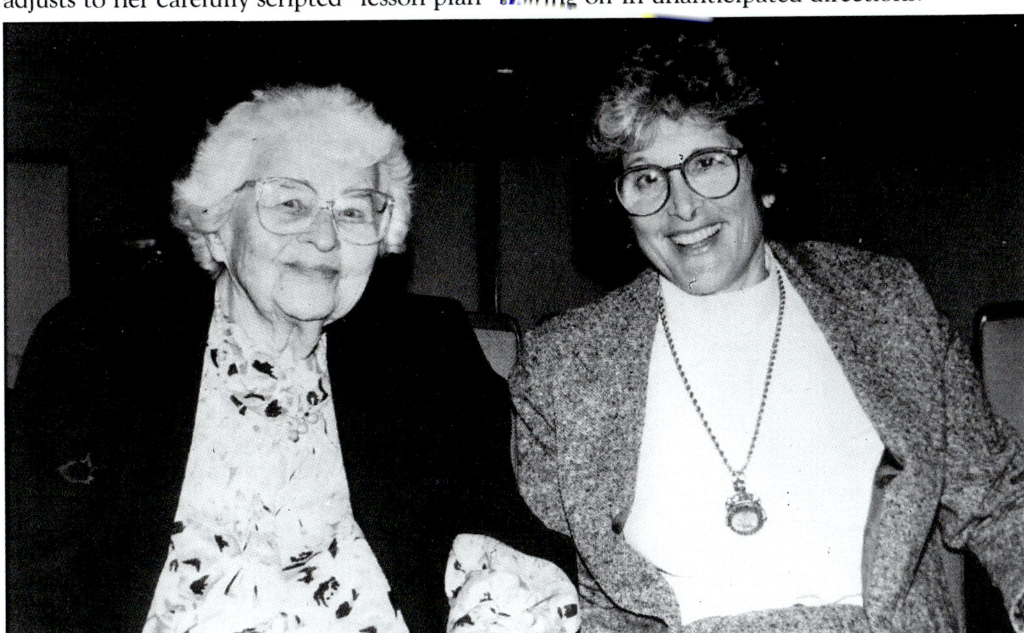

The Confidantes. New Hampshire Poet Laureate Maxine Kumin rejoices in her friendship with Dorothy Harbison (Mary Fosher's mother), following a local reading. Sharing a fierce love of horses, Maxine Kumin wrote a poem for Dorothy Harbison called "The Confidantes," in which the older woman, then 91, remembers a lost world, and bliss, in the nuzzling of a filly. "It was all horses then . . . All horses. Heavenly. You understand."

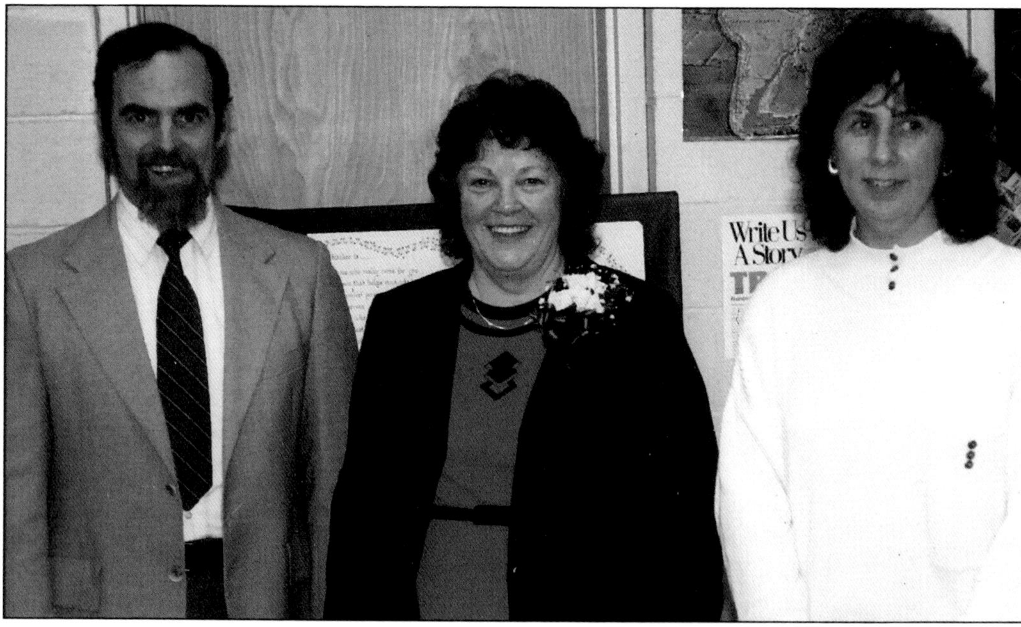

Three Teachers, 1992. The new Surry School had stood at this location only 42 years, but these three teachers had already logged 50 cumulative years at the time of this recognition ceremony in 1992. Accepting the plaudits are, from left to right, J.C. Russell (fifth and sixth grades), Marilyn Jarvis (first and second grades), and Patricia Small (third and fourth grades). (See Ruth Connors's comparable achievement one generation earlier, page 99.)

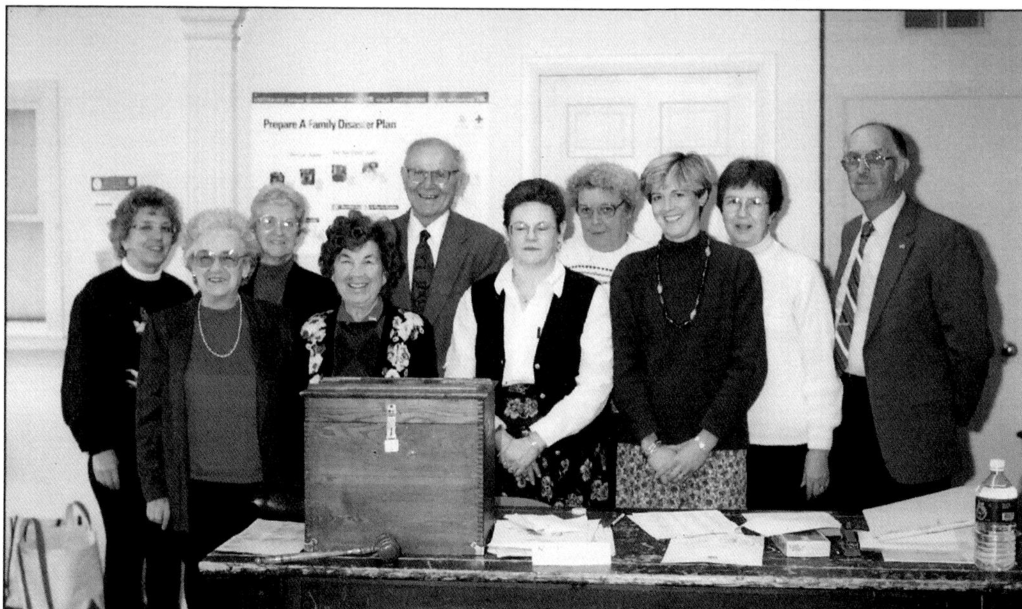

The Officers, 1998. The election staff prepares to receive voters at Surry Town Hall for the quintessential act of representative government, casting of ballots to choose who shall govern. Shown, from left to right, are Mary Nadeau, Ruth Frink, Mabel Rhoades, Rachel Arnold, Calvin Frink, Carolyn Berglund, Virginia Clark, Katherine Richardson, Beulah Smith, and Hugh Clark.

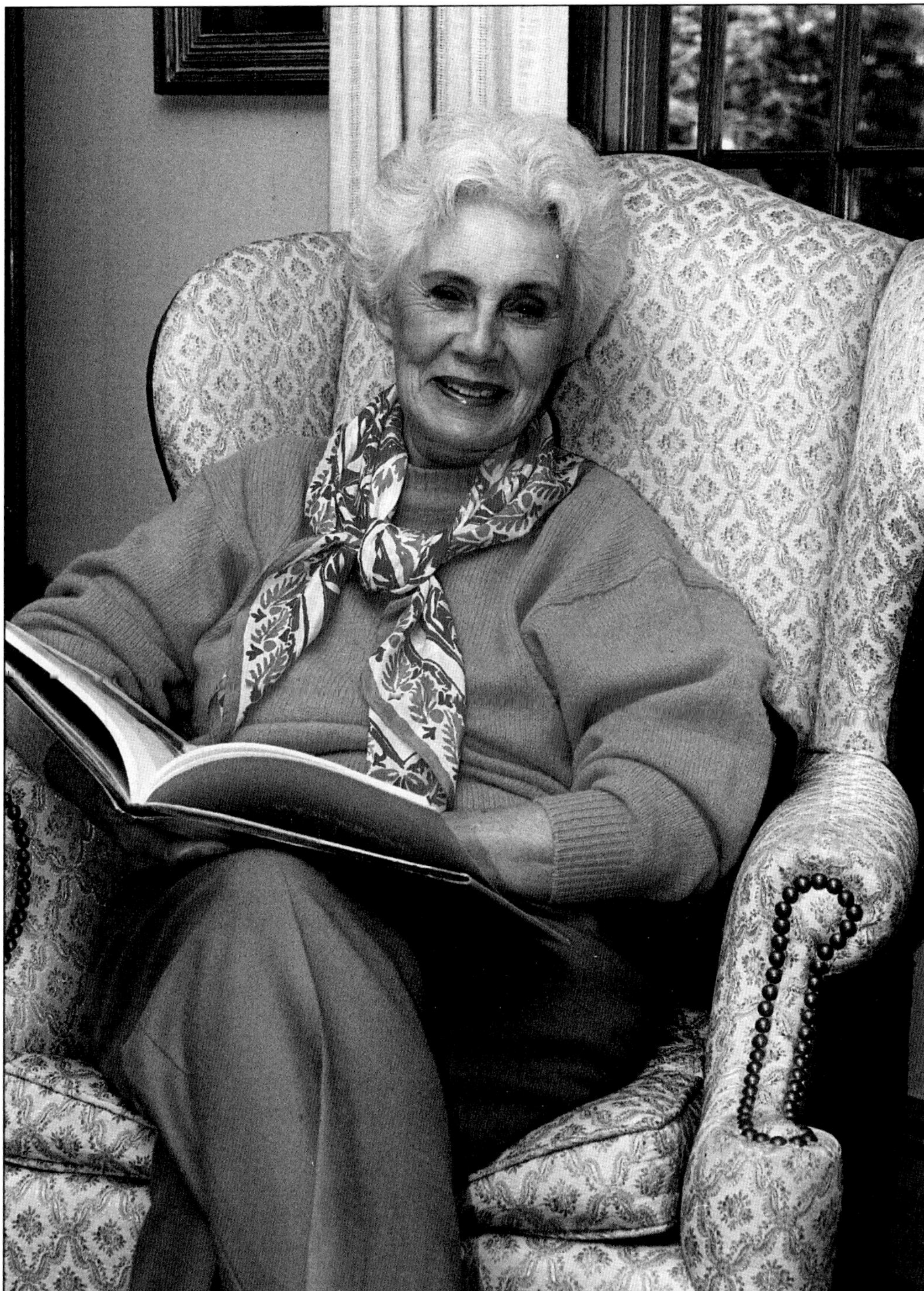

The Hospitaler. Cecile Jennings was recognized as U.S. Caregiver of the Year 2000 for the strength and warmth she brings to hospice work for families coping with cancer. A survivor herself, she has given selflessly for 20 years to others confronting what she has endured. Caring for the sick and needy is the root meaning of "hospice," "hospital," as well as "hospitality." (KS.)

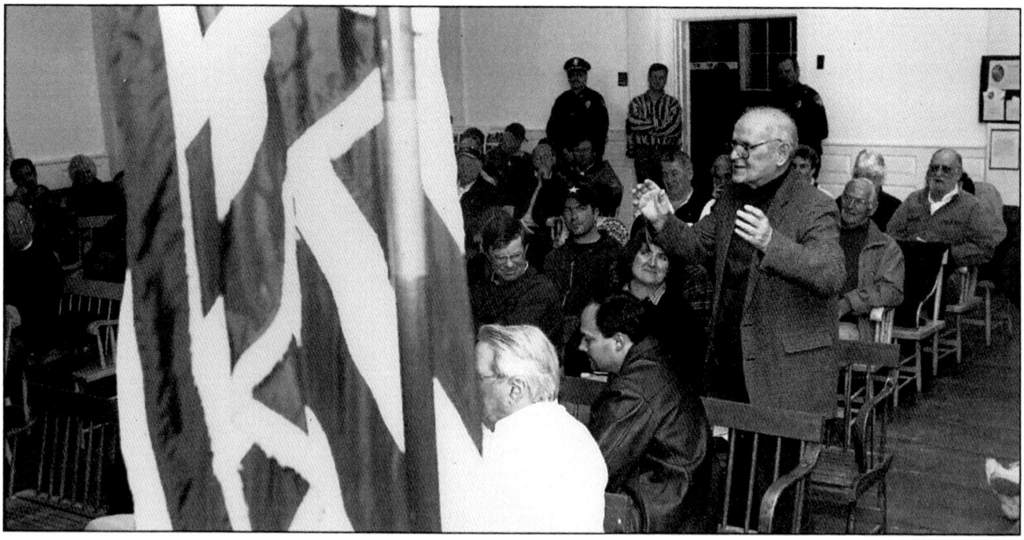

CALVIN FRINK AND SURRY HISTORY, 2001. Calvin Frink makes a funding proposal to town meeting 2001 for support of this publication and the subsequent update of the Frank Kingsbury history. Voters approved the motion. Frink first convened a group to update the history in August 1990. The group met and conducted research continuously from that time. Calvin Frink exemplifies a laudable pattern of Surry citizens who contribute years of their lives to the good of the community, accepting appointments when asked and sparking civic initiatives when inspired. He has logged more than 120 service-years to his town. He served as town moderator (19 years), fire department (45 years, cofounder), conservation commission (17 years), selectman (two years), school board (four years), budget committee (one year), forest fire warden (25 years), and history committee (11 years). Descended of a pioneer settlers of New England, he was born in Keene in 1922. A small-business owner, he has been an incorporator and trustee of Cheshire County Savings Bank and a director of the successor Cheshire Financial and CFX Corporations. He was a trustee of Cheshire Hospital through its transition to regional medical center. He served as governor's representative on the Northeast Forest Fire Protection Commission through five administrations. He is treasurer-trustee of the Historical Society of Cheshire County. (KS, both photographs.)

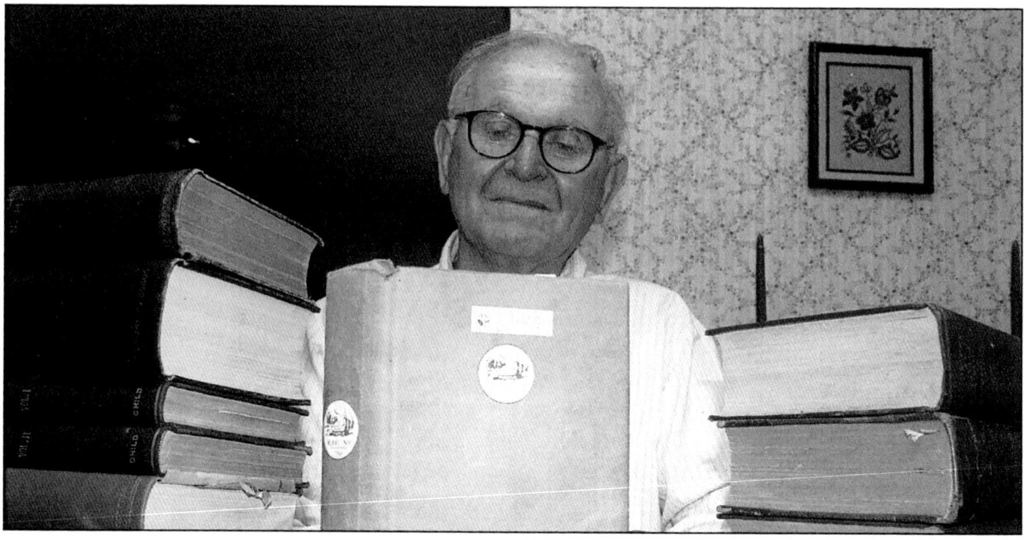

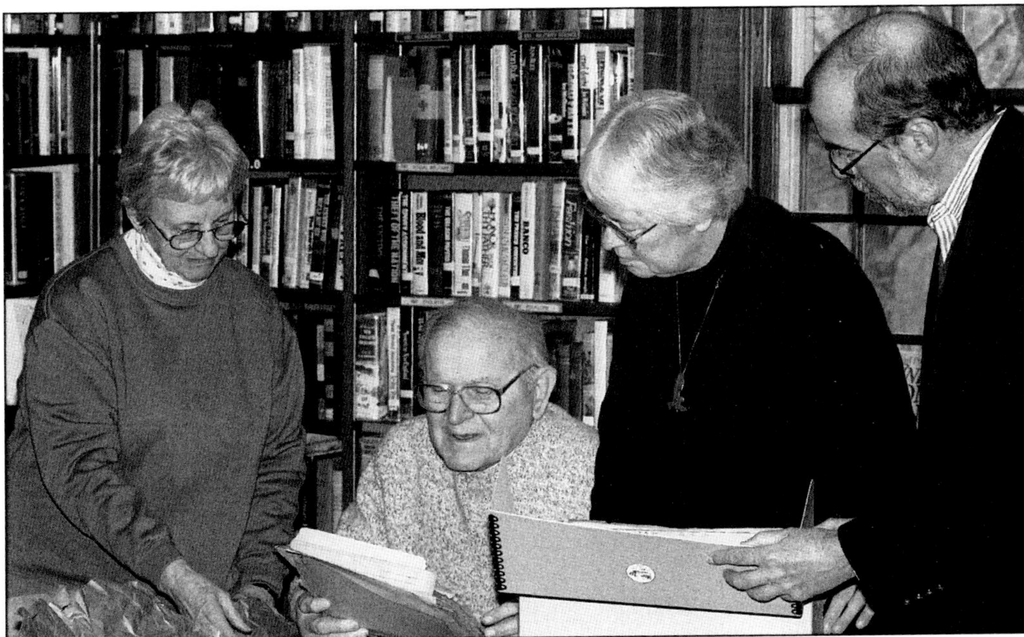

The Surry History Committee, 2000. Culminating 10 years of compilation and research, the Surry History Committee opened the sealed manuscripts of Frank Kingsbury's *History of the Town of Surry* (1925), stored for 75 years in the town vault, and transferred all materials to archival (acid-free) containers. Mabel Rhoades, chairman Calvin Frink, Mary Fosher, and consultant Richard Scaramelli evaluate the documents.

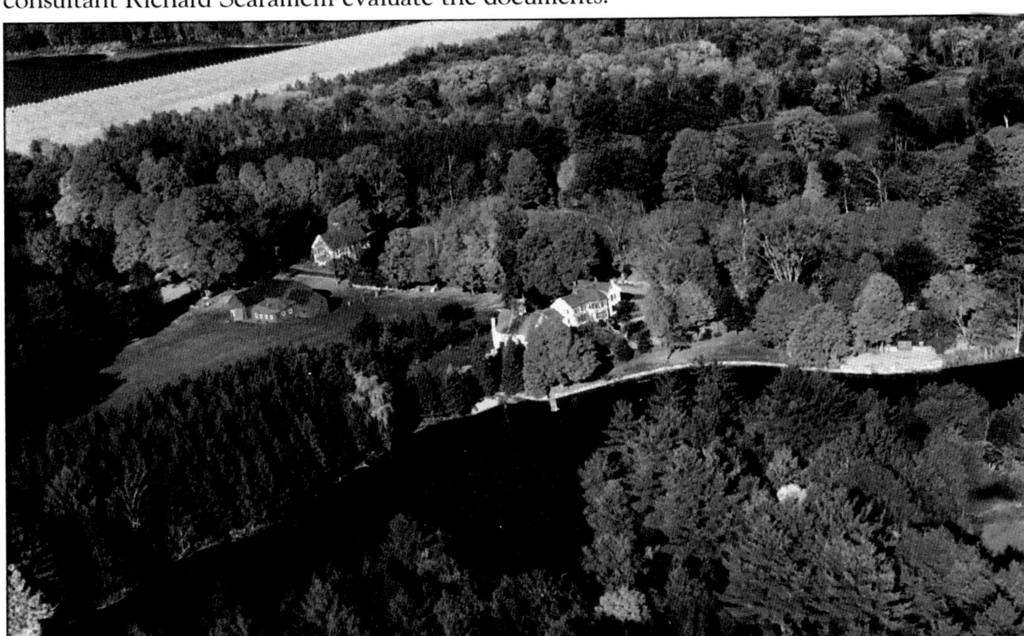

Below the Dam. This beautiful foliage photograph shows Surry Mountain Dam and reservoir at the upper left, Rogers Pond at the bottom, and the Wilbur-Arnold Farm. Surry entered its third century with a cultivated base and optimism like that of the tree farmer who set out the plantation seedlings (lower left) for a future generation.

ACKNOWLEDGMENTS

The Surry History Committee records its appreciation for the assistance of many individuals in creating this compilation of photographs of historical and contemporary Surry. Principal acknowledgment must go, however, to the institutions without whose cooperation the book would not have been possible: the U.S. Army Corps of Engineers office at Otter Brook Dam, which provided ready and complete access to the files concerning land acquisition and construction of Surry Mountain Dam; the Keene Sentinel, which afforded similar access to the negatives file of Wallace Baker, its first staff photojournalist; and the Historical Society of Cheshire County, which generously made accessible its outstanding photograph collections of 10,000-plus images. The contributions of each are noted in the text as ACE, KS, and HSCC.

The committee thanks the following individuals for their help, whether in the loan of a family photograph or in extended telephoning to chase down a fact. Heading the list is David Harvey, committee member and grandson of photographer James E. Harvey, whose outstanding work makes up the earlier sections of the book. David Harvey entrusted all to the project.

Earl Anderson
Rachel Arnold
Wallace Baker
Hazel Scripture Balch
Victoria Ball
Ruth Kelly Balla
Ellis Barrett
Laura Barrett
Matthew Barrett
Beth-El Bible Church
Roger and Elaine Bienvenu
Maureen Bigelow
Peter Bissell
Constance Blewett
Sheila Breton
Frederick Breton
Mary Malcolm Carey
Eric Carlson
Leslie Carlson
Kiki Chakalos
Hugh Clark
David Crotto
Bill Fosher
Frederick Fosher
Mary Fosher
Calvin Frink
Herbert Frink
Ruth Frink
S.R. Gilcreast Jr.
Allison Gleason
David Harvey
Edith Hasbrouck
Historical Society of Cheshire County
Steven Hooper
Marilyn Jarvis
Keene Sentinel
Maxine Kumin
Michael Moore
Tony Nappi
Jeannie Perry
Harold Pike
Reed Free Library
Mabel Rhoades
Clayton Robbins
Stanley Scripture
Bruce Smith
Kenneth Smith
Lawrence Sportello
Beth Stillings
Surry Conservation Commission
U.S. Army Corps of Engineers
Vivian Wallace-Britton
Christopher Warman
Dorothy Wilbur
Howard Wilbur
Yankee Inc.
Lynn Zimmerman